One Foot in Heaven

Finding Hope in the Hopeless

(A MIRACULOUS TRUE STORY)

Sheila Preston Fitzgerald

Selah Press
PUBLISHING

James —

Blessings and honor from heaven about upon you

my friend !

Sheila

One Foot in Heaven
By Sheila Preston Fitzgerald

Editor: Lisa Blevins May
Cover Design: Christine Dupre, Vida Graphic Design
Author Headshot by: Nikki Hollis Photography

ISBN: 978-1733327107

For information email: 1FootNHeaven@gmail.com

Unless otherwise noted, Scripture is taken from THE HOLY BIBLE, NEW INTERNATIONAL VERSION®, NIV® Copyright © 1973, 1978, 1984, 2011 by Biblica, Inc.® Used by permission. All rights reserved worldwide.

Printed in the United States of America

Disclaimer: The author and publisher have left out names and identifying details to protect the privacy of individuals. The author has tried to recreate events, locales, and conversations from the author's memory of them. In order to maintain privacy the author and publisher have in some instances left out the name and identifying details of individuals. Although the author and publisher have made every effort to make sure all information is correct at press time, the author and publisher do not assume and hereby disclaim any liability to any party for any loss, damage, disruptions caused by stories with this book, whether such information is a result of errors or emission, accident, slander, or other cause.

What people are saying about
One Foot in Heaven...

"Incredible story...incredible lady...a must-read!"

Manny Sethi, M.D.
Author of *The American Dream in Tennessee*

"*One Foot in Heaven* radiates light and hope in our world where darkness seems to take so much. Sheila's attitude, stemming from her incredible faith, cannot help but inspire everyone who encounters her. Sheila's misfortunes could have taken her joy and livelihood, but instead she let God take hold of her story and transform it into a powerful testimony. Now she encourages others to follow her incredible example."

Ginny Priz
Co-Host of *Bloom Today* TV Show and
Author of *Ditch the Drama*

"While Fitzgerald may have *One Foot in Heaven*, she lives wholeheartedly dedicated to Christ here on earth. With a natural humor and lighthearted spirit, this author shares the tragic details of her recovery from a motorcycle accident and inspires readers that they can face their own struggles with a heart of grit, grace, and gratitude. Through Fitzgerald's journey, God shows each of us He can transform our most hopeless and cocooned places into something as transcendent and beautiful as a butterfly. You will laugh, you will cry and you will walk away with a deeper faith and a greater hope to face the challenges in your life!"

Lisa Murray, LMFT
Author of *Peace For A Lifetime: Embracing a Life of Hope,
Wholeness and Harmony Through Emotional Abundance*

"Oswald Chambers writes, "A spiritually vigorous saint sees every situation in which he finds himself as the means of obtaining a greater knowledge of Jesus Christ." In this world of upheaval and loss, many of these situations that Chambers refers to are those in which we would not willingly put ourselves. Sheila Fitzgerald's story exemplifies one of the more extreme cases of this, while also holding true to the idea that God is the very essence of grace and love. Her story is one of healing and joy procured against all odds that has led to a fuller understanding of who He is as both God and Father."

Rhonda Madge
Author of *Hindsight*

"I can't imagine facing the trauma and heartache Sheila Fitzgerald chronicles in her inspiring new book, One Foot in Heaven. Her incredible story beautifully illustrates how, even in the midst of tragedy and heartbreaking loss, God is with us every moment. She has experienced relentless pain and major life change but at the same time her story will fill you with faith and point you to the only one who can sustain us when life falls apart. One Foot in Heaven will make you laugh and cry and most importantly, fill you with hope."

Kate Battistelli
Author of *The God Dare* and *Growing Great Kids, Partner with God to Cultivate His Purpose in Your Child's Life* and mom to GRAMMY-award winning artist, Francesca Battistelli

"Tragedy is a part of this Earth-life. Sheila Fitzgerald is a woman transformed. Her journey from tragically broken and permanently altered to a woman boldly dependent on Jesus has brightened my life. Sheila's *One Foot in Heaven* tells all, and with gentle humor bears much pain—yet has overwhelmed me with the beauty of God's grace and unending love for us!"

Beth Leonor Dukes
Author of *A Day Without Mama*

"Sheila is one of the most inspirational women I have ever met. Her ability to motivate and encourage others, in spite of challenges and obstacles in life, is a gift from God."

Sue Jeffers
2018 Spring Hill (TN) Woman of the Year

"Sheila's unbelievable journey of struggle and perseverance is like few I have ever known. She's a lady who has managed to maintain an attitude of optimism and hope with her unwavering faith in the Lord. Read Sheila's incredible story, *One Foot in Heaven*, and you will be encouraged and inspired by the life of 'one special lady.'"

Larry Adamson
Author of *Just Some Thoughts*

"Sheila is a living miracle! Her story of not only overcoming but thriving after disaster is a testimony to the power of God! Her talent of sharing her story with grace and humor is a blessing to all she encounters. *One Foot in Heaven* will change lives giving the reader the courage to not only continue on in the midst of a roaring battle but to live life to the fullest even through the pain."

Hope Beryl-Green
Author of *To Tell the Truth*

"My dad always called her 'Sunshine,' and that she is! Through God's redemptive healing, Sheila continues to shine, even when unimaginable tragedy struck her life. Her bubbly personality, her positive attitude, and her love for Christ shines through. Sheila's inspiring true story is filled with INCREDIBLE HOPE, even in life's hardest moments. Shine on my friend! Shine on!!"

Dianna R.
Reader Review

"Sheila has been through a harrowing life experience yet is one of the brightest and most optimistic people I know. Her zeal for life usually doesn't follow a tragedy the magnitude of what she experienced..."

Rick Cua
Pastoral Care Pastor, Grace Chapel, Leiper's Fork, TN

"From Sheila, I have learned perseverance and keeping a positive attitude even when things seem tough. This lady has shown me the strength of a champion."

M. Jackson
PT, MSPT, CEAS Vanderbilt

"The story of Sheila's life-altering accident is one of courage, determination, and resilience. It's filled with honesty, frankness, and HUMOR! Even as she details the numerous setbacks and excruciating pain…she does so with remarkable spirit and faith. You end *One Foot in Heaven* not feeling sorry for Sheila, but sharing her joy of being alive, rejoicing in God's love, and learning to take one day at a time."

J. Smith
Reader Review

"As a guest speaker to a group of students in an alternative high school setting, Sheila Fitzgerald challenged the students to view their school suspensions as catalysts for positive options as they go forward, to 'choose happy not crappy.'"

Peggy Elliott
Retired Educator

"…I can't believe how much faith is inside one person, especially when Sheila has gone through so much…incredible testimony!"

Kylee May
Published Journalist

"Sheila's inspiring story, *One Foot in Heaven*, is one of survival and renewal, and is the product of her introspection and deep faith. She is the proverbial silver lining to your dark cloud. She has been there, lived it, and survived it. Her extraordinary character, strong faith, truth to her word and indefatigable approach to life is utterly amazing."

Stryker Warren, Jr.
Healthcare Executive

"Sheila Fitzgerald is a shining example of a woman who praises God through the trials and tribulations of life and unapologetically yet tenderly, humbly, and lovingly speaks and represents the Truth at all times. A woman of honor, integrity, and wisdom, Sheila showcases the glory and loving kindness of the Lord simply in her smile and profoundly in her testimony. To know this warrior of a woman is to love her! It would be impossible not to be impacted by Sheila's bravery."

Amy K. Weber
Founder: THE pow{h}er METHOD, {r}elevé One Foundation, and Pow{H}er 432 Ministries

"Sheila's story, *One Foot in Heaven*, is one of perseverance, strength and never ending faith. She has a joy for life. As a kidney recipient, it haunted me that another had to die in order that I might live. Sheila's story reminded me of the goodness of life and the glory of what is to come."

Brigid Halama
Transplant Recipient

"The students in my kindergarten class thoroughly enjoyed their time with Miss Sheila. She did such a wonderful job explaining her disability in such a hands-on way, through children's books, a special bear, and kid friendly language. She has such a presence with adults, but also with children! They absolutely loved her and talked about her for days!"

Jennifer Boyette
Metro Nashville Public Schools

"Personally, as both a kidney transplant recipient and an amputee, *One Foot in Heaven* has inspired me. She tells a story filled with faith, love, perseverance, and encouragement. By telling her story, she will help many overcome their own obstacles in life, and ultimately find a closer relationship with God."

Michael Brookhart
Amputee and Transplant Recipient

"Sheila Preston Fitzgerald has a unique capacity to love others well and relay her redeeming story, *One Foot in Heaven*, of God's healing and grace to all ages! You will be motivated and encouraged by her words that are truly inspired by God."

Kathy Cook
Executive Director
Pregnancy Centers of Middle TN

"Even in the darkest moment, having survived a near-death motorcycle accident, Sheila exudes an unwavering positivity, and has shown she has the heart of a fighter."

T. Stevens
Executive Director TN Chiropractic Assoc.

"I do not know any other person who has suffered so much with a victorious heart. I believe *One Foot in Heaven* will touch countless people who are suffering with a message of hope and encouragement. Sheila is a gifted woman who has proven her courage in the shadow of death. What she has to say is important."

Helen Andrews
Director
Fresh Approach Ministry

"What an amazing book written by an amazing woman. Sheila's journey is like no other, and *One Foot in Heaven* is like no other book you will read. Her inspiration, motivation and strength are contagious. No matter what gets in the way she has proven that with God on our side we can conquer any challenge!"

D.L. Bolton
Reader Review

"My wife and I have been privileged to know Sheila for years and have personally seen how her story has transformed lives; first her own, and then all those who are fortunate enough to come into her orbit of influence. Sheila's life and her story are gifts to a world in desperate need of hope!"

Dean Barham
Spiritual Life Minister Fourth Ave Church
and Community Chaplain

Dedication

One Foot in Heaven is dedicated to those who step out, and step up to help others every single day. Your servant hearts make this world a better place. May God bless you abundantly!

In Loving Memory of My Parents

Dave and Joan Preston

Matthew 19:19, NIV
Honor your father and mother,
and love your neighbor as yourself.

Foreword

Over the last fifteen years of pastoral ministry, I've realized that many of us have stopped believing that the grace of Jesus is sufficient for us. Christian communities are filled with grumblings of discontentment and dissatisfaction. The heaviness of life's disappointments and the things we wish for is a heavy burden that we weren't meant to bear. There's a reason why Jesus said, "my yoke is easy, and my burden is light" (Matthew 11:30). Every now and then you meet someone that lives under that easy yoke and carries with them what Jesus called, "the light of life" (John 8:12). They live with a contagious joy, an unwavering optimism, and an enduring hope that few people truly have. Sheila Preston Fitzgerald is one of those few. Her story is filled with suffering, surrender, and sorrow. Yet Sheila Fitzgerald has allowed God to bring her glorious triumph out of her tragedy.

Sheila has endured years of agonizing loss, physical and emotional pain, heartache, and walked through the darkness of a broken marriage. This is a woman who had every reason to raise her fists in the air toward God and yell (like many of us would), "Why me!? If You loved me, how could You let this happen to me? If You cared about me, why didn't You prevent all this?" As Sheila will tell you, she's had her moments, but the beautiful thing about her story is that she didn't stay there. She's wrestled through it; she's walked through that valley and come out on the other side better and brighter.

One Foot in Heaven is a story of the courage to continue, to take another breath, another step, and to lean into the sufficiency of Christ in all things. The truth is, when you have the Light of Life living within you, you may stumble but you won't stay down. Jesus says, "Whoever follows me will never walk in darkness, but will have the light of life" (John 8:12, NIV). Sheila Fitzgerald is a genuine follower of Christ who has lived through horrendous darkness, but not lost the Light of Life.

One Foot in Heaven is a story of one person's refusal to filter tragedy through the lens of bitterness, anger, regret, shame, or resentment. In all of our own sorrows and suffering, we need stories like this one to remind us that we're not alone, that God's grace truly is sufficient for us, and that we follow a God who draws near to the broken-hearted. My prayer for you as you read Sheila's story is that God ignites in you a defiant joy in the face of a broken world and that you too will carry the Light of Life.

Associate Pastor Rob Rogers
Grace Chapel, Franklin, Tennessee

One Night That Changed Everything

On a beautiful fall evening, without warning, my world suddenly changed forever...

I was riding my motorcycle home when an oncoming driver failed to yield, at an intersection, crashing into me.

As I lay conscious on the pavement, unable to move, yet fully aware of everything around me, I believed that the good Lord was coming to take me home.

Chapter One

My life was full of love, hard-work, beauty, and adventure before that one fateful night that changed everything. As a young girl, I grew up in the foothills of the beautiful Colorado Rocky Mountains. My daddy taught us all to love, appreciate, and respect what he termed "God's Country."

We were a typical middle-class family. My parents instilled in us a hard work ethic; teaching us to mind our manners and to do a job well, which meant going above and beyond whatever was asked.

I was nine years old when I first started working for pay. My parents, along with my aunt and uncle, owned a couple of western wear and boot/shoe repair stores. My love for boots, shoes, and all things western stemmed from being at the stores. I also loved playing 'store' and the game Monopoly. For me, working in the shops was the best real-life combination of both. I'm pretty sure that was long before child labor laws. Regardless, I loved it. (It didn't matter the tasks—sweeping the floors, stocking shelves, polishing boots, cleaning bathrooms, cashing out customers, or hauling trash to the dumpster), I was happy. I don't remember too many times receiving money as compensation for hours worked, rather an exchange of my time served for something I desired at that moment.

In the early years, that exchange usually meant a trip to Burger Chef®. Now, for some of y'all, that may sound like I got shortchanged. Hardly! We were a blue-collar family that worked hard for everything we had. Eating out was an extremely rare event when I was growing up. It was a treat for us to have a frozen, store-bought pizza (when on sale, of course) and Kool-Aid® on a Friday night. What was so special about Burger Chef® you ask? For those who aren't familiar with the former Midwest burger chain restaurant, they had the coolest condiment bar. I'm not talking about one of those little stands where you find ketchup and mustard packets. I'm talking about a big ol' bar filled with huge bins of lettuce, tomato, onion, mayonnaise, mustard, ketchup, and dill pickles. Oh, the dill pickles! I'd order burgers for

Daddy and me, carry them to the condiment bar and dress Daddy's burger with a little of everything. Mine? You guessed it. More sliced dill pickles than burger and bun combined.

I couldn't wait to get back to the shop to devour the burger. Over time, as my skillset improved, I'd earn a pickle burger and a little spending cash as well.

It didn't take long for me to learn that the harder I worked, the more I accomplished, the more I sold, and the more I earned. At a very young age, I learned this "work thing" wasn't all bad.

In time, I'd truly learn what a gift it was to have been raised with this strong work ethic, and how it would help me with life beyond work.

~ ~ ~

All but a year or so, my nurturing mom worked from home. I could say she was a stay-at-home mom, but her duties were WAY beyond that. She was a cook, a baker, a house keeper, a financial guru, a gardener, a canner, a hostess, a server, a wanna-be seamstress, the most gifted at making a dollar stretch until the end of the month, and of course, a mom to my siblings and me.

Daddy worked outside the home to make money. Mom did everything she could in and around the home to make the money go as far as possible.

My dad, and later my brothers, would hunt while Mom and us kids raised a giant garden. Working together, our freezers and cellar were always full. We may not have had conveniences and luxuries, but we were blessed.

Both my parents taught me the value of learning. I don't necessarily mean book learning, although that is important. I'm referring to life learning—learning from trying, failing, and trying again, and again, and again. Wow, did that persistence become a key part of my journey as well.

My cowboy dad was raised way down south near the border of Mexico. Tough, south Texas ranch life will make a man out of anyone. He was raised with a farm-ranch mentality: get creative…figure it out. I think the phrase "duct tape and bailing wire" was coined for my daddy. Back when he was growing up, they lived far from a decent-sized town. When things broke down on the ranch, you'd figure out how to fix it with whatever you had lying around. He was a tough man, but he solved problems and loved the best way he knew how.

Although Mom grew up a city girl in a Philadelphia row house, her life was no picnic either. At the age of fifteen, and the oldest of six kids, her mother passed away from cancer. It's safe to say, my mom was a mom, in some capacity or other, her entire life. She mastered it well.

As a young girl, I didn't understand all the wonderful life lessons my parents taught me through daily, hard work. I didn't always respect my parents back in those rebellious teenage years. I guess you could say that some of their "be independent and self-sufficient" teachings backfired a bit when it came to me, but...decades later, those life lessons would truly become life-giving.

~ ~ ~

After I graduated from high school, I attended York Christian College in York, Nebraska, about six hours from home. York was a great atmosphere for me. Especially after coming out of those rebellious teenage years. Don't get me wrong, I wasn't doing anything illegal. Nope. Just plain ol' teenage know-it-all stupidity.

I loved college life. Mine was a very small school, even smaller than my high school. Some dear friends, brothers, and upperclassmen at the time, pulled some strings to get me in. I had a small scholarship, a student loan, and for the rest, I worked two jobs—one as a switchboard operator for the college, and the other as a waitress nights and weekends. It was a full load, but I liked being busy. Guess I've never been a fan of sitting around wasting time.

Speaking of upper-class men, I met and fell head-over-heels in puppy love with a fella. I call it "puppy love" because we were pups in love—not a care in the world, and oh, so naive about life. Less than two years later, we married. Less than five years after that, we were divorced. In many ways, we were still pups even after the divorce. We had no business getting married so young. That was over 30 years ago. I'm grateful God has blessed us with His grace of forgiveness, reconciliation of friendship, and a rear-view mirror that sees past hurt and shame. Those images get smaller and smaller as we move farther and farther away from them.

~ ~ ~

One of the greatest gifts from my first marriage is that it brought me to Tennessee. I absolutely love living in middle Tennessee. It offers beauty like none other. The acres and acres of lush pastures, the picturesque rolling hills, and all the lavish green trees and foliage take my breath away. The only things more beautiful are its precious southern people. Thank You, Lord, for planting me here decades ago.

When I first arrived in Tennessee, I worked in private practice healthcare administration. The first doctor was kind enough to give this inexperienced girl a shot. (No, not with a needle.) She saw my can-do attitude and eagerness to learn. Soon, staff members at a larger clinic stole me away. Okay, not really stole me away, but urged me in their direction. It was a decision I'll never regret. Dr. David Pence not only trusted my abilities but also he encouraged my passion, creativity, and desire to achieve and grow personally, in his clinic, and in the Chiropractic profession as well.

As the Founder and past President of the Chiropractic Assistants of Tennessee, I, along with a handful of gifted ladies, created a statewide educational program for Chiropractic staff in Tennessee. We started small with very limited funds to work with. The program quickly blossomed. I'm proud to say the blood, sweat, and tears of a few strong, willing, and able ladies helped create one of the most well-respected associations in the Chiropractic industry today.

Tiffany, one of those gifted ladies, turned out to be one of the dearest friends I'll ever know. What started out as a relationship between respected, dedicated colleagues, has, over time, grown to so much more.

I thank God that He allowed our paths to cross all those years ago.

Our friendship would be greatly tested in the years to follow. Tiffany's love, support, and dedication would go above and beyond the call of duty.

~ ~ ~

While working in Dr. Pence's office, I met a real nice fella. He was reserved, quiet, and a southern gentleman. After his appointments, he seemed to hang around the office a little too much (if you get my drift).

Before you knew it, we were dating. A year and a half later, we were married in a sweet, front porch, country-style wedding. He was a dedicated firefighter and an active Rotarian. One of the area's civic Rotary Clubs founded the local rodeo over 70 years ago. It's been a popular community event ever since. My husband's involvement with the club helped satisfy his desire to be a part of the local rodeo. Having grown up around rodeo (I have an uncle who was a rodeo clown), it was a natural fit. We spent years working and honing our individual careers and enjoyed the occasional rodeo together in our free time.

Several years into our marriage, he started a family business with his uncle and cousins. They were the labor, sales, and workforce; I was all administration: office, clerical, bonds, insurances, etc. The business was doing so well that it became too much for me to handle along with my other full-time work. I chose family over my career and resigned from the Chiropractic industry. Not long after I resigned, I was approached to serve on the Chiropractic Board of Examiners for the State of Tennessee. I was honored to serve several Governor re-appointments, for a combined fourteen years of volunteer service to the great state of Tennessee.

Unfortunately, as many family businesses do, they closed the doors a few years later. All wasn't lost—at least not for me. The biggest blessing of that business closing? The entrepreneur bug hit me hard!

In many ways, I felt like I was a kid again. Yet, more. I didn't want to work in a family business that kept me closed up in a one-person office. I missed people and wanted to build my own business. At about that same time, I was cleaning out a closet when I came across an old high school journal. In it I had written, "When I grow up, I want to be a beautician." Well, because of my weird sensitive skin and other circumstances, I never pursued a field in cosmetology after high school. That was nearly 20 years after my high school graduation. Dare I go back to school and be the "old lady" among the kids?

With a renewed vigor and hopes for a new career path, this "old lady" bit the bullet and went back to school. Obtaining my cosmetology license for a professional manicurist came easy for me. Logging the required hours for the state was the frustrating part. My desire and passion for the trade made learning a new skillset an easy task. Only being allowed by the state a maximum of eight hours per day, slowed this girl down. Shoot! If they'd have allowed me to do twelve hours a day, I could have graduated in a third fewer days. Can you see a pattern with time-management and work ethic learned in my youth? Thank You, Lord, for blessing me with parents who instilled those skills in me. They've served me well.

I was SO excited to be a part of an upscale salon, working with clients, and helping folks take care of their hands and feet. Not only did they look good when they left but also they felt good, and, in a small way, I helped them feel better about themselves. God blessed me big by allowing me to do a job I truly love.

A Lifetime Friend...

On my first day in my new career I met a fun-loving, beautiful lady named Tammy. She, too, was a professional manicurist—way better than I was at that time. Her years of experience and expertise in the industry set her far above all standards. My parents raised no fool. Tammy had a successful, booming business—exactly what I wanted. I immediately hitched my little wagon to her star. She was sweet and gracious, patient, and oh, so encouraging. I watched, listened, and learned from a master. Before long, I too had a full schedule of clients on my books.

Tammy and I worked really well together. Quickly our work relationship grew into a wonderful friendship. Although we're close in age, she's the big sister I never had. No matter the topic, issue, or concern, when I confide in Tammy, she's a straight shooter—all in love, but grounded in truth and honesty.

I thank Jesus for placing me in that salon at that exact moment in my life. Little did I know how important Tammy's friendship would become to me.

~ ~ ~

My husband and I never had children. It just wasn't meant to be. The older I get, the more I wonder what it'd be like to have kids and/or grandkids. I like to think I'd have made a great mom and an even funnier Ya-Ya. Although I don't have children of my own, I'm blessed beyond measure by nieces and a nephew. They're biological so they have to love their Aunt Sheila (kidding—they're all very loving to me). I'm not sure if it's because I don't have any family living near me or because I'm the childless, cool aunt, but I've had several youngsters call me "Aunt Sheila" over the years. There's nothing more precious than a child running towards you with outstretched arms, with a smile from ear-to-ear, yelling "Aunt Sheila!" (My heart is smiling as I write this.) Kids can't fake that kind of stuff.

I admit it, I may not be smarter than a fifth grader. Unlike most of y'all who've had kids, you learned things for yourself in fifth grade. Then you learned those same things again when your children went through school. And now, if you're grandparents, you get to learn it all one more time. Me? I learned it once, and fifth grade was a very l-o-n-g time ago for this girl.

An amputee, cowboy friend of mine taught me a marvelous new mindset when it comes to not having children of my own. While out horseback riding one day, I asked him, "Why is it that you don't have kids, Lantry? You seem so good with them." Without missing a beat, he quickly replied, "It wasn't for lack of tryin'!" Slapping his britches, he threw his head back laughing so hard I thought he'd lose his hat. He slowed his horse from a jog to a four-beat walk. I did the same.

As our horses fell into step, side by side, Lantry shared with me a beautiful story of what he referred to as "God's Reasoning." This man longed to father children of his own, but even after two marriages, that dream never happened.

Years later, a friend of his suggested that maybe God's reason for his never having children was because God knew if he'd had children of his own, he'd spend all his time with only those children. Since he didn't have children of his own, he's been able to mentor, train, and raise-up dozens of boys and young men through his ranch and ranch rodeos.

"I love that!" I replied.

I learn so much from kids, or as I tend to call them, "little people." I mean no disrespect to anyone, of any size. It's just that children, to me, are people too. They're just little in size. In my lifetime, I've learned some of the greatest lessons from the mouths and minds of little people. Their genuine honesty and simplicity helps to keep me grounded and rooted in this faith journey.

Like a child, I'm still learning... a forever work in progress.

The Reality of a Rodeo Marriage

Our marriage was one many admired. For nearly two decades we had what appeared to be a perfect relationship. In many ways, it was. We were both thriving in our careers. We traveled the country on great vacations, hosted all kinds of entertaining events at our home, competed in local 5Ks and 10Ks, supported our community, regularly attended church, and loved on our pets beyond measure. We loved, supported, and encouraged each other. Never, in nearly twenty years, did we raise our voices—let alone argue or fight.

Everything seemed perfect. The problem with "perfect" is that it's rarely reality. In our case, the reality was that things were far from perfect. For me, all the wonderful things about our marriage had been slowly taken over by all things rodeo. My husband's passion eventually turned into an obsession. I take full responsibility for my years of loyalty, dedication, service, and support of his passion for rodeo. I loved rodeo too. Still do. What I didn't see happening was that of an unhealthy balance of rodeo in our marriage. It was like being on a see-saw with too much weight on one end, carrying the load, or in this case, the burden, while the one on the other end keeps rising higher and higher. My "Rodeo Meeting Widow" button—originally worn in good, clean fun—became a sad reality of our marriage.

Once I finally figured out what was happening to our marriage, I sought professional counseling. Eventually, my husband joined me though he seemed to be threatened by the idea. My husband kept saying "If you'd just go back to how you used to be, everything would be just fine." For me, that wasn't an option. In my mind, that meant that it was all about what he wanted with no regard for me, my thoughts, my feelings, or our marriage. Through my eyes, all I saw was my beloved husband choosing the rodeo over me. I was no longer his top priority, or his first love—a huge blow to my ego, not to mention my heart. We sought individual, friendly counsel...not a good thing. Friends mean well, but most of the time, they have no idea what's really going on behind closed doors. They hear one version of the story. We all know, there are three sides to every story: yours, mine, and the good Lord's truth. Turning to the wrong people for wise counsel turned out to be a horrific mistake. At least for me it did.

I tried and tried to right the imbalance in our relationship. However, due to my crushed spirit, my attempts came across in an attitude of frustration. When frustration meets defensiveness, it's a combination for anger and aggression to explode. Once that ball gets rolling, it's extremely hard to stop, let alone reverse it. The old saying "hurting people hurt people" is so true. Sadly, we became masters at hurting each other. Like a lot of married couples, we played the game well. From the outside, things still looked pretty darn good, but oh, the inside was a HUGE mess. Lord help us.

Makes me think of several folks I've known over the years. They look all put together—smiling and bubbly on the outside. All the while, their hearts are breaking, and they don't know how to fix it.

I, too, was one of those broken people.

A New Ride

We also sought marriage counseling. One of our marriage counselors (sad, but true, we had more than one) suggested we try something new together—a hobby, sport, craft, etc. I don't remember how we chose motorcycles, but we did. I was so excited! I couldn't wait for us to get bikes. I thought riding would be a great way to spend time together, but with not so much face-time in each other's personal space, which typically ended in arguments. My hope was that we'd eventually find our way back to each other without the constant fighting. He'd never ridden before while I grew up riding dirt bikes with friends. Oh, the muffler burns…manually pushing the bike…jumping on and popping the clutch to jumpstart the thing…those were the days.

Riding has always been relaxing for me—be it a motorcycle, a four wheeler, a jet ski, horseback, a snowmobile, or a vehicle. If I'm in the driver's seat, I can either hammer down, or put it on cruise and enjoy the ride. That's my daddy in me. We logged a lot of miles in a short time on our new bikes—some together, some separately. The counselor was right. We were able to do something new together and it was fun. The fact that we were on our own bikes allowed us to spend time together, yet not so much that we would fight and argue.

Looking back now, we might have been together, but we were far from "connected."

~ ~ ~

Like most riders that time of year, I enjoyed the freedom of the open road commuting via motorcycle. For me, it was one place I could escape modern technology and enjoy the beauty of God's creation. I'd put on my riding gear, pack my saddle bags with a sun dress and fun sandals, and head to the salon. Once at the salon, I'd change from denim and leather to dress and heels, fluff my hair, and start my day's work. At the end of the day, I'd do the superman clothing change, or in this case "salon girl," and ride home.

Chapter Two

On Thursday, September 29, 2011, after working all day at the salon, we met some friends for dinner at a local Mexican restaurant. Many have asked, "Had you been drinking?" No, I rarely, if ever, drink when out and never when I rode. That night was no exception—no alcohol. As my husband and I left the restaurant, I distinctly remember a sweet friend saying, "Y'all be careful. I'll say a prayer for your safety." Her husband was in a tragic, life-altering, motorcycle accident years prior.

Before leaving the parking lot, I donned my leathers and a full-face helmet. From head to toe, I was more than appropriately attired for riding. It was a gorgeous fall night. Clear. Peaceful.

As I approached a local major intersection, I let off the throttle, noticing an oncoming vehicle making a left turn in front of me. Unfortunately, there was a second car that followed. The driver never slowed down, accelerating through the turn. For a brief moment, I thought to lay the bike down and slide, rather than take the full impact. There was no time for options.

The initial impact pinned my lower left leg between the front bumper of the other car and my bike. My body landed on the hood of the car; my head hit the windshield. The lateral impact of my head to the windshield caused me to black out for a few seconds. During the momentary blackout, as I flew through the air like a rag-doll, I completed not one, but two summersaults in which my boots flew off. (I can't believe I was unconscious for my one and only gymnastics moment of glory!) Sadly, I "stuck" the landing alright. With my right leg—mostly my right knee and right femur. My final resting place on the pavement came with such force that when my head hit the ground, the impact forced my full-face helmet off my head.

In a matter of seconds my husband, who was on his bike behind me, was at my side. His years of expert training and experience instinctively took over. He immediately held my head and neck in cervical traction, hoping to lessen any further movement or damage. Assessing my injuries and yelling out for someone to call 911, he stayed with me until the paramedics arrived a few minutes later.

I remember it all. Every vivid detail. The horrific crushing impact, the sounds, the smells, the tastes, people touching me, my husband yelling, over and over, "I'm sorry. I'm sorry. I'm so sorry!" Other voices screaming…"Oh my God!"…"It's a woman!"…"Where's her foot?!"…"Soft weeping"… "Gasping"…

The chaos around me was real. And VERY loud!

~ ~ ~

As I lay on the pavement in the middle of the intersection unable to move and feeling no pain, I presumed I was paralyzed from the waist down. Most of my life I've prayed two consistent prayers. One, please give me the heart of a servant, and two, when it's my time to die, please, God, don't let me suffer. In that moment, I had no doubt it was only a matter of time. It was then that I began my bargaining with God. Y'all know what I'm talking about. We've all done it at one time or another in our lives. Mine went something like this:

I'm not asking for myself, Lord, but for my folks. What are the odds that one set of parents could have two children (my hero, and younger brother, is a quadriplegic from a swimming accident many years ago) to become paralyzed from accident related injuries? Ya know, God, that wouldn't be fair to them. So if that's the case, please just take me home now.

That prayer was answered beyond my wildest dreams. It would take years before I would share my amazing spiritual journey with the rest of the world.

As my husband continued to hold my head and neck still and I lay kind-of on my right side with my legs behind me, I slowly removed my leather riding gloves—removing one finger at a time, laying the gloves on top of each other on the pavement beside my face. I said, "Get my purse. I need my purse." Ever the organized one, it was routine for me to put my riding gloves in my bike mounted purse. My husband asked someone to find my purse. "It's on the windshield," he said. A moment later, I saw a woman's hands. She oh, so gingerly, laid the windshield from my motorcycle on the pavement near my face where I could see it.

My purse was still attached to the windshield. I asked her to take it off. She didn't seem to know how. Seeing her hands shaking, I told her, "Open the flap and on the inside, on the back of the purse are two toggles. Turn those and it'll release from the windshield." She did as I asked.

It would be the only part of my beautiful bike that I'd ever see again.

I heard a soft, young voice praying. Someone gently touched my left shoulder.

"Don't touch me!" I yelled.

Although I didn't feel pain in my body from the accident, I felt horrific, shocking pain when anyone touched me. Half of my body was mangled which caused massive, open nerve damage. When someone touched me, the electrical current sent ghastly, sickening pain throughout my entire nervous system, causing unbearably raw torture.

The first responders arrived on the scene. Being a fire department officer's wife, I knew a lot of the responders. My main paramedic was a gem. Chad and I chatted all through the assessment, at times laughing. As far as I know, I never lost consciousness or went into shock. I was, and did, carry on normal conversation. I could sense a heightened anxiety from the first responders. This was, after all, "one of their own"—something they didn't know until they arrived on the scene. I was determined to keep it as light as possible for them. They had enough pressure on them already.

Chad was wonderful, his voice calm and steady, yet firm when need be. As they began to assess the situation, I heard a voice I recognized. Straining to look up, without moving my head or neck, I made eye contact with Joe, the officer on duty. It was the first eye contact I'd made with anyone. It was in those kind blue eyes, looking back at me, that I knew. It was going to take a miracle if I was to survive.

"Sheila, we're gonna have to cut your jacket off," said Chad.

"NO! Don't cut the coat! I can move my arms. It's a 100 year anniversary Harley Davidson leather riding coat. DON'T CUT THE COAT!" I yelled.

"We have to cut the coat. We can't allow you to move," replied Chad.

"Well, then at least cut it on the seams!" I responded. (I figured if they did, my talented girlfriend could put it back together for me.)

Yeah, apparently my request was unrealistic. They cut the coat...into pieces!

Next, Chad said to me, "Sheila, we're gonna have to cut your top off."

"Of course you are. It's new, not to mention my new favorite."

At that point, I'm thinking I sure hope that's all they cut off.

Chad was in control, doing his thing. The other first responders created a team effort around us.

Chad said, "Sheila, we've got to cut off your chaps."

With a razzing attitude, I replied, "Of course you do. You realize they have zippers ALL the way down them, right?"

Yep! You guessed it. My leather chaps became scrap leather.

Please let me make one thing perfectly clear. I have the utmost respect, admiration, and love for all civil service personnel. Especially these fellows. My razzing them was to help lighten the extremely tense moment, for all of us.

Picture this: I was in the middle of one of the busiest intersections of the city, surrounded by dozens of personnel, many of whom I knew well. All the while, I was half naked!

"Sheila? We're gonna have to cut your jeans off," said Chad.

((SILENCE))

Umm...do I tell him now or let it be a surprise?

Going with option A, I whispered "Ahh, Chad? This may not be the best time to tell you this, but...I'm goin' commando."

He looked at me for a moment, then chuckled. Fearing that my previous attempts at "keeping things light" may have caught up with me, I whispered again, with a serious tone, "Chad? I'm NOT kidding."

Thank God, at that very moment, the Good Lord revealed to Chad the need to cut my jeans off was far from necessary. Truth be told, I later discovered, Chad heard a silent voice specifically instructing him not to move my legs. If they had removed the jeans, or straightened out my legs, I'd have bled out at the scene of the accident. My femoral artery had been severed, and the twisting of the tight denim jeans in multiple compound fractures of the femur created natural tourniquets.

Isn't it cool how God uses even the simplest of things, in the worst tragedies for good?

All Is Calm...

I felt a strange sensation in my legs—like someone poured hot molten lava down them. Oddly, it wasn't painful. It was almost soothing as I started feeling very cold all of a sudden.

I had the first of many miraculous encounters from God, that beautiful fall night, at the scene of the accident.

As I lay on the pavement with the first responders working around me, the most amazing peace came over me. I don't recall the exact time frame, and quite frankly, it doesn't matter. I've learned that God's clock is beyond my comprehension. In one way, it was as if time stood still. Yet, in another way, it felt like a parallel universe. Please know, I've prayed fervently about sharing my spiritual journey with others through this book. This part of my journey is the greatest gift I've ever received. I pray that my feeble attempt at putting it to written word touches your soul.

In the midst of the chaos around me, I felt my body being cradled. I, Sheila, a horrific sinner by all standards, with a mangled body, lay in the middle of an intersection in the gentle, loving arms of God. He chose to be with me. He loved me enough, even at my very worst, to cradle me in His arms—His comforting arms.

I wish I could describe it, so you'd know, truly know, how it feels to be in the arms of God. As a child, think of a special person who loved you no matter what. Who gave the best hugs ever. Who was always there for you. Whom you felt safe in their arms. As a parent, there's no way in this world you'd let anyone or anything harm your precious child. Multiply that to infinity and beyond and you'll just barely grasp what it feels like to be held in the arms of God. It's an endless love like nothing we can imagine. An indescribable intimacy in the depth of your being.

I looked up as far as my eyes would allow. There was the most vibrant, fluttering blue I'd ever seen. A color of radiant blue that we don't have the words to describe. In an effort to help you understand the depth of this color, maybe this will help.

There's a beautiful, bright, almost iridescent blue butterfly: the blue morpho butterfly. When the sun hits it, the shimmering blue is beyond magnificent. Multiply that to infinity and beyond, and you'll barely grasp what it feels like to be surrounded by the Holy Spirit. The color that radiated above and around me makes the stunning blue morpho butterfly look like horse manure. I wish our language had the words to describe the vibrant, glorious color that surrounded me that night. It's a color so warm and comforting, yet so bright and calming. The atmosphere was beyond peaceful. I will never forget it!

I felt a gentle, yet intentional, touch on my right forearm. When I looked up, my eyes met the most compassionate eyes I'd ever seen— deep, beautiful, warm, loving, forgiving, caring, compassionate eyes. Eyes that held a depth so deep there was no need for words. I knew I'd met my Savior, Jesus Christ.

All Fear Was Gone…

The kindest voice spoke to me in a southern drawl, because He knows that's what I understand.

"Honey, there's nothing to fear. We've got this. You're gonna be okay."

I couldn't take my eyes off His face. He was so calm, so peaceful and SO loving. While kneeling beside me, with His left hand still on my forearm, He slowly raised his right hand upwards towards the heavens.

My mind told me, "Yes! I'm going home. They've come to take me to heaven. I can't believe it. Yes!"

Just as Jesus' arm stretched out above Him, I heard "whop-whop-whop-whop-whop-whop…"

It was the greatest God encounter of my life. Some folks may question or doubt my experience and that's okay. All I know is no one will ever convince me otherwise. God, Jesus, and the Holy Spirit are real. They do exist, and they're still performing miracles every day. I should know…I'm one of them.

It can't be measured or explained… it must be experienced.

"Sheila, it won't be much longer. We're waiting for the ambulance to arrive, so it can transport you to where the Life Flight chopper is waiting," said Chad.

By the way…there was no record of a call to Life Flight! They just happened to be in the area! They just happened to be empty! They just happened to be a trauma crew! They just happened to be female nurses on board, (remember I was commando under those jeans?) and they just happened to land without being dispatched! I don't care who you are, there's no "just happening" in any part of that. God orchestrated every single part of the plan!

To this day, the sound of a helicopter warms my heart to its core. I've become pretty skilled at pinpointing which chopper it is by each distinctive sound—be it media, military, or medical helicopter—it's always a kiss blown and a prayer lifted for the last two.

With all the commotion and chaos, we didn't know it or realize it, but for Life Flight to have arrived before an ambulance was not normal procedure.

"Sheila, the ambulance has arrived. I'll stay right with you. I'll make sure you get loaded into the ambulance, and I'll ride with you to the helicopter," said Chad.

Chad was awesome! True to his word, he stayed by my side, talking to me the entire time. The paramedics in the ambulance arrived with the gurney. Once locked and loaded, Chad explained to me what to expect next. The ambulance ride wasn't far. A few blocks, maybe. Several intersections in and around the scene had been shut down, causing traffic to back up making it difficult for the chopper to land any closer.

Time out. The two medics in the ambulance were a hoot! One was behind the wheel, the other in the back with Chad and I. Chad was respectful of the professional boundaries. He'd speak to me, but not interrupt or interfere with the two in the ambulance. The situation turned comical. These two fellas were fussing (for those who may not know, that's southern for bickering) at each other about how to get to the chopper. I felt like I'd stepped into the middle of an *Odd Couple* episode.

"If you'd just pull forward a bit you could turn around."

"I'm going to back up this way and then get turned around."

"It'd be faster and easier to pull forward. There's more room than to back up your way."

"Who's driving? You or me?"

I wanted to giggle over these two, but thought it best to pay attention to Chad.

Little did Oscar and Felix realize, they would not only lay a foundation for my recovery but also they'd later play a key role in my journey.

I knew the moment the ambulance doors were open. The wind sound was deafening.

My body never experienced pain that night. It's amazing how the brain can flip a switch to protect oneself, yet turn other sensors way up.

My sensory nervous system was running at lightning speed.

At the scene of the accident, I could taste the road. It was nasty! Mind you, neither my mouth nor my tongue ever touched the ground, but I tasted dirt, dust, road oil, gasoline, tar, and something that tasted like what you'd think a dead animal would taste like. Disgusting!

And the smells! Pee-yew! I smelled many of the same smells that I tasted, but they were stronger. I could also smell all the medical stuff the guys were using—different material smells, but I mostly smelt strong plastic and medicinal smells.

The accident occurred at about 8:30 pm, so it was dark outside, yet it seemed extremely bright to me. The lights from the fire trucks, the police cars, and the intensively bright spot lights set up all around the crash site were blinding. The interior ambulance lights? Wow! One could do surgery on an ant inside one of those things, it was so bright.

Before the first responders arrived, I didn't want anyone touching me. I remember repeatedly yelling "Don't touch me!" I wonder if the gloves the first responders wore blocked the horrific nerve pain I previously felt when others touched me with skin-to-skin contact?

I'm not a medical scholar, so I have no idea how or why my sensory nervous system was in hyper mode. Maybe it was the lateral whiplash on the other driver's car windshield? Maybe it was the blunt impact trauma to my head when I hit the pavement after being airborne? Maybe it was because my legs had been mutilated? Who knows? Whatever it was, it was very strange and very real.

Between the gusts of the chopper blades and the roaring of the engine, I thought I was headed into a tornado when the ambulance doors opened.

"Sheila, it's really loud," said Chad. "We're taking you to the helicopter. I can't go any farther. Don't worry. They'll take great care of you. You're gonna be okay."

Ya know, I never felt a bump or a single jarring during any of the transfers. Not from the pavement to the back board, not from the backboard to the gurney, not from loading the gurney into the ambulance, not from unloading the gurney from the ambulance, and not from the gurney into the helicopter. Maybe it was because I couldn't feel pain. No, that wasn't it. My sense of touch was extremely heightened. These guys were simply perfect at their profession.

Once in the helicopter, the atmosphere took a huge turn. Within seconds, literally less than three or four seconds, the gurney was secure, the engine got louder, and my bra was cut off me as the chopper blades went faster. All of a sudden, something very warm and soothing invaded my body.

Everything went black.

Life, as I knew it, ceased to exist.

Chapter Three

Time, for me, stopped on September 29, 2011, at 8:30 pm. It would take years before I'd have the chance to restart it.

~ ~ ~

"Is she going to die?"

"Will she bleed out before they get her to the hospital?"

"Is she paralyzed?"

"Will she ever walk again?"

"Does she have head/brain trauma?"

"What about internal injuries?"

All the answers would come, but it would take days, weeks, months…even years.

~ ~ ~

I was life-flighted to the world-renowned Vanderbilt Hospital in Nashville, Tennessee. I was later told, in that short flight—less than 20 miles, I stopped breathing, and had to be intubated for life-giving resuscitation. My body had finally gone into shock.

The incredible emergency room staff at Vanderbilt hospital quickly went to work assessing my injuries and immediate needs: tests, scans, X-rays, paging the trauma surgeons, etc. Friends began to gather with my husband in a private waiting area. "Private," in this case, meant we don't know if she's going to make it or not waiting area.

After the trauma surgeon on call that night completed his initial assessment of my compound injuries, he went to the private waiting area to speak with my husband.

"We have some good news. There's no sign of head trauma or internal injuries. However, the bilateral (both legs) compound femur fractures are life threatening. If she makes it through this first surgery, she has a very long road ahead of her with many more surgeries. This first surgery is critical in saving her life. Would you like to see her, briefly, while I get prepped for surgery?"

My husband said yes. Looking to Tammy, he asked her to go with him.

With each step, toward the ICU pre-op holding room, my husband and Tammy tried to prepare themselves for what could be their final goodbyes, neither of them quite knowing how emotional it would become.

~ ~ ~

"Stop!"

"Stop yelling!"

"Don't touch me!"

"Get out of my face!"

"I can't see!"

"Stop touching me!"

"Must you keep yelling?!"

"Stop shaking me!"

"Please, just leave me alone!"

I can't feel anything.

"Oh, God!"

"Where am I?"

"Who keeps talking?" They're making my head pound.

"Please, make them stop!"

Someone was holding my left hand, squeezing so tight, it hurt. I tried to pull away. I tried to block the blurred images that kept hovering over me. No one was listening to me. I kept yelling for them, whoever "them" were, to leave me alone. It's as if no one could hear me. There was activity all around me—super bright lights, machines blinking, humming and clicking, bodies moving around, and the smell —disgusting! Had I been kidnapped and drugged? What is wrong with me? Why can't I move? Why can't I speak?

Oh God, please help me.

~ ~ ~

"Back away, give her some space." I heard a soft but firm female voice say, "Sheila, it's Tam. Can you hear me?" as she gently touched my right hand. "If you can hear me, squeeze my hand," she said.

Nothing.

Tammy later shared with me, "I was freaking out, but I knew I couldn't let it show. That's not Sheila. Those aren't Sheila's eyes. Oh, God, is this it? Is she gone from us?"

"If you're in pain, squeeze my hand," said Tammy.

With resistance, due to the cervical immobilizer, I slowly shook my head "No."

My eyebrows furrowed. Apparently, that was the only thing on my body that worked.

"Don't get so close to her. I think it's too much for her." Tammy said to my husband.

"I'm not leaving," he replied.

My brows again furrowed.

Tammy whispered into my ear still holding onto my hand, "Are you okay?"

I wiggled my hand free from hers as I frantically, with deep intensity, began to sign into her palm.

"Slow down," Tammy said aloud, "start over and go slow."

I began, slowly, but with full intention, or as she describes it, "with great force," finger spelling "W-H-A-T-S W-R-O-N-G."

I'd taken an introduction to American Sign Language course years before, though I'd never used it until that night. To be honest, I don't know that I even knew the entire "sign" alphabet. Tammy? She didn't know sign language either. She'd learned the alphabet as a kid, but remembered very little of it. Somehow, some way, she knew what I was spelling in the palm of her hand.

"What's wrong?" she asked.

Again, Tammy leaned down near my right ear and whispered, "Honey, you've been in a really bad motorcycle accident. You're in the hospital. You do not have any head trauma or internal injuries. Your legs are mangled, but you're gonna be okay."

Tammy watched my face, and especially my brows, for my response.

Knowing can be a huge part of any battle for me. If I can wrap my head around the facts and marinate on them for a bit, I can usually get through it. Hearing from a dear and trusted friend, "you're gonna be okay," gave me the confirmation I desperately needed in that moment.

Calm settled over me.

I don't remember every detail of every situation throughout my journey, especially those first few days. The recollection of those who were there, combined with the daily journaling I did for several years after the accident, have helped piece the story together.

Before leaving me, for the trauma team to begin the first of many surgeries, my husband was handed a bag. In it contained the remainder of my clothing that the emergency room crew removed from my body upon arrival.

Back in the private waiting room, overcome with grief and shock, my husband lost it.

"Where're her rings?"

"She had two rings. They're not in here!"

"She had a wedding ring and an antique ring. Did one of the nurses take them?"

I can't imagine what all he was experiencing in that moment. First, he saw, live and in person, his wife of over 20 years go through a movie scene like that out of a deadly James Bond film. Then, he saw the gruesome injuries up close and personal while he waited on the first responders. And now, he'd just come from what he thought was his final goodbye.

Always level headed in a crisis, Tammy says, "Here, give me the bag. I'll check the pocket of her jeans. Maybe she took them off before riding."

Taking the bag of clothes, reaching in, she easily found the pocket of my jeans. Sliding her hand into the pocket, she felt something wet. Slowly, in horror, she pulled her hand out. It was covered in blood. Not wanting to further stress out the others in the room, Tammy quickly grabbed another friend, and carrying the bag of clothes with them, they found a restroom. After washing and drying her hands, Tammy put on a pair of plastic gloves. She slowly removed the blood-filled, ripped, scissor-cut jeans and laid them on the floor. She laid them out and opened the pant leg that had been scissor-cut by the hospital staff. Amongst the blood saturated denim and flesh that looked like raw hamburger meat, was what she described as 'an explosion of chunky white glitter'.

My other girlfriend, in the restroom with Tammy, kept repeating "Oh, God! Oh, God! Oh, God!"

Flabbergasted, Tammy tried to wrap her brain around it all. 'How can this be? What kind of impact must that have been for Sheila's bones to literally shatter like this?'

They never found the rings.

The only thing I would eventually come home from the hospital with would be a tiny, manila envelope about the size of a business card.

In it contained…a beautiful pair of sapphire blue earrings that I'd been wearing the night of the accident.

Life or Death…

The first surgery lasted roughly eight hours. The surgical trauma team, led by Dr. Manish Sethi, did all they could do at that point to stabilize my life-threatening injuries. The next forty-eight hours were critical. Fear of infection, continued blood loss, persistently low blood pressure combined with my body constantly fighting against the pain, created an atmosphere of looming death for family and friends both near and far.

What I remember most of the next few days was a feeling of nothingness. I don't know if the medical team kept my body in a semi-comatose state, or if my body chose it voluntarily. I didn't want to do anything, and I mean anything. I had no desire to live or breathe let alone open my eyes. Communication of any kind was out of the question. I could hear activity around me. Sometimes it would be so loud and intense I'd want to yell "Go away and leave me be!" Sometimes, though, it'd be so quiet and still I wasn't sure where I was. It was a weird feeling being so far removed mentally from my body. It's hard to explain. The entire situation was extremely unfamiliar to me. That, in itself, brought about its own fear, anxiety, frustration, confusion, despair, heartache, indifference, loss, etc. I was mentally and emotionally beyond overwhelmed. I no longer cared. More than that, I didn't really know that I no longer cared. Looking back, I realize my brain shut down in many ways. Not because of injury or damage, but because of its innate protection mechanism. God created our brains to automatically know when to block out pain be it physical, mental, or emotional—or in my case, all three combined.

There would come a time when the horrors of my accident would be revealed to me. Like all the trauma to my physical body, the extensive trauma to me mentally and emotionally would take weeks, months, and years to recover from.

A couple of days later, they removed the breathing tube. That, in itself, was overwhelming—not because it hurt to remove it, but because now everyone would expect me to participate in the chaos around me. I'm not sure I was ready to participate or converse with anyone, and I sure wasn't ready to make logical decisions. That first step of engaging was tough. I'm so very grateful for those who stepped in for me. Between my husband and two dear friends, Tammy and Tiffany (TNT), among others who never left my side, I didn't have to engage much. They took care of everything.

When TNT are combined, these two incredible women are beyond explosive—all in a good way! They don't let obstacles or walls stop them from doing what's right. I wouldn't be alive today without them. One or both of them, along with my husband, routinely became my advocate, nurse mate, organizer, liaison, confidant, encourager, cheerleader, joke teller, memory maker, beautician, body bather, clothes dresser, personal shopper, prayer warrior, and overall self-sacrificer.

My time in the ICU Pit, a medical term for the most intensive of ICU, as well as my time in the ICU Step Down Units were the most emotionally challenging for my husband, parents, and girlfriends. They never knew, literally, from minute to minute, if I'd survive.

~ ~ ~

Pain. Horrific pain. Unbearable pain. Never-ending pain. Why-couldn't-I-have-died pain.

I was given regular, routine high doses of oral narcotics every few hours. Plus, they had an IV pain pump attached to me so I could self-administer additional IV opioid doses every ten minutes. It still barely touched the excruciating pain. I couldn't understand why they couldn't stop the horrific pain. Everyone tried, but we quickly realized overcoming pain would turn out to be my greatest battle.

Please don't misunderstand me. I'm no sissy when it comes to pain tolerance. I've had dental work without Novocain, I've had stitches without numbing agents, and I've had slivered glass in my eye. I was in the best physical shape of my life—power walking four to six miles every day at eleven- to twelve-minute miles, including hills. I was far from a wimp.

When I was flown into Vanderbilt Hospital, the team of specialists would discover a lower left leg amputation held on by a very small piece of skin and one visceral artery, multiple compound fractures in both femurs, multiple breaks to the left tibia and fibula, and a crushed right knee. Plus, extensive vascular and soft tissue damages on both legs from the hips down.

The massive, multiple, compound orthopedic, vascular, and extensive soft tissue damages were beyond the 1 to 10 pain scale. By the way, I hate that scale. To me, it's not logical or accurate, and definitely not effective. For those who've never experienced the modern day medical survey question: "On a scale of 1 to 10, how do you rate your pain?" let me just say, in my experience, it's the most inconsistent tool to be used in the medical field. My 1 may be your 10. And, for the nurse or practitioner who's determining the pain medication dosage, my 10 may be their 1. Unless there's some routine and consistency throughout the patient scenario, it's totally ineffective. In my experience, in a high trauma injury situation, within a 24/7 hospital environment where staff changes take place several times a day and several times throughout the week, it's extremely difficult to maintain any level of consistency, let alone create a standard of 1 to 10 pain scale for each individual patient. I'm not sure what the solution is. Maybe one day there'll be a device that actually measures each patient's pain level.

Please know, I'm beyond grateful for each and every person who was, and is, a part of my medical team. There were dozens and dozens of gifted, talented, and caring professionals along my journey. I thank God for each and every one of them.

The battle to stay ahead of the pain was constant. It didn't take long for that battle to become a full-blown war. The enormous amounts of opioids, oral and IV, combined with the constant IV antibiotics wreaked havoc on my digestive system.

Chapter Four

Let the Game Begin...

My loyal crew, my husband, and TNT, took the challenge to find something—anything—that I could eat and enjoy. I had zero appetite and even less chance for food to taste good. Remember, my senses were on overdrive (which included the taste and smell of food). Absolutely nothing appealed to me.

Friends were cute.

"How about a milkshake?"

"What about pizza? Yum!"

"You love grilled chicken. I could go get you a grilled chicken salad, yes?"

"Wait! I know. You never turn down Mexican food. What would you like?"

Bless them! They could have gone through the entire food chain, in every possible combination, and nothing would have sounded good.

My body began to shut down. My heart rate dropped. My blood pressure plummeted. Light headedness turned into mild blackouts. Soon, my speech slurred. Then everything went black.

I'd later learn that I'd been losing blood. Not sure where I lost it. I don't remember bleeding anywhere. Maybe my body was using/absorbing it? Who knows? Low blood levels would be yet another battle in the war to survive.

If you're a blood donor, or if you donated blood in my name, God bless you! Blood is life. The average adult human body has six to eight pints of blood. Over the course of my recovery, I'd receive enough donated blood to fill four adults. I believe that those who donate blood do it out of compassion and kindness for others. There's got to be a depth of love within each donor to give so unselfishly. I also believe that such love, compassion, and unselfishness is passed on through their gift of life-giving blood. Our local American Red Cross was flooded with blood donations in my name. Some have reported that it was a record for local donations. Regardless, this recipient is eternally grateful for your love and kindness.

Round Two...

The second surgery would be five days later, on an early Tuesday morning. This would be a "twofer," two surgeries back-to-back. First, they'd go in and check the left femur where they'd rebuilt it from the hip down with interior-bone, titanium rods. Then, they'd de-breed the dead and dying tissue on the lower left leg. They'd also install a "wound vac"—a medical machine designed to pull out excess fluid in hopes of reducing further infection. Staying on top of infection was my trauma team's number one priority. One of the best ways to do that was to continually clean out/remove any dead/dying tissue and pockets of infection that kept pooling up.

Debridement was painful. It was raw, scary, and a battle that was ongoing for me. I knew it was serious, not to mention life-threatening, when the infectious disease specialist got the CDC (Center for Disease Control) involved.

My body was fighting so many different infections at the same time that we didn't know if I would survive. There were common infections they could identify: skin, blood, staff, etc. The hardest ones to identify were those I tagged "roadkill infection." Scientists and researchers were frantically trying to determine what infections I had. Time was of the essence, and the sooner we knew what we were dealing with, the better they would know how to fight/treat it. The science of medicine can often be a practice of elimination—determining what it is not. Well, apparently when it comes to "roadkill infection" it's a long list of what nots. Think about it. On any open road you could have dead animals, bird droppings, untold numbers of things tracked on the road via tires and/or animals, trash, food rubbish, settled air pollutants, animal waste, or human spit, to name several. No wonder they called in the CDC for help.

Fighting infection was one battle. Treating it was another. Beating infection requires a clean, healthy source. Every moment was a battle for my body. I struggled with intense pain, very little productive sleep, poor nutrition due to absolutely no appetite, almost no circulation as I couldn't move from the waist down, and dangerously low vitals and blood levels. Having just one of these inhibits healthy healing. Having all of these makes it nearly impossible.

The first time I remember opening my eyes and seeing my legs all I could think was, *I look like a mummy—a really swollen mummy—and why are there two long pieces of re-bar bolted to the outside of my right leg from my upper thigh to just above my ankle?*

After taking post-op X-rays of the right leg, my awesome orthopedic trauma surgeon said he was very pleased to see how my femur went back together.

Unfortunately, his next sentence wasn't as welcoming. "It'll be at least three months before you can put any weight on it."

"What? Three months? That was supposed to be my good leg!" I replied.

Dr. Sethi showed us the post-op X-rays. WOW! It looked like someone had dumped a can of screws into my right knee. Plus, there was a long plate and several more screws holding my femur together. Apparently, that re-bar bolted to the bone on the outside of my right leg was a stabilizer until the bones grew back and held together on the inside.

It had been a week since the accident. I became more and more aware of life around me. Well, as much life as there is in a hospital room. The battle to stay ahead of the pain never stopped. The fight to win over infection was relentless. The never-ending nausea and lack of appetite remained. Nights got very, very long and extremely lonely. The days were filled with various kinds of physical therapy training, working on things as simple as learning to sit up and learning to dress without moving from the hips down. Both were agonizing and frustrating.

What an infant or a toddler could do without much thought, I had to retrain myself how to do. One would think it would be easy. The hard part wasn't the relearning. It was learning to do a previously mindless task that now had to be done in a whole new way. Once I wrapped my head around that new concept, things got a little easier. Most of the time, I'd let my creative side come up with a fun way of tackling what needed to be relearned, challenging myself to do more the next time: more reps, longer times, etc.

With the use of a handy, long-handled, grippy thing and a way too baggy pair of shorts, I managed to dress myself. Nothing stylish or feminine, but I was getting the job done. Most of the time, I didn't waste my time with shorts unless the physical therapists were coming in for a session to practice transfers. Before the accident, I had no idea what a transfer was. At that stage of rehabilitation, for me, it sounded pretty simple. "Sheila, we're going to practice transfers today. You're going to learn how to transfer from the hospital bed to the bedside potty," the therapist said.

Always eager to do what I can, I replied, "Okay, let's do it!"

How hard could it be to slide from one to the other? I thought to myself. Oh, my gosh! I quickly learned why there were two therapists. Any movement I made had to be done strictly with just my upper body. My legs had to remain perfectly still and straight out in front of me. I looked like a 90° angle all the time. When I slept I wasn't much more than 100°–110°. It would take years before I could sleep stretched out, let alone on my side. Even now, I can only sleep on my right side. After much sweat and a few tears, I finally made it to the bedside potty...backwards!

That's right. I learned to do a backwards transfer. Sounds advanced, huh? Hardly. Basically, using only my upper body, I'd hand-walk myself backwards to a perpendicular position on the hospital bed. Once that was complete, I'd wipe the sweat from my hands, then continue hand-walking backwards until I reached the bedside potty.

Oh, sorry. I forgot to mention, someone would have to first place the bedside potty perpendicular to the bed, lock it in place, and then stand behind it so I wouldn't tip it backwards. My core center was off a bit in the beginning. Have you ever tried going to the bathroom with both of your legs sticking straight out in front of you while sitting in a 90° angle? Try doing it without leaning back. It's not as easy as one might think. Great core workout, though.

Next came the tough part. Hand-walking back into bed, feet first. Not easy. We eventually learned to raise the bed a couple of inches past the bedside potty when going in reverse—hand-walking backwards to the potty. Then, we'd lower the bed a couple of inches below the potty, getting back into bed. I never imagined I'd cry so hard from going to the bathroom. Many times those tears would be from pain and exhaustion. Pain was constant. Add movement and the pain levels rose considerably. Sometimes pain would hang around at a level 7 or 8. Occasionally, it would drop to a level of 5 or 6, but mostly the pain would stay at level 10–12 on a scale of 1–10. There were tears of joy from simple successes too. I was a quick learner. Knowing it could take ten minutes or more, literally, to get to the bedside potty, I learned quickly that when the urge hit, there was no time for dawdling.

Next, the physical therapist wanted me to learn transfers into a wheelchair. That was a bit more challenging. Initially we did bed to wheelchair transfers similar to the perpendicular potty transfers. However, that meant that the therapists had to hold my legs, one on each leg, while a third person gently eased the wheelchair backwards until the therapists holding my legs would rest my legs on the wheelchair leg risers that had been fitted with soft pillows. In time, I'd worked up to sitting in a wheelchair for an hour or so a day. It sounds simple enough, but I'd hurt and hurt through that hour. Not sure if the movement caused circulation to stir up nerve pain or infection to shift during the movement. Whatever it was, it was extremely painful.

I'd soon master the bedside potty as well as wheelchair transfers in a quicker time frame than expected. Maybe not with grace and poise, but it would be effective nonetheless.

My reward? Sunshine.

Sunshine...

Folks who know me well, know I LOVE sunshine. My body craves it. I'm prone to S.A.D. (Seasonal Affective Disorder) in the dreary, grey months of winter. Light therapy boxes and a trip or two to the beach during the winter months get me through.

It was a gorgeous, sunny fall day outside, and I couldn't wait to be out in it. I was exhausted from yet another wheelchair transfer, but hopeful that some all-natural Vitamin D would be worth it. Oddly enough, leaving the safety of my hospital room for the first time was a bit scary. Sensing my anxiety, my husband slowly wheeled me outside. I could feel every tiny variation in the floor as we made our way to the elevator and then outside. As soon as I felt the sun on my face, big crocodile tears began to fall. I remember thinking, *I'm gonna be okay, not sure when or how, but I will eventually be okay.* That was definitely a breakthrough moment for me.

Within mere minutes, sensory overload kicked in. As people walked by I could smell their deodorant, body soap, lotions, foot spray, sweat, bad breath, perfumes, leather shoes, starch in clothing, ladies makeup, etc. All the intense odors heightened the already pain filled legs. It had only been ten minutes but I had to get back to my room—pronto!

Recess was over.

~ ~ ~

My number one goal over the next few days was to conquer the checklist of functions I'd need to do for myself in order to be released from the hospital and go to Stallworth Rehabilitation Center. My orthopedic trauma team continued to daily monitor my injuries. We—the orthopedic resident, my husband and I—would take a photo of my lower left leg and send it to my lead orthopedic trauma surgeon for his evaluation. He was so good about staying on top of the infection. He used the phrase "cautiously optimistic" a lot.

A "suck it up buttercup" family environment taught me to do all I could to see past the pain as if pain were temporary, and the faster I figured out how to get through it, the faster I'd stop hurting. I won't say that particular mindset wasn't beneficial in my recovery. However, it was really tough to stay in that frame of mind when dealing with multiple, compounded, pain-filled situations. It didn't take me long to learn the difference between bone pain, muscle pain, joint pain, surgical pain, infection pain, or nerve pain. (The last two being the worst and most consistent for me.) Combine all of them together and it becomes a tough war to win.

Graduation Day…

Ever the over achiever, I managed to conquer all the requirements to make the move to the rehabilitation facility much faster than the physical therapists expected. We didn't have to go far. It was basically across the street. I'd soon learn how comforting the term "location, location, location" would become.

The move was exhausting—physically, mentally, and emotionally exhausting. I was excited, which made me eager to take the next step on my road to recovery. A huge benefit in my rehabilitation was that, prior to the accident, I was in the best physical shape of my life. As a matter of fact, I was registered to compete in my first ever half marathon. Sadly, the accident occurred nine days before the race. I don't remember who, but someone picked up my race packet and brought it to me. I still have the bright lime green running shirt in my closet. It's a bittersweet reminder of a past life.

The staff at Stallworth Rehabilitation Center were very kind. I liked their process of a detailed schedule. It made this li'l organizer girl very happy. The goal was for me to rehab extensively for ten to fourteen days so I could go home. I like goals. I like a schedule for tasks. I like an organized system, and, I loved that there wasn't a CNA (certified nursing assistant) or an RN (registered nurse) coming in every hour, all through the night. Ahh…rest.

It was also the first time my husband, family, or friends couldn't stay the night. They had strict visiting hours. I liked that too. Please don't misunderstand me. I loved having visitors. It was my connection to the outside world, but I was tired. I worked hard all day with four to five therapy sessions, never stopped hurting, and rarely slept more than a couple of hours at a time. A little down time was necessary. The rehab's goal and my goal were the same—focus. Do the work and go home!

While at Stallworth Rehabilitation Center, I had to wear real clothes. No more gowns allowed. Sounds like a good thing? Well…it should have been. However, for me, "clothing optional" became my new slogan. Initially, I didn't completely realize what I was doing. One of the side effects of the pain medications was dramatically increased body temperature—without warning! While in a private hospital room, where the door was usually closed because of my high risk for infection, I'd strip off my gown, toss the sheet aside, and grab a hand fan. It didn't matter who was in the room. I was on fire and needed to cool off right then and there.

Things were a bit different at Stallworth Rehab. For one, I shared a room. Two, the door was always open. Three, a continuous line of staff and guests paraded up and down the hall outside our open door all day long. Lastly, my bed was next to a wall of windows (yay sunlight) that looked out onto a busy street and sidewalk. You know it's bad when a nurse says to you, "Oh, I know you. You're the stripper!"

Apparently, my 'stripping' wasn't limited to strictly interior locations. Cheri, a sweet friend of mine, later shared her 'stripper' story with me:

> I went to visit Sheila the day she was being transferred to Stallworth Rehabilitation. After leaving the nurses station where they told me Sheila had been released to rehab, I walked outside and just happened to see Sheila on a gurney. It was a beautiful, sunny day, and Sheila was really soaking it all in.
>
> I spoke to Sheila, and she acknowledged me. However, I don't think she really knew what all was going on. Without notice or warning, Sheila removed the blanket and sheet

covering her. She didn't stop there. She started taking off her gown saying she was burning up.

Being a retired nurse, I knew the signs. No need to argue or fight with her. I did my best to keep her covered as I distracted her with random conversation until the ambulance arrived. Sheila is one very impressionable friend!

~ ~ ~

Up to that point, my husband and my girlfriends did all the status updates on social media and the Caring Bridge sites for me. Not until writing this book did I learn that the very first blog update from me, directly, would be the following:

Tuesday, October 11, 2011
Praying for 'Wonder Woman' strength…

Good Morning!

Please let me start by saying how grateful I am for the outpouring of love, support, and prayers from each and every one of you. I am SO tremendously blessed! Next I probably need to make note of what I refer to as my "Narcotic Disclaimer."

As most of you know, it's rare for me to take an aspirin. So, needless to say, the effect of the pain killers on me can be quit amusing. I'd like to apologize, up front, if I say or do something that's offensive to anyone. With that said, the upside of the drugs have given others great amusement. Apparently I've recreated some of the English language (I am not surprised!). What I didn't know was that the pain killers cause my body temp to rise, sometimes rather quickly. What's the problem with that, you ask?

Well…I became a bit of an exhibitionist and peeled off ALL clothing without warning or notice—and without regard to who's around. This is where I pause and apologize to anyone who's had to witness that. Sorry, Mom. I know you raised me better. I promise, it's the drugs. I love you all! Sheila

~ ~ ~

All in all, my first day at rehab went well. The therapists were pleasantly surprised at how much I could do, complementing me on my strength and determination. My upper body strength developed quickly while still in the hospital. I awoke from the first surgery with a trapeze bar above my head. If I wasn't already using my hands to move about the bed, or if I wasn't asleep, I'd practice pulling my full body weight up via the trapeze bar above me. It didn't matter if I was in pain. Once I realized the pain was a given, that it would be constant no matter what I did, I had to find a place deep within myself and push through it.

Speaking of pain, I had, yet again, another setback with pain medications after my first day of rehab therapy. Fortunately, they were able to remedy the issue fairly quickly. They also started me on a regimen of Pregabalin, a drug designed to effect the chemistry in the brain that sends pain signals throughout the nervous system. They said it would take about three days for the drug to make an impact. The seventy-two hour countdown was on.

Sadly, the lower left leg wasn't looking good. The skin and tissue all around the calf and shin were dying. We knew there was a razor-thin battle line drawn between old tissue dying off and new cell growth trying to take its place. My constant prayer was: *Please Lord, more new healthy cell growth under all that which was dying, and please no more infection.*

As I worked as hard as I could in rehab, several teams were volunteering their time and talents to rehab our home. We were blessed to live in an open floor plan, one level, ranch-style home. However, there were steps getting into the house. Knowing that I'd be wheelchair bound, we needed to find a way to have a ramp entrance built and a roll-in shower configured in our master bathroom.

Our local community went above and beyond. Volunteers, craftsmen, vendors, and businesses donated time, materials, and discounts to have these two projects completed. The Franklin Fire Fighters Association and the Franklin Noon Rotary Club would lead the way, succeeding in record time. They were amazing. Thank you from the bottom of my heart!

Best Therapy Ever!

My husband and I had read in the rehab center's rules and regulations that pet visits were allowed with prior approval.

"Oh, my gosh! PLEASE?!?! I so need to see my li'l Daisy!"

In reality though, we were afraid of what she might do to me in her excitement. It had been more than two weeks since I'd last seen her. She weighs about seven pounds, but she's a bundle of energy when excited. Matt, a dear friend, blessed us by moving into our home, for as long as needed, after the accident. What a gift! He took care of everything at the house, including the dogs. This gave my husband the ability to stay with me while I was in the hospital.

When they brought Daisy into the room, I cried with pure joy. She has always brightened my day. The first time I saw her after the accident was the most joy she has given me. She, too, was crying with excitement. Her tail was wagging the dog. She does this cute thing where she smiles at you when she first sees you. Sure, she's showing her teeth, but the whole time she's wagging her tail, and wiggling so much, there's no way she looks vicious. We were afraid she'd hurt my legs if she got too close to them. Her habit, at that time, was to lie on my lap, between my legs—she would not be able to do with me any longer. Y'all, I kid you not, she knew—we didn't have to train her. Never once did she touch my legs or even attempt to sit on my lap. After kissing my entire face, she lay on my left side, next to my left leg that had been horribly crushed. To this day, years and years later, she continues to do the same. Yes, she knows.

~ ~ ~

Up to this point, it had been more than two weeks since I'd showered. Not pretty. My sweet caregivers would sponge bathe me daily, which helped, but, I so wanted my hair washed! Tammy made several really comfortable all cotton headbands out of old t-shirts to keep my hair out of my face and to camouflage my pitiful lack of fashionable hair. Have y'all ever heard of a shower cap shampoo? It's about as comical and ineffective as it sounds. At least it was when TNT tried it on my head. Following the directions the nurses gave them, they warmed up the sealed bag, gently opened it, and placed the bag over my head. Next, they massaged the bag into my hair and scalp. All the while trying not to let it run into my eyes, ears or down my back.

"How's it feel?"

"Like I'm wearing a heavy, crunchy plastic bag on my head." I replied.

"Does it feel clean?"

"Hard to tell. The plastic is so thick and crunchy."

We crunched and massaged according to the directions given by the hospital staff. After removing the shampoo bag, the girls towel dried my hair. Holding their breath, they handed me a mirror. Running my hand through my hair I said "Ladies, it looks and feels worse than before we started." We all busted out laughing. They're so sweet. Neither wanted to hurt my feelings by saying the same thing.

We sat around for hours sharing our complaints and confusion about the pitiful shampoo-in-a-bag. We even asked a nurse or two about them. The nurses raved about them. Weird. Why didn't it work for me? I had rather short hair. I could see it not really working on long hair. You know that saying, "when all else fails, read the directions"? In our haste to give me clean hair and scalp, we followed the verbal directions from the staff rather than reading the written manufacturer's directions. After retrieving the used bag from the trash and reading the directions, their version of rinse-lather-repeat went like this: wet the hair/scalp with a wet towel, apply shampoo-in-a-bag, massage well, remove bag, apply clean wet towels to remove residue. Basically what we did was apply residue. No wonder my two-week-old dirty hair looked like it'd just had an oil change! The girls did their best to convince me it was their version of a hot oil hair treatment.

Learning new ways to address personal hygiene would continue to give us many challenges, test our creative skills, and make us laugh until our sides hurt.

Chapter Five

Beautiful Butterflies...

Cards, calls, emails, flowers, food baskets, and balloons arrived in abundance from friends, family, and the community. I was overcome with love and kindness from so many generous people. There was a constant recurring theme among the gifts—butterflies. Lots and lots of butterflies. There were butterflies on cards and in cards, and in floral arrangements. There were butterflies as focal points in handmade artwork sent to me from little children. There were butterflies on wrapping paper, on stationary, and on books. They were everywhere. Not that I was complaining. Heavens no. At that time, no one knew my connection to butterflies. How on earth did so many people know my deep, inner longing for the joy that came from a single butterfly? Each and every butterfly, especially the blue ones, would take me to a place I'd one day hope to share with the world.

After learning and experiencing the impact on me when I saw butterflies, Tiffany took it upon herself to find a unique butterfly to hang in my hospital room. She found the prettiest, giant, blue, three-dimensional butterfly that would travel the journey with me. It went with me from room to room to room in the hospital.

Speaking of rooms, I think I was in eight or nine different rooms throughout the hospital during my initial stay. One of the rooms we dubbed the broom closet. It was tiny. I promise you, Tammy and/or my husband would, literally, climb over the edge of my bed to get to the reclining chair so they could sit or sleep. The staff making rounds would make jokes about my "broom closet" room. I wonder if I got a discounted rate on the tiny room? Thank goodness my trauma surgeon took pity on me and helped remedy the situation. Still, regardless of the different rooms, the different floors, or the different wings in the hospital, the giant blue butterfly would be there.

God is so cool! As I'm writing, with soft instrumental music in the background and my li'l Daisy resting at my feet, I look out the windows of my office. A bright yellow butterfly dances playfully—another confirmation that I need to share my journey with the world.

Just when the caterpillar thought the world was over, she became a butterfly.

I have a serious allergy to latex and adhesives. Neither are fun when it comes to medical care. My latex allergy started years ago as strictly a topical allergic reaction. Over the years it's become a respiratory allergic reaction. Anaphylactic shock is no laughing matter. Fortunately, nowadays, most medical facilities have rid themselves of latex gloves. However, it can still remain in other medical supplies. For example, the rubber tourniquet strap used to draw blood, replace an IV, or put in a PICC line, can still contain latex. The hospital had signs on my door, on my bed and on me that stated SEVERE LATEX ALLERGY. They even had a special non-latex medical supply cart for my room.

I guess we're all creatures of habit, especially in our daily routines. Although I spent a great deal of time heavily medicated—and not always in my right mind, I recall hearing my patient advocates speak out for me on several occasions. They would need to remind staff not to use latex materials around me and to remove them from my room.

Speaking of latex—I love balloons! They're so happy and carefree. Who doesn't love them? Before people were informed of my allergy, balloons arrived for me at the hospital. The delivery would be stopped at my room door. I'd take a quick look. My heart would smile as would my face. Then they'd be carried away to the nurses station. Most floral arrangements would be treated in the same fashion. Any arrangement containing pollinating flowers would make their doorway debut, someone would take a photo and I'd usually cry happy tears. They too would go to the nurses station. It didn't take long for the nurses station to look like a floral shop.

"Wow! There's sure a lot of people who care about you," nurses commented.

That's when I decided it was time to pay-it-forward. We started asking the nursing staff, "Who needs cheering up? Which patients are without family or friends with them? Who hasn't had visitors?"

"That's so sweet!" they responded.

"It's the least I can do. Besides, I've already been blessed by seeing them. I have the cards and photos I'll forever cherish. Please distribute the arrangements to others who need a little 'happy'."

Topical adhesives are another no-no in my world. Fortunately, my allergy to adhesives isn't life threatening as latex is. However, it does leave a permanent impression on my body. In most cases, if an adhesive-backed wound dressing is left on my skin longer than an hour, the skin begins to blister and burn. It's taken years to lessen the scarring caused by the Steri-strips® used over sections of staples and stitches on my legs. Early on, the scars looked like rail road tracks down my legs. Life threatening trauma, infection, and pain are enough to battle. Add in all the residuals that occurred almost daily, and it was enough to wear anyone down.

God sees much beauty in the broken.

I'd been in the rehabilitation facility just over a week when my orthopedic trauma surgeon came in for his evaluation. Not good. The tissue, in and around the lower left leg, was dying. Have you ever seen dead or dying skin? It's grotesque! There's no better word to describe it. To look down and see most of your pale white leg below the knee in varying shades of dark grey to ash, to jet black is creepy. I needed to look at it in order to understand what was happening to my body. I didn't want to focus too much on it for fear it would mess with my head.

At that time, I don't think I realized the magnitude of my injuries and the degree of serious infection my body was fighting. I could feel my body slowing down. I thought I'd overdone it in physical therapy. I'd find out soon enough that it would be the farthest thing from what was really happening.

So long, rehab center. Back to Vanderbilt hospital and back into the operating room. Again.

That night was extremely hard. The nights were tough every night, but that night was different. My mind wouldn't stop racing. I could feel the pain getting worse. My body temperature was rising, and for the worst part, I was all alone. In the deepest part of my being, I knew I was headed towards the fight of my life.

It would be a fight I'd battle for years…

God wasn't punishing me, He was training me.

I'm not sure why, maybe because I was no longer an in-hospital patient, but when they transported me back to the hospital they had us sitting in the general waiting area with a couple of hundred other people. We waited in that general waiting area for more than four hours. The entire time I was sitting at a ninety-degree angle, in a rigid wheelchair, with both my legs sticking straight out in front of me. No food, no water (pre-op requirements). As time slowly clicked by, I felt my body get weaker and weaker. The pain medications had worn off. I could feel the infection gaining on me. That feeling of "not caring" was taking over. I was too weak, too tired, and in way too much pain to care anymore. Lord, help me!

I was finally taken to pre-op. All I could think of was "Thank God.

I can finally lie in a bed." The surgical team and I were prepped to start surgery when all of a sudden the train came to a complete stop. Someone, not sure who's responsibility it was, but someone failed to book an operating room that'd been cleared latex-free! There's a step-by-step system the hospital does to void an operating room of latex spores. It takes a while to complete the process.

What was supposed to be a morning surgery didn't start until around 6:30 pm. The infection in my body was winning, and I no longer cared.

The surgeon's post operating report confirmed what my body was telling me. The lower left leg, and now the heel too, were full of infection. The surgeon's hope was that the debridement of all the dead skin would lessen the infection pain. What he didn't really prepare me for was the intense pain from all the raw, openly exposed parts below my left knee. Basically, the only thing that remained of my lower leg was the metal that was used in the first surgery to re-attach my leg, and very little bone above it. Remember all the chunky white glitter they found in my jeans the night of the accident? That crushed section of my leg along with all the soft tissue, muscle, veins, nerves, etc., was gone. What little skin tissue I came in with the night of the accident had died from infection and was now gone.

I can't begin to describe the pain. You'd think if something had died it would no longer hurt. Sadly, the bazillion nerve endings that were severed, were now openly exposed. Their raw, tormenting pain NEVER stopped.

I was living in a hell right here on earth.

The infectious disease team, the orthopedic team, and now the plastic surgical team, was meeting to create the best plan of attack. The infection was winning. They couldn't seem to pinpoint exactly what it was. Cultures, labs, and blood were tested throughout the next day. My numbers were all over the board.

The infection was in overdrive.

Initially, the plan was another debridement surgery to remove newly formed dead skin and infection. Then, give my body three days to recover and go back into surgery again for more debridement. Unfortunately, with the infection taking over so aggressively, I'd go back to surgery less than forty-eight hours from the previous one. Their greatest fear was coming true. The infection was dangerously close to invading my bone and they had every intention of not letting that happen.

My hero and younger brother Jake is no stranger to the effects of infection on the body. He was paralyzed at nineteen from a routine dive into a familiar swimming pool. A freak accident. Too much inertia behind the dive. He dove in an athlete, and surfaced a quadriplegic. He is AMAZING! He's nothing short of a miracle. At the time of my accident, Jake had been paralyzed for over twenty years. He's taught me so much about how to handle catastrophic adversity with grace. It's not easy for either one of us. For both of us, infection can be our greatest fear. The major difference between Jake and I? He can't feel the pain, which means he may not know he has an infection until it's life threatening. Me, I felt and still feel pain…every single day.

Job Security…

On most days, either my husband or friends who came to visit were given jobs. Albeit small jobs, they were pretty much constantly on duty. Because of the depth and amount of injuries my body had endured, I rarely, if ever, could get comfortable.

My loyal and dedicated caregivers would spend day-in and day-out doing all they could to help me fight against the constant pain.

Pillows became one of our greatest tools. We had pillows under me, beside me, and around me, for support and comfort. Unfortunately, no sooner would someone get one pillow in the perfect spot when another area would hurt. There were hours on end that my husband or girlfriends wouldn't even sit down because of the constant need to adjust and re-adjust pillows. Each wanted so badly to be the one to find the perfect spot for a pillow, if only to see a brief moment of relief wash over my face. For them, that look was worth its weight in gold.

The nurses station became very familiar with my dear friend Tammy. Poor Tammy, one day she couldn't take it any longer. Watching and listening to a loved one writhe in constant pain finally took its toll on her. She promptly marched herself to the nurses station, firmly and with great authority said, "I'm here for Sheila. I don't think you understand the extent of trauma she's been through on top of the added trauma from multiple surgeries. She's GOT to have some pain relief."

A nurse replied, "Someone will be in as soon as they can."

"Great! I'm not leaving this station until they do," said Tammy as she stood her ground.

Tammy stood there, solid in her convictions. It didn't take long before she was following a nurse into my room.

I thank God for the precious gift of strong, tenacious and loving friends!

Here We Go Again...

The next debridement surgery, scheduled for the following morning, meant no food or drink after midnight. The surgery schedule also played havoc with my scheduled narcotic regimen. My body was in yet another cycle of mass confusion. After all the shuffling of my medication schedules, the surgery wasn't going to happen—"a mix up in communication among staff and scheduling," we were told.

Unfortunately, by the time we were notified, my pain was off the charts. Once again, the pain got ahead of me. When that happens, your body becomes ultra-sensitive, and the complete feeling of utter despair overcomes your mind. Since surgery wasn't happening that day, they took me for a CT scan. No big deal, right? Hardly! All the extra transfers, from beds to gurneys to tables and back again, increased my already horrific pain levels. My poor body. It was fighting between massive amounts of pain and in most moments...no longer caring if I lived or died.

Sometime during one of my transfers, my IV was compromised. The IV pain medication I was given to help "catch up" from being behind schedule never made it into my veins. So, now I was doubly behind in pain meds. The needle was still under my skin but had somehow come out of my vein. My hand and arm were swelling up with the pooling of IV medication and IV fluids just under the skin. I'm so grateful for my husband's training to see and recognize what was happening to me. He was boldly adamant that the IV needed to be addressed immediately. In a very small way, it was nice to know I wasn't completely losing my mind. I knew my pain was climbing higher and higher even after they'd given me the "catch up" dose. Disastrously, that dose was wasted. Unlike dogs, we humans must receive medications and fluids in our veins to be affective.

I'd had so many different IVs by that time that my veins were shot. Small veins, collapsed veins, and not being able to put needles in the bends of my wrists or elbows, I soon ran out of options. I even had IVs in my neck—that was creepy! Sometime during the chaos and confusion of the days crazy events, it was decided that I'd have a PICC line installed in my chest.

For those who may not know, a PICC line is a peripherally inserted central catheter. For me, it meant no more daily needles.

Of course, the PICC line had to be ordered by a physician—more hurry-up-and-wait time. More transfers, more movement, and nothing but oral pain medications that did absolutely nothing for the immense amount of pain I was in. After a day of constant moving, scans, setbacks and debacles, my body started shutting down yet again.

By nightfall I had a functionally installed PICC line and finally received heavy IV narcotics for the crazy intense pain. My blood counts plummeted yet again. Thank you, blood donors, as I needed several more units.

Back to the Operating Room I Go…

The next day I went back again to the operating room for another debridement surgery. Fortunately, that would be one surgery that wasn't too extensive. Phew! Maybe because it took most of the previous night to catch up on the fight against pain and low blood levels, or…maybe I was so worn out that a few extra hours under anesthesia helped my body rest and settle down a bit. Regardless, it was nice to have a reprieve, even if it was only temporary.

We took advantage of that reprieve with a mini spa day being brought to me. Anytime one is bed bound in the hospital like I was, creativity of any kind can make a world of difference when trying to cope. Some dear soul designed a really cool bed-bound shampoo tray, which allows the water to drain into a large trash can that's placed next to the bed. Oh, how good it felt to dig my own fingernails into my hair and scrub my scalp clean. I won't lie, it was a bit weird—lying in bed washing my hair. Loved that shampoo bed-tray contraption almost as much as I loved finally having clean hair. No more shampoo-in-a-bag for this girl. Woohoo!

The same day I was rejoicing with clean hair, we became aware of a problem with the wound-vac system. Every few hours, the liquid that my body would excrete had to be removed from the wound so that it could stay as clean as possible to avoid infection. Thank God for the wound-vac system—although, it sometimes malfunctioned—and that day was one of those days. We reported it to the nurses as soon as we discovered it. They, in turn, reported it to the doctor on call.

It was after suppertime before the on-call doctor came in to examine the wound vac and my legs. Oh, y'all, I pray you never have a doctor treat you like he treated me that night. He wasn't unethical or negligent, but rather brutally aggressive, jerking both my legs and everything around them. It takes a lot for me to cry from physical pain. In that moment, I couldn't decide if I wanted to punch him or openly cry. Not wanting him to be even more aggressive with me, though I don't know how that could have been possible, I chose the latter. Tears fell. It was a fairly good day, up to that point, in the fight against pain, but no longer.

Everything from my waist down was on fire. We begged the nurses for some kind of pain relief. Of course, their hands were tied. All they could do was to put in a request. After waiting as long as I could, my husband called my trauma surgeon and explained the situation. No sooner was he off the phone than a nurse came in with extra authorized pain medication.

I should probably clarify the pain versus prescribed narcotics. Most of my time in the hospital, I was on both oral and IV narcotics at the same time; most of the time, the dose was the maximum allowed. However, there would be several times to come when my situation would require a prescription beyond the norm. That night was one of those times, and I'm so thankful for my amazing trauma surgeon who not only trusted his own expert medical knowledge but also trusted and believed in my knowledge of my own body and what it needed.

All indications were that the teams of specialists' plan to attack the infection sooner, rather than later, turned out to be a good thing. My body was exhausted. Two surgeries in less than seventy-two hours on a body that was knocking on death's door yet again had more than taken its toll.

Nights were hard. REALLY hard. The atmosphere was so different. My husband, or whoever was staying with me, was usually fast asleep. The night nurses were much less interactive with patients than daytime nurses, so conversations were non-existent, and I don't watch television. So what's a girl to do? My mind tends to come alive when the rest of the world goes to sleep at night. All those long, lonely nights, I'd spend talking to God. I'd look at the beautiful, blue giant butterfly hanging from the ceiling, close my eyes, and drift back in time. I'd journal. Oh, how I'd journal. What a gift that would become. All night, every night, I'd fight between pain, a pain-medicated stupor, or moments of mental clarity. I'm surprised I have half a brain left.

Blessed is the one who endures trials.
—James 1:12, NIV

Treating the infections involved super strong IV antibiotics. Different antibiotics were used to treat different infections. Some worked. Some, not so much. Oh, the lovely side effects of high doses of IV antibiotics.

Ladies, many of you will be able to feel my pain with this one. I'd never, in my 46 years of life, had a yeast infection. Ever. Well, I'm here to tell you, I had a Paul Bunyan sized yeast infection. From the rounds and rounds and rounds of IV antibiotics, my body was covered in yeast from my arm pits to my knees—from the front to the back!

One more battle in the war. TNT once again stepped in. "I just knew you'd be scarred from it. It was awful. You were covered in an open skin rash. Your skin looked like raw meat it was so angry. You looked like a burn patient." Tammy said. The girls made it their mission to win the yeast infection battle. Several times a day they'd make me eat yogurt, made sure I was taking high quality probiotics and nursing my topical body rash with creams and powders. Did you know one can purchase Desitin in big tubs, rather than the standard tubes? Ask Tammy, she knows where to find it. The girls applied it to my body by the handfuls!

Medically, the hospital had me on a Diflucan regimen. It can take seven or more days to cure yeast infections in normal cases. Mine? There was nothing normal about it. It was ongoing. It took weeks to clear up most of it. Unfortunately, I'd fight it in some capacity for months, even years.

The roller-coaster ride continued. Not only was my body in the fight of its life against infection and horrific pain, I fought massive amounts of inflammation. Having had so many surgeries in such a condensed time frame, my body never got a chance to recover from the anesthesia from one surgery to the next. As y'all know, inflammation is a booger on the body—joint pain and stiffness, loss of function, erratic insulin levels and hormones in wick-whack, to name more than a few of its symptoms.

~ ~ ~

Surgery number six—a total reconstruction of my lower left leg— took place nearly four weeks after the accident. The surgical procedure had several surgeries combined in order to obtain the desired goal.

Each surgical specialist had presented to me their specific role in the procedure. My mind was spinning. So much information to try and process. Once again, my mind became a debating "what if" machine that night.

What if their plan doesn't work?

What if I bleed out again and they run out of blood?

What if my body can't take any more anesthesia?

What if they give me too much anesthesia?

What if the infection gets into my bones before they can stop it?

What if I never walk again?

What if the electricity goes out in the middle of the surgery?

What if they run out of anesthesia and they have to finish without it?

Crazy, huh? Maybe, but very real. I spent the whole night in a battle of the mind. I'd pray and pray and pray.

Lord, help me! Please turn it off. I'm SO tired. Tired of physically fighting to survive. Emotionally exhausted trying to stay positive for all those around me. Mentally drained from trying to understand what's happening to me.

In that moment, I was even spiritually drained. Don't get me wrong. I wasn't doubting God or His plan. Rather, I was surrendering and didn't know it. I didn't think I had any other options; and maybe, I didn't. It was as if every compartment of me was empty—physically, emotionally, mentally, spiritually.

Sadly…I no longer cared.

~ ~ ~

The next day was extremely long for everyone. The team of specialists—orthopedic, vascular, neurological, and plastic surgeons came together for a ten-hour group effort to rebuild my lower left leg.

The plastic surgeon made a long lateral incision in my lower abdomen to remove a lateral abdominal muscle he would use as soft tissue filler around the hardware in the lower left leg. I never did get a good answer as to why they didn't do a tummy tuck while they had me sliced open. You'd have thought after everything I'd been through they'd have helped a sister out. Ha!

The vascular team worked to repair and re-attach the arteries, veins, and lymphatic system all around the newly-created leg.

Plastics also performed the skin grafting. Oh my gosh! If you're not familiar with the process, let me help you understand. It's basically like using a sod cutter on your skin. They take crisscross layers of healthy donor skin from one area of your body and attach the healthy donor skin to an unhealthy area. Because my injuries were so extensive, the plastic surgery team had to take all of the healthy layers of skin (subcutaneous layers) from my right thigh, from my knee to belly, and from my outer hip to inner groin—a huge area! The skin from all those areas was then used to wrap the new bone and non-functioning abdominal muscle to recreate the missing section of my lower left leg skin.

It's fascinating how surgeons can rearrange body parts to rebuild a mangled body.

It's how we repair our mistakes that defines us.

Life in Surgical ICU...

Surgery number six was in the medical history books. As for me, the struggle only got worse. Originally, when I was flown into Vanderbilt the night of the accident, I had a lower left leg that was a dangling amputation, multiple compound fractures in both femurs, and a crushed right knee. Six surgeries and several weeks later, I still had all those massive injuries, plus a whole lot more. The most recent surgery added a long abdominal incision and a belly that felt like I'd been repeatedly kicked in the gut. My entire upper right leg was literally blood red and raw from being a skin donor area. Then, there was the lower left leg. Oh, y'all. It was horrifying. I wasn't at all prepared to see what I saw when I recovered from anesthesia and opened my eyes for the first time. I thought looking at dead and dying infected skin was gross. My leg was freakishly deformed. From below my knee to my ankle was wrapped in grafted skin. I'd never seen grafted skin before. It looked like blood red snake skin attached to my leg with big staples. In one section, it was bulging like the 'snake' was pregnant with twins.

(That was my abdominal muscle which was used as a soft tissue filler.) Even though the whole rebuilt area was swollen, it was far from proportionate to my right leg.

The worst part, the rebuilt leg was constantly in my line of vision. I couldn't not look at it. I didn't understand why it wasn't bandaged, or at least covered with a sheet. Holy moly! One touch of the sheet, or anything for that matter, and I'd scream out in blood-curdling pain. My leg had to remain elevated above my heart for at least two weeks to eliminate blood clots or excessive swelling. The reason it was completely exposed was to give it oxygen for cellular regrowth and healing.

I had wire and tubes coming from all parts of my body. No doubt, I looked like a science project. I guess I kind of was!

Every hour a nurse or doctor would come in and check the doppler machine that was attached to my rebuilt leg. I hated that thing! It was hard enough battling all the physical pain, and then I had to add to that the emotional struggle of looking at a grotesque leg anytime my eyes were open. That annoying doppler sounded off with every single heartbeat. Combine that with the constant nausea from massive amounts of narcotics and medications…I was done. I'd had enough! Something had to give. I could feel myself sinking into depression. The *I don't care anymore* thoughts had turned into *I'm SO done*! Fortunately, my husband recognized my unspoken cry for help.

You can't start the next chapter of your life if you keep rereading the last one.

"I can't look at it anymore. It's making me sick." I'd said.

It took a little trial and error, but soon my husband had built a tent around the openly exposed elevated leg. He used pillows and loose pillow cases to drape over the pillow fort to block my view of the grotesque leg. The pain from the occasional slip of the pillow case touching the exposed leg was worth it. Anything so I didn't have to look at my freakishly grotesque leg.

What I experienced next still makes me hurt to this day. Anytime I'd bump or move my right thigh, the pain burned like fire. The grafted skin donor site was like a hot plate set on high. It was covered in a burn gel goo-like solution, then wrapped in a clear silicone or plastic looking see-through material. The resident physician that came in to clean the donor site and change the dressings must have missed the course on bedside manner. Either that, or she'd chosen to remove all emotional connection to not be affected by what she had to do in her profession.

Her very first question, "When was the last time you hit the pain pump?"

"A few minutes ago." I replied, thinking *this doesn't sound good.*

She waited until I could push the pain medication pump again. The pump was regulated for dosage allowance. I could hit the button all day long, but it would only push the IV narcotics through about every ten minutes.

Once I hit the button again and it dispensed a dose, she said she'd work quickly, as it could be painful changing the dressing and cleaning the donor site.

OH, MY GOD!

Again, I'm not a sissy when it comes to pain tolerance, especially if I can go to my mind's happy place. Happy place or not, the pain that I had to endure was off-the-charts, out-of-this-world insane.

She removed the outer dressing. It hurt, but I survived. Next, she took what looked like a soft sponge and s-l-o-w-l-y dragged it across my raw, blood red, donor site. I would say she dragged it across my skin, but there wasn't any skin there.

I have no doubt every person in the hospital could hear me screaming out in pain.

I grew up with a mom who liked to cook in a cast-iron skillet. After she'd use it, she'd clean it and then set it on a hot stove burner to completely dry it. That was her way of ensuring it was fully dried so that any water residue wouldn't turn the skillet to rust. There were times when she'd put the skillet on a hot burner, walk away to do another task, and come back to find her black cast-iron skillet turning orange-red, because it was so hot.

As I cried and screamed, clenching my fists onto the bedrails until they hurt as the resident physician continued to s-l-o-w-l-y drag the sponges across the donor site, over and over, until all the gel goo was removed. Every swipe felt like a red-hot, cast-iron skillet was repeatedly, ever so slowly, being dragged across my leg. I now knew what it felt like to be a burn victim. God bless any of you out there who have or are enduring that kind of pain.

I don't remember how often the resident physician would come and clean the donor site. I know it was several times, but beyond that, I'm unsure. Interestingly, I didn't journal about it. Going through it once was more than enough for me. I had no desire to relive it. Even if it was only on paper.

The next couple of days were unbearable on the poor hospital staff. Trying to manage my case became a juggling act of epic proportions. We could never get ahead of the pain. When we'd get close, I'd get so sick they'd cut back on the narcotics. The constant nausea made it hard to get in the nutritional calories and protein for my body to heal. It had been four weeks since the accident, and I felt like I was on a carnival ride spinning out of control.

Eight-hour Vacation...

After four days of the ever-spinning, faster-and-faster Tilt-A-Whirl™, a pain management specialist came in to see me. He offered several options. After careful consideration and prayer, I chose to have a nerve block. Since all my injuries were below my waist, having a groin nerve block was a huge risk for further nerve damage or paralysis. To me, it was worth it. After a month of fighting and never conquering the pain, my body was beat. The doctor told us the nerve block typically lasted up to twenty-four hours. The plan was to utilize every moment of that twenty-fours in changing my pain medicine regimen to a different combination that my digestive system could tolerate. We had tried previously to make some of those changes, but some of the pain drugs couldn't be given with or on top of other pain medications. It's a crazy, confusing cycle with even crazier side effects. I was a little nervous about having the block done. That all changed in a matter of minutes.

Oh my! It had been four weeks to the day since I'd last smiled. Hallelujah for nerve blocks! It was the first time since the accident that I had pain relief. It wasn't completely gone, but compared to the "off-the-chart levels" I had previously experienced, I was in heaven.

Some things you never get over... you just get through them.

Why Was I Not Surprised?

The nerve block that the doctor and I hoped would last closer to twenty-four hours wore off after a mere eight hours. Heart broken, I felt all the pain return with a mighty vengeance. The new pain regimen they had started me on earlier in the day had yet to take effect.

Oh Lord, please. Not again.

I'd also been moved from a regular ICU room to a step-down ICU room. I wasn't in the step-down room three hours before they were moving me to yet another room. Put together the not-yet-working pain medications, the constant monitoring of my vitals, the leg doppler readings, ongoing nausea and the increased pain from changing rooms, not once but twice in a matter of hours, I was beyond exhausted.

"Just seeing the hurt in her eyes breaks my heart," a friend said.

"She's an amazingly strong lady to go through what she's going through," said another.

The pain management team increased the new pain medications. It would take a couple more days before they became effective. Sadly, every time they moved my left leg, the pain would take over again. Fortunately, we were learning when and how often to request additional narcotics to stay on top of it.

I was asked by a lot of people, "How are you?"

"You've been through so much. How are you REALLY doing with all of this?"

I couldn't lie. It had been an extremely difficult journey. I hurt ALL the time. Sometimes worse than others. I taught myself to find joy in those rare moments of what I call tolerable pain.

I'd been blessed beyond measure to be surrounded by loving family and friends who rarely left my side; I was in one of the greatest trauma hospitals in the world, and people from all walks of life were praying for me daily.

I'm not sure why I didn't have a complete and total nervous breakdown. My best guess…at that time, I didn't have the strength, time, or energy for it.

There would come a day…

Sometimes we don't learn the value of a moment until it becomes a memory.

What a difference forty-eight hours can make. I was a week out from the reconstruction surgery. It had been a few days since the nerve block and the newly increased pain medication regimen. The Pregablin drugs were finally building up in my system—reducing the horrific nerve pain to almost tolerable. Combine all that with a full week of no surgeries, and my body was thrilled! It was finally able to start doing what it was designed to do if given the chance—heal.

Don't get me wrong, I had a VERY L-O-N-G road ahead of me. There was a certain peace that came from finally, after a month of fighting every single second to survive, to no longer be standing, or in my case lying, next to death's door.

It was the first night since the accident that I would truly rest.

Chapter Six

Wait...What?

No sooner had I wrapped my mind around the idea that I could and would survive, the hospital was releasing me—to go home.

"What? What about rehabilitation?"

"You're too high risk for further infection to go to a rehab facility."

How could this be? I still had wires and tubes in my body, massive open wounds, and I couldn't use or move my lower body. I tried my best to be excited, but I was a nervous wreck inside. I'd been under the constant care of some of the greatest medical professionals in the world. The safety of the cocoon I'd been in for nearly five weeks was coming to an end.

I now had two constant battles. Pain, meet your best friend...fear.

Even when you lose everything, you can't let fear win.

My mind raced out of control all night long,

How on earth are we going to do this?

I'll no longer have access to professional help at the press of a button.

What if the home nurses are rough?

What if the narcotics stop working?

What if the PICC line clogs up?

What if my blood levels plummet again?

It's only been two days since we finally stabilized the pain medications.

What if things go south again?

What if I can't do everything they think I can at home?

What if the home-bound hospital bed hurts?

What if the home therapists are mean?
What if the home delivery of refrigerated IV antibiotics doesn't arrive on time?
What if the fridge stops working?
What if the electricity goes out?
It's crazy how the mind messes with you.

Worry is meditation on crap.

It was sometime in the early morning hours. The night nurse had just made her scheduled round with me, charting vitals and monitoring IV levels.

"Try and get some sleep," she whispered the commonly used phrase before she left the room.

The hospital, in general, was quieter at night and whoever was staying the night with me, usually my husband, would be sound asleep in the hospital recliner in the corner of my room. I tried and tried to read as I used to enjoy it. I couldn't concentrate. I'd read and reread the same sentence over and over again. Sometimes I'd figure out that all I was doing was rereading the same sentence. Sometimes I couldn't even figure that out. I'm not sure if it was the countless doses of heavy narcotics, the massive hours of anesthesia or the damaging side effects from the trauma and infections, but it would be three years before I would be able to comprehend reading enough to enjoy it again.

In those dark, long, lonely hours of night, I'd pray and I'd write. Most of the time, tears of some sort would accompany the writing. It's fascinating, to me, how therapeutic writing combined with prayer can be for someone in the midst of trauma, struggle, pain, and recovery. I spent months, in some cases years, working through issues of my life during the middle of the night while the rest of the world was asleep.

For the first time, I began to understand Psalm 46:10.

Be still and know that I am God.
—Psalm 46:10, NIV

There's No Place Like Home...

After nearly five weeks in the hospital I was finally headed home. My last night in the hospital held very little sleep with the fear and anxiety of leaving my cocoon of medical safety, but in any new beginning, a first step must be made. Although I didn't sleep much the night before, I awoke with a sense of peace—a confirmation of *you're gonna be okay* in my spirit. I had no idea how that would happen, but for some reason, the how didn't seem to matter. I was going home. I couldn't wait to snuggle with my sweet dog, Daisy, start in-home physical therapy, enjoy the smells of home rather than the medicinal smells of the hospital, see much better views than a roof top or commercial buildings, and last, but not least—no more hospital food!

Arrangements were made for me to be transported from Vanderbilt hospital, via ambulance, to our home in the next county south. Imagine my shock and surprise when I found out who'd be my paramedic chauffeurs for the ride home. Y'all remember Oscar and Felix? The same fellas who took me on the ambulance chariot ride from the scene of the accident to the helicopter, took me home! What a gift! I got to thank both of them, in person, for their role in saving my life. We had such an enjoyable ride. We chatted and laughed the entire time. Two very kind gentlemen.

Thank you Lord for placing them in my path, not once but twice.

Blessings abounded that first day at home: the warmth of the sun on me for the first time in weeks, the gorgeous autumn leaves of Tennessee, the sweet "welcome home" balloons on the mail box, the fantastic wheelchair ramp the Franklin Fire Fighters Association built—so smooth and easy, the overabundance of puppy kisses from Daisy—all day long, family and friends greeting us when we arrived, friends grocery shopping, another running all over town to see that all my prescriptions were filled, my parents bringing dinner, other family members had cleaned the house, and most of all…the comfort of being home.

There's no place like home.
—Dorothy, *Wizard of Oz*

Remember my missing rings? They were found right where I left them—on my bathroom vanity. Thank You, Lord!

~ ~ ~

Reentry was tough. I was home, but NOTHING was the same as it was before the accident—at least not for me. I never served in the military, and I'd surely never compare my situation to what soldiers experience in war time. Yet, after all I'd been through, I could empathize. My life would never be the same, and I really had no idea how to handle it.

I was living in the middle of our large, open great room. So grateful we had a home that fit my physical needs as well as it did. My in-home hospital bed was in the center of the room, allowing me to see out both the front and the back windows of the house. I was surrounded by a large bedside potty, a wheelchair, a rolling hospital bedside table, containers of extra dressings and medical supplies, plus all the regular furniture and decor that was in the room before the accident.

Clutter and chaos was all around me. Sure, it was the same way while in the hospital, but that was the hospital's space. I had no control over that. Surrounded by so much stuff, all out of place, in my own home, and knowing there was absolutely nothing I could do about it, taught me a huge life lesson:

I can't control that which I cannot change.

In that moment, I realized I could change very little in my world. I couldn't change the fact that I was stuck in a hospital bed or a wheelchair, that my legs were still stuck straight out in front of me, that

I was still on massive doses of heavy narcotics and multiple daily doses of injectable antibiotics, that pain was my constant companion, or that fears of the unknown still haunted me every second of the day.

There seemed to be only one thing I had any control over—my attitude. My personal motto became "choose happy not crappy." It was a simple saying I could easily remember without writing it down. I can't tell you how often I'd repeat those words to myself. Over, and over, and over again.

In time, over the years, that simple slogan would grow and flourish into something much stronger…and definitely much deeper.

Boot Camp Routine…

Calendars, schedules and timers became the new norm in my world—a never ending daily cycle of:

- Dispensing prescription drugs
- Monitoring narcotics
- Multiple IV antibiotic infusions throughout each day
- Physical therapy sessions with home therapist
- Physical therapy sessions on my own
- Bathing
- Visitors
- Meal deliveries

New day, same routine. Repeat. Day after day, it was the same ol' thing. Occasionally, the daily routine would be shaken up with a trip to one of the medical specialists.

My husband was a trooper during those first couple of months. He rarely left my side. He, along with countless girlfriends, were my greatest healthcare advocates. It takes a lot to help nurse a loved one back from an illness or accident. My situation wasn't easy on anyone. We had a written daily schedule for everything and for everyone who helped out in an effort to stay on top of things. I was busier than a termite in a saw mill. I've often heard "it takes a village." For this girl, it took villages, and I'm grateful for each and every one. I love my village people!

It's not our job to mold another, but rather to help unfold them.

Gift of a Brand New Car...

Okay, before y'all get too excited, we were not given a brand new car. Not really. However, a dear friend who owned several local auto dealerships gifted us the use of a new van for as long as we needed it. What a HUGE blessing! You see, my husband and I both drove trucks at that time. The trucks were too high for me to get into, even with the use of a transfer board. Why would I need to leave the house, you ask? For follow-up doctor appointments—lots and lots of doctor appointments...with the orthopedic trauma surgeon, plastic surgeon, infectious disease specialist, primary care doctor, and my chiropractic physician.

But first, I'd need to master transferring from the wheelchair to the van, all without moving or hitting my legs that were sticking straight out in front of me.

Several friends and family just happened to stop by the house for a visit as I made my way outside to practice getting into the new van.

Oh, Lord. Pressure's on with everyone watching. Focus, Sheila, focus!

The original plan was to put me and my wheelchair parallel with the van's side door. I would then use a transfer slide board, a smooth piece of sturdy wood that bridges the gap between the wheelchair and the van. The middle van seats were removed, and I was to slide straight in. (Easier said than done.) I was to hand-walk my bum to the opposite-side sliding door to transfer back into the wheelchair once we arrived at our destination.

My first moment of doubt came when I looked down between the wheelchair and the van. It was huge! From my view point, it might as well have been the Grand Canyon. Finding that suck-it-up buttercup spirit, I was determined to make it happen.

I thought to myself, *don't look down, don't look down*, as I grunted my way. Using just my hands and arms, I moved my body along in a super-slow motion. After what seemed like an hour, I finally made it into the van. I was exhausted physically and emotionally, as were the other adults around me from holding their breath so long. We all needed a break, or a stiff drink!

Once I was finally all the way inside the van, we realized that that particular technique wouldn't work long term—at least not at that point in my recovery. Yes, I completed it, but at a huge cost to my body physically. We had to figure out a different approach. Unfortunately, I had to first get out of the van.

You guessed it. I did the same exact thing getting in the van as I did to get out of the van, but now I was doing it in reverse. While I sat there sweating from the circus act of getting in and out of the van, I could see the wheels turning in the minds of those around me. Every van door was open and seats were moved to every possible position. Two heads, or more in this case, really are better than one. With the rear van door open, and the rear van seat folded down flat—making it almost level with the bottom of the van floor, my wheelchair was oh, so close to the same height—about three inches different in height.

My sweet neighbor Michelle, who works for a local church daycare, says "Hey, what if we put a tumbling mat down in the van cargo area? Would that work?"

"Worth a try," my husband replied.

My neighbor quickly ran to the church while the rest of us visited outside. When she returned with the mat, not only was it the perfect height, it was the perfect width of the cargo area.

Yay, God!

With the wheelchair parallel to the back of the van, I could easily, without the use of a slide board, make the transfer. Woohoo! We all clapped and cheered over the victory.

"Wait! What about a seat belt?" I heard someone ask.

Looking at my husband, a friend asks "Yea, how are you going to secure her in?"

They all stood around the back of the van looking for ways to strap me down like cargo.

"Seriously?, I'm not going anywhere. I'll hold on here, and brace myself with my other hand. Besides, I've been through way worse than a little jostling in the back end of a van." I told them.

All of a sudden, my husband closes the van door. If those outside of the van were emoji's, they'd have been the big eyed "Oh my gosh!" ones. I'm not sure what they could see from their point of view. From inside the van, all I could tell was my head was barely visible out the van's back door window. I waved and started making faces as they all burst out laughing.

Oh, the fun I'd have with that one. Can you imagine what you'd think if you pulled up to a van and all you saw was the head of a grown woman in the back end?

From time to time, I'd be so exhausted I'd lean my head against the glass and fall asleep. I'm surprised we were never pulled over.

The Little Engine That Could...

I had yet to see, let alone use, the newly remodeled roll-in shower in the master bedroom. My husband couldn't stand it any longer. He had to figure out a way for me to see it.

"Pictures don't do it justice," he'd said.

Because both of my legs were elevated straight out in front of me, it made me and the wheelchair too long to make the turn into the bedroom from our long hallway. My determined husband decided if I'd transfer to the shower chair, which was not only narrow but also had four-wheel steering, and then prop my legs on a separate all-wheel rolling stool, he could get me in to see the new roll-in shower. Once I was in the shower chair, I put my legs on a rolling stool that was brought in from the shop.

Oh…I'm not so sure about this, I thought to myself as I rolled one way and my legs rolled the other. Fortunately, our sweet friend Pat was there visiting and helping us. She took the lead, guiding the rolling stool that held my legs, while my husband steered the shower chair. Like a very short train, we slowly rolled down the hallway. We did really well until we reached the bedroom doorway. As the three of us held our breaths, we gingerly inched through the turn. Phew! We made it. The new roll-in shower was beautiful.

Sadly, it'd be a few more weeks before I'd receive medical approval for a real shower. I began counting down the days.

Let It Shine...

My dear friend Sondra, whose husband Kit ran a local gymnastics facility called Let It Shine offered to build me a home physical therapy table. It was awesome! Perfect dimensions for my needs. I would transfer from the hospital bed to the wheelchair. Then, I'd slide out of the wheelchair directly onto the physical therapy table. I wasn't assigned home physical therapy yet, but we knew I needed to practice all that I'd learned while in the hospital and the rehab facility if I was going to maintain any kind of body strength.

This girl wanted way more than to just maintain. We created some great upper body and core workouts. The goal was to be as strong as possible in my upper body so that once my legs healed, after being immobile for months, I'd be able to hold myself up with at least my arms. To the crew at Let It Shine who built and delivered the physical therapy table, it was no big deal. To me, the recipient, it was a life changer. I had no excuse to lie in a hospital bed for months on end turning into mush. From the bottom of my heart, thank you!

~ ~ ~

My first post-op appointment with the plastic surgeon went pretty well. In general, he was pleased with how my body was healing—in both the skin-donor site of my upper right thigh and the entire lower left leg. He described the donor site as "a bit angry." Not sure what he meant by that, I asked, "What does that mean?"

"A couple of areas are inflamed and oozing more than they should be. Chances are, you've bumped those areas. Even a slight touch can cause irritation or break down of your skin on your wounds at this point."

I had no idea how sensitive skin grafting was. Both the skin donor site and the skin graft recipient site would forever be fragile areas. It's been years since those surgeries, and those areas of skin have yet to see the light of day.

My skin-donor site—my entire upper right thigh—is the whitest of white skin. The only bit of color in that area are random dark spots that resemble age spots. They aren't age spots. They're scarring from those early days of minor bumps—most of which I never knew happened.

The donor recipient skin site hasn't seen the light of day either. The skin in that area is super thin. I had a medical specialist describe donor skin as "virgin skin," like that compared to foreskin on a newborn baby. In the beginning, the donor skin was so thin you could see through it. Years later, it's still super thin though stronger. The texture appears a bit like snake skin. It's definitely got its own unique style.

I've often said, these legs look like a cross between an old patchwork quilt and a great road map, and like an old quilt and a road map...they've got stories to tell and places still to go.

The more broken we are...the more light that shines through.

Chapter Seven

DeeDee the Designing Diva...

I'd been home from the hospital for a week when a childhood friend came to visit. DeeDee and I grew up in Colorado, moved away, got married, and both moved again. Through it all, we remained dear friends, sometimes closer than others. Regardless of time and years, we had a special connection.

It was great to have her visit, even if only for a week. She was a huge help! Her being there gave my husband a chance to leave, doing things he needed to do. In addition, she and I visiting helped take my mind off my situation. It was beyond therapeutic to talk about the good ol' days. I needed that more than she'll ever know.

DeeDee is a gifted seamstress. I don't think there's anything she can't create or sew. She shared some of those talents while at our home that week, creating a gift for my legs like none other.

The more time I spent in the wheelchair, the more my legs would hurt. The elevated leg risers on the wheelchair had two small, thin pads; one on the bottom, basically under the calf area, and the second pad for the outside of the calf. Nothing was on the inside calf area to keep the leg cradled. Because of the massive trauma to my lower left leg, I had to use pillows around it to cushion it, which made the leg roll inward. That hurt!

DeeDee designed the coolest horseshoe-like cradles for my legs. They were made from heavy foam. She sewed custom fit covers made of soft leather Naugahyde® so they could be cleaned easily. Oh, y'all, they were amazing! They all but eliminated the extra leg pain when in the wheelchair. My legs no longer rolled inward and fell off the leg risers. Plus, my legs didn't bounce around like before with the standard leg riser cushions. Not only did these awesome cushions help with my current situation at that time but also they allowed my left leg to be independently supported when the time came to start lowering the right leg.

I thank God for DeeDee's skill with a needle and thread, and for her precious gift of friendship.

Little did I know how her gift of friendship would later save my life.

Day Forty-eight...

A monumental day for me. What happened on day forty-eight? A shower—a REAL shower!

It felt amazing to be clean again—not just soap and water clean, but scrubbed from head to toe losing layers of built up, dry, scaly, dead skin. I think I lost a pound or two in dead skin with that first shower.

There was nothing simple about my first real shower. It was far from easy. One could compare it to an episode of *Laurel and Hardy*, or something straight out of *I Love Lucy*.

Let me set the stage. Remember, my legs still remained elevated, basically straight out in front of me at all times. With that said, we couldn't get me, in my wheelchair with my legs sticking straight out, down the long hall, and around the turn into the master bedroom and bath. That didn't stop my determined husband.

First, I transferred from the hospital bed that was out in the open great room into the shower chair. Then he brought in a rolling office chair. He put a towel on the seat of the chair. I put my legs on the toweled rolling chair. Oh! I almost forgot, I placed my unprotected, un-bandaged, still raw and painful wounds on the toweled chair! Any slight movement or touch caused my body to cry out in pain when bandaged and supported. I wasn't sure if I'd be able to endure the pain from all the jostling about without the protective bandaging. Somehow, someway, I'd reached down and found the strength to overcome the pain. I'd silently repeat to myself, over and over, "You'll feel so much better after a real shower. You can do this!"

With me in the shower chair, and my legs resting on the rolling office chair, we began our second slow roll down the long hall. Our little mini train was followed by the cutest caboose, my li'l Daisy! She never left my sight.

Once we made it to the roll-in shower, we had to trade out the office chair, which was cloth, for the heavy plastic bedside potty. You're probably wondering why we didn't use the rolling shop stool like we used it the first time I'd seen the new roll-in shower. That was because I continued to fight serious infections. We chose not to use a dirty old shop stool that may or may not have unknown contaminants on it—especially since I wouldn't be protected by heavy bandaging this go round.

The finagling of the different chairs and different levels of leg elevation, along with the physical strength needed to make all the transfers, had me plum worn out, and I hadn't even felt the first drop of water!

While I did my own, hands-on, cleansing of my hair and body, I'd need my husband's help in handing me stuff like soap, shampoo, conditioner, a wash cloth, and a razor for my under arms. There'd be no need for leg shaving for a very long time. He also needed to hold the shower nozzle and hand it to me intermittently throughout the process. He decided since he had to be in the shower with me, he'd shower as well. Made sense. For about ten seconds.

I tried hard to be patient, but pain and numbness were winning. My hind side was numb from sitting in one position on the hard shower chair, while both legs were past numb from being elevated on the potty chair. Did I mention the potty chair was several inches taller than the shower chair? No wonder my legs had completely fallen asleep—to the point that they hurt and I was certain they were going to fall off numb.

I'm sure he was doing his best to shower quickly. Me? I was still trying to be patient—it was not as though I could go anywhere. As I sat there shivering, I started thinking, *Didn't you already wash that area? Is it really necessary to rinse that long? Good grief, can you just hurry it up! I'm freezing over here.* Being the good wife, I didn't verbalize a single word to him. Rather, I continued practicing patience. The key word—practice.

Somehow I survived the shower, and all without getting Daisy wet. With it being a huge, roll-in shower, she thought she should be included in the party. Silly dog!

As I towel dried, a renewed vigor came over me. We did it. Another step on the road to recovery. Yes!

Then reality hit. Oh, crud! We've still got to get me back down the hall, transferred back to the hospital bed and put on clean, new surgical dressings on both legs.

Obviously we made it, but like most things at that point in the journey, I'd learn, yet again—*Be patient, Sheila!*

How long did it take for that first shower? Over two hours. It was strictly a shower only. No primping, no make-up, no hair styling, etc. Just the basics.

So, the next time you jump in the shower, be grateful you can hop in and out in just a few minutes. Not everyone shares the same luxuries in life as others.

Speaking of the new roll-in shower…it was perfect! Thank you to all the volunteers who designed and built it. Y'all rock!

The Blessing of Receiving…

Blessings come in a multitude of ways. For us, especially in the beginning, they were poured out upon us.

My whole life, from the time I was a little girl, I was raised as a giver. Combine that with a family heritage of get 'er done and a can-do spirit. It's beyond humbling to be on the receiving end of life.

It was the week of Thanksgiving. Less than eight weeks since the horrific motorcycle accident that turned my world not only upside down but inside out.

Friends, family, colleagues, the community, civic organizations, and others reached out to help us. The Franklin (Noon Rotary) BBQ Society stepped up big time. This group, along with the Franklin Firefighters Association, held a community-wide fundraiser. For several days, they smoked hundreds of beef tri-tips and sold them to folks eager to help the Sheila Fitzgerald Recovery Fund.

On one particular day in late November, I wanted to stop by and thank, in person, all the wonderful volunteers for all they were doing with the BBQ fundraiser. It was a cold day. Having grown up in Colorado, I understood the importance of properly dressing for the elements, so I bundled in layers.

I was far from prepared for the dramatic changes a body goes through after a major physical trauma when it comes to dealing with cold temperatures. What used to feel like cold now felt frozen, and what used to feel frozen now felt beyond rigid arctic freezing. The cold temperatures, although in reality it wasn't all that cold that day, were wreaking havoc on my body. I've learned over the years that once my body gets bone cold, it can take days to recover. It's not fair, but it's part of being a survivor.

As humbling as it was, it lifted my spirits to hug necks and shake hands with volunteers and community supporters. I also learned a very valuable lesson that beautiful, albeit cold, autumn day. When others, especially strangers, do something in kind for you, be genuinely grateful. Don't take away their blessing, their joy in giving of themselves. I pray whether you're the giver or the receiver, that next time and all the rest of the times, your heart is in the right place—grateful.

Let your outer reflections mirror your inner intentions.

Out of the Mouths of Babes...

My sister and her oldest daughter, three years old at the time, came to spend Thanksgiving with us. It was common for all my family to gather at our home for the holiday.

To be honest, I don't remember a lot of things during that time.

I'm eternally grateful for the gift of daily journaling. The hundreds and hundreds of pages journaled, especially the first few years after the accident, have not only helped me to heal inwardly, but blessed me with memoirs for this book you're reading. Thank you Jesus for the gift of pen and paper, for the ability to put my thoughts into written word, and for the courage to share them with the world.

Apparently, I encouraged my family to still come to our home for Thanksgiving. Sounds like something I would say. However, it doesn't sound like something someone in my condition should have said. I'd only been home from the hospital a few weeks. I was basically confined to a hospital bed in the middle of the living room, living the life of a heavily medicated, several times a day IV antibiotic infused, recovering trauma patient with very limited mobility. I was absolutely, positively no help whatsoever. My sister, Amanda, was a trooper. She dove right in and took care of everything.

That day, the home health nurse was scheduled to evaluate my wounds, clean and service my PICC line, draw blood, and complete a weekly analysis for all the medical specialists to review. When the nurse arrived, she began setting up her supplies. My little niece, whom I'd spent every waking moment with, however few they were, playing tea, suddenly became silent. She knew her Aunt Sissy was hurt really badly, but until that moment I'm not sure she fully grasped what it all truly meant.

Typically, the home health nurse would draw blood from my PICC line once she cleaned and flushed the line. For some reason, the PICC line wasn't cooperating for a blood draw that day. This meant the nurse would have to stick me. To this day, I'm still not a huge fan of needles. However, after surviving all my body had been through, including dozens upon dozens of needles, one more stick of a needle was a piece of cake.

Standing and watching from a safe distance, my niece's eyes got as big as saucers. She pointed to the drain tube and said "LOOK!" as she watched my blood being drained from my body into the various tubes. I was so proud of her. No fear. Only curiosity. Mind you, she still stood at a safe distance. Smart girl!

Once the nurse finished her routine procedures, it was time for me to put clean dressings on both my legs. I found it to be much less painful if I did my own dressing rather than any medical staff doing it. At one point, I needed some assistance so I enlisted my sister. Once Amanda was hands-on, that gave my niece the confidence to come closer. Watching her see my injuries, up close and personal, my niece showed nothing but sweet genuine compassion as she said, "Owwee. Ouchie." With tears in her eyes, she asked me, "Does it hurt, Aunt Sissy?" At that moment, it took all I had to remain strong. I knew if I let my emotions show by crying, she'd probably get scared. I couldn't and wouldn't lie to her.

"Yes, honey, it hurts, but Aunt Sissy will be okay. It's just gonna take a long time to heal these boo-boos."

After receiving truth she could understand, she turned back to her tea set.

It was then that I heard a precious, little voice singing and praying—asking God to heal her Aunt Sissy's boo-boos.

It was my turn to shed tears.

What a beautiful spirit in a tiny soul. Out of the mouths of babes...Or as Jesus said in Matthew 18:4, "...the greatest in the kingdom of heaven."

God Wink...

It was the Saturday after Thanksgiving and my younger brother and his angel-sent-from-heaven wife loaded up their conversion van for the long drive back to their home in Kansas. There's usually tears shed when they leave, but this time was different. There's a new and special bond he and I share. It's hard to explain. Maybe because I don't know exactly what it is myself. Although I'm older than he, he is much wiser in years than I. He's truly my hero. There's no way I can comprehend the hurdles and obstacles he's endured in his journey as a quadriplegic. My injuries and limited mobility give me a mere glimpse into his world.

It was fifty-nine days post-accident…The first recorded day of a day filled with melt downs. A day filled with tears, lots and lots of tears, (cleansing, yes, but pain-filled nonetheless.)

The last words my brother spoke to me as he rolled out the door were: "Be Strong."

On that day, I felt anything but strong. I had held my head high, tried to be positive in every struggling situation, and did the best I could, knowing how to give the rest over to God.

Day fifty-nine post-accident was sunny and gorgeous, which usually lifted my spirits. Nine weeks prior, I power walked eleven miles. On day fifty-nine I cried—no, I bawled—when I saw folks outside walking. Nine weeks prior, I could get myself a drink whenever I wanted, I could walk to the bathroom, shower myself, wear two shoes (cute ones at that), and drive. On day fifty-nine I cried not only because I couldn't do any of those things, and so much more, but because I missed taking care of myself. I missed taking care of others. It was as if my servant's heart was stolen from me. Tears flowed uncontrollably at the realization of the loss. I think it was the first time I comprehended the depth of the accident. It was one thing to suffer physical loss, but losing a part of who I was—who God designed me to be—that's a hurt deeper and stronger than I cared to admit.

Things change…and they change you.

I'd received a sweet note of encouragement from a dear friend that day. Their final words to me were the same as my brothers: "Be Strong!"

Lord, I'm trying, but God, it's SO hard!

Later that same day, Susan, a precious former client who lived out of state stopped by the house for a brief visit. While I don't remember much about the visit, I'll never forget those final words she whispered in my ear as she hugged me goodbye, "Be Strong."

Like most things said or done during the first few years of my recovery journey, it took me a bit to comprehend what all happened that day.

Not once, not twice, but three times during that no-good, really horrible, very bad day the Holy Spirit whispered in my ear..."Be Strong."

When I later shared it with a girlfriend, she said, "Honey, that's called a God wink."

Look up, pay attention. God winks are all around.

Pain, Pain Go Away...

From the moment I was lucid in the hospital, after the accident, pain was my constant companion. It didn't seem to matter how much pain medication I took or how often I took it—IV, oral, or both at the same time, the pain NEVER left me. It didn't matter—day or night, with movement or without movement. It hurt to simply breathe. I even tried holding my breath, thinking I'd get a reprieve from the constant battle with pain if only for a minute or two. No luck. There was no escaping the pain—ever.

There was surgical pain. There was traumatic injury pain. There was nerve damage pain. There was muscle pain. There was infection pain. There was joint pain. There was pain from swelling and inflammation. There were medication side-effects pain. There was pain from eating, and there was pain from not eating.

Absolutely everything hurt all the time. From time to time, one area of pain would be less painful than another, giving me a temporary break from the all at once pain.

Unfortunately there was never a time when one or more of the above listed areas were not causing excruciating pain. Maybe that's why I struggle with the medical world's pain scale of 1 to 10, with 10 being the worst. At any given second, my muscle pain may only be a 6 or a 7, but the nerve or infection pain would pound hard at 10+. It would take years for my body to adjust to the ever-changing, roller-coaster ride of pain management.

Sadly, pain management, still, to this day, several years later, is a constant battle in some form or another.

There's no shame in being broken.
What matters is what you do with the pieces.

Chapter Eight

My Achilles Heel...

According to Webster's Dictionary, the meaning of Achilles heel is "a weak spot, a flaw, vulnerable."

I could relate. Literally. I'm not exactly sure how my left heel pad was ripped from my heel, but it was. Maybe it was from the massive force impact of my boots flying off when my body went airborne, doing two summersaults before landing on the pavement.

Regardless, my left heel pad—all the skin down to the heel bone—was ripped off. It looked kind of like peeling back a pull-tab lid. The skin was still attached at the toe end. Good thing. That gave the trauma surgeons the option to re-attach my own skin to my own body. The giant flap of skin was pulled and re-attached surgically all around my heel—up and including to my Achilles tendon on the back of my left foot. The plastic surgeon, in a later surgery, would use some harvested donated skin to help close up the remaining open areas.

Little did we know what kind of nightmare my Achilles heel would truly become. My body would struggle and fight numerous infections over the next several months. My team of medical specialists and I would be blessed by conquering one battle, only for another one to rise up against me.

Sadly, infection never left that area.

Please, Make It Stop!

I've never been a fan of carnival rides. Just ask one of my first childhood boyfriends. We were at the local county fair and rodeo. He had an hour or so until his next ride in the high school rodeo competition. As we strolled through the carnival midway, he kept asking me to ride one of the rides with him. Trying my best to convince him "I don't do rides," he wouldn't take no for an answer. It could have been his adolescent hormones thinking he could sneak a kiss in on me once on the carnival ride, or it could have been his macho, cowboy way of coercing me onto the ride. After all, he was a rough stock contestant. I'm teasing. He was a nice fella, but still not willing to take no thank you as my final answer. The carnival operator must have had a temporary moment of insanity as he just laughed when my date dragged me up to the ride. I told him, "I don't do rides. I promise you—I get sick."

What is it with the male code? The grown man operator winked at my date, all the while laughing, as he replied, "You'll be fine. Just have fun."

It wasn't so bad the first time around. The cage rocked back and forth like a hard, rigid rocking chair. The second time around was faster. My cowboy fella date put his arm around me saying he'd protect me. Ha! The third time around, the ride was going around one direction and our individual cage was spinning in another direction entirely. I'm sure I took a chunk out of his thigh, as I clawed into him like a cat in attack mode. He yelled. I yelled. Change that—I screamed!

I was begging the operator to please stop, yelling at him, "I'm gonna get sick!" Again with the male code. What the heck?! Maybe his ears were full of wax and he couldn't hear me screaming? No, that wasn't it. People began to gather around to see what all the commotion was about.

It's bad enough when a fourteen-year-old male chooses not to listen to a silly, young girl, but a grown man? Shame on him! The operator chose to send us on a bonus ride. Not a smart move on his part. It was worse than any bad scene in a romantic-comedy movie. I felt so sorry for folks in splatter range as they had nothing to do with it.

My date and the carnival ride operator—neither took too kindly to my "I tried to tell you." I was mortified, as we were both covered in shook-up, spun around, splattering barf. The operator spewed obscenities at us as we crawled out of the puke covered cage. I gave him ample warning. He chose not to listen. It also meant, he had to clean up the mess. The cowboy? Thank goodness he had a clean shirt for his upcoming ride in the rodeo performance.

Funny…we never really hung out after that. Go figure.

My ever-changing, always turning, making sudden stops in its tracks, life of recovery I continue to live in, makes that carnival ride of my youth seem tiny by comparison.

I still don't like carnival rides, and although I've been riding the toughest ride of my life every single day for many years, there are still times when it takes all I've got not to hurl.

~ ~ ~

It was early December 2011. Much had happened since the accident on September 29, 2011. I'd had six surgeries; one to save my life, the others to save my legs. I was doing everything I possibly could at home to gain strength and mobility. I still resided in the hospital bed in the middle of the living room floor. My husband went back to work after taking two months of Family Medical Leave. Every third night, when he was on shift at the fire station, I'd have a girls' night at our house. That sounds way more exciting than it really was. I had a written schedule of babysitters. They were awesome!

As wonderful as my husband was those first couple of months, we both needed a break from the 24/7 togetherness. Please do not misunderstand me. I'm so grateful for his help, his support, and his dedication to my initial recovery. I think it was perfect timing when he chose to go back to work. I was becoming more self-sufficient, which seemed to bother him from time-to-time. I told myself it was all in my head, like many things after the accident.

Most of the babysitters were actually former nurses or medical personnel. Babysitting me was a piece of cake for them. I tried to prepare them ahead of time of the various tasks I'd need help with. Most were simple—fill my water bottle, fix me something to eat, help Daisy get on or off the hospital bed, take Daisy outside, etc. There were a couple of tasks that required a stronger frame of mind. Assisting with the PICC line IV antibiotic infusion made most ladies a bit apprehensive. It's not that they couldn't perform the necessary steps, but rather they'd be afraid they'd mess up something or hurt me. We fumbled a time or two but never caused any real harm. The other big scare for my sweet sitters was protecting my legs. Rarely did I need help with wound dressing changes. Though on occasion when a sitter was there, I'd hit one of the wound areas. Always fearful of messing something up and not knowing it, my brain wouldn't let it go until my sitter and I would take the dressing off and be sure everything was okay.

You know, I'm not sure I truly realized the extent of my injuries until folks, outside my circle of medical specialists, saw the extensive damages to my legs. Friends and family did their best to be strong, desperately trying not to show emotion on their faces. When the mind tells the body to gasp—it's gonna gasp. For those who held in the audible gasp, it showed all over their faces.

It's truly humbling to have a girlfriend assist with a bedside potty. Sure, us girls usually travel two or more going to a public restroom together, but in all my years, I've never had a girlfriend join or assist me in the stall. I guess I lost all inhibitions and modesty after my "stripper" days in the hospital. It's one thing to have a girlfriend take the potty pail of urine to one of the toilets to flush and rinse. It's entirely another when it's poo. Now, that's a real friend!

When later asked, every single babysitter said spending a night with me was not only easy, it was fun. Apparently I can be quite entertaining when on prescription narcotics. Once word got out, the list of sitter volunteers quickly multiplied.

Ladies, I may not remember a lot about our girls' nights...but I'm sure thankful for your selfless love.

Loss teaches us greater love.

Cold Turkey...

A lot was happening with my body. One of my surgeons said I no longer needed the heavy narcotics. Actually, he said, "You can stop taking them."

My eyes as big as saucers, I asked, "Cold turkey?"

"Yea, you don't need them anymore," he replied.

If there's a spot in the brain labeled "freaked-out," I'd found it. I'm thinking, *Oh, my God! What?! Are you kidding me?! Do you have any idea what my body's been through?!* I've heard and read stories about people becoming addicted to narcotics. I always told myself, *That'll NEVER be me.*

I'm here today, to share with you how insanely crazy narcotics can be on the mind. Those who know me, know I'm rather strong willed. (Y'all be nice.) My will and determination to not be controlled by a controlled substance was a huge priority for me. There was no way I'd let drugs take over me. Even if they were necessary and legally prescribed. Having been on heavy, up to 80mg Oxycontin daily, the battle to overcome was on!

Every moment, even in my sleep, my mind was battling against the drugs. The drugs convinced my mind that there was no way I could endure the pain without them. At the same time, my mind would argue and battle against those evil thoughts. It was insane! My mind fought against the "cravings" for weeks. The physical effects weren't much better.

If I understand correctly, detox symptoms can vary from person to person. I had trouble sleeping due to weirder than weird nightmares. My skin itched like I'd bathed with mosquitos, it felt as if bugs were crawling over my entire body, my neck, shoulders, and hands hurt constantly, I had a heightened sense of fear and anxiety, and I couldn't drink enough water—I was so thirsty.

All of this was on top of the multitude of issues my body was already battling. The skin graft on my left heel didn't take—leaving another open wound that required a special step-by-step treatment regimen.

Knowing there'd be another surgery in the near future, I was doing all I could to physically prepare my body with several daily workouts.

I'd been released to begin putting weight on my right leg, which meant I needed to master the use of a walker. I hated that thing! It was so cumbersome. That strong will came in handy as I quickly mastered standing on one leg while using the walker for support.

For grins one day, I wanted to see if my left foot would move at all. My trauma surgeon was sure to let me know it may not function like it used to. "Chances are, you'll need to wear a brace on it the rest of your life. Hopefully it'll flex, but it may never extend," he told me.

"It's alive!" I screamed, as my left foot slightly flexed. Crocodile tears of joy flowed as the left foot not only flexed, but it ever so slightly extended. I could actually see the tendon at work through the grafted skin. So cool!

The psycho, nerve pain, which started while I was in the hospital, never let up. Added to it, I also had involuntary nerve movement. Or so I thought. There really wasn't any actual movement going on. I thought the drugs made me nutty. (I was afraid to say anything for fear of being sent to the psych ward.)

One day while doing physical therapy, Elisabeth, my in-home physical therapist, noticed me freaking out. As I lay on the therapy table, resting between reps, my eyes suddenly flew open wide.

She asked, "What's wrong?"

I tried to hide it, but there was no denying it.

"It feels as if my lower left leg is sticking straight up in the air. Not my entire leg. Just the part below the knee."

Elisabeth looked at me as if I'd lost my mind, and for a minute, I wasn't sure I hadn't. It's not physically possible for a leg, midway between the knee and shin to bend, let alone stick up perpendicular to itself. I was freaking out! The sensation lasted about a minute. Once it subsided, the sweet therapist gave me my first phantom pain lesson: "It's real, it's weird, it's tough to describe, and sadly, it would only get worse."

Life is full of the unexpected. Embrace it!

New Year, New Goals...

Although my road to recovery had a long way to go, I was making, and actually taking steps, in the right direction. My right leg was getting stronger and stronger in spite of the bucket of screws holding the knee together, and the titanium plate and screws holding the femur together. It took a couple of weeks to gain enough strength to take that first step.

Every step in the right direction meant one step farther from the wrong direction.

On January 14, 2012, with the assistance of a walker, I took my first step. More like a hop. I was still non-weight bearing on the left leg. For the next four days, I pushed myself, working and strengthening the right leg. Why only four days you ask?

Surgery Number Seven...

Back to Vanderbilt Hospital for surgery number seven—bone grafting. Once my body basically healed from the previous reconstruction surgery, I went back to the hospital for the bone graft procedure. My talented orthopedic trauma surgeon did his best to prepare me for the procedure—explaining how they'd do the bone graft. By then, he and I were friends. We'd been through so much together, we'd learned each other's basic strengths. He knew I had a keen awareness and connection to my body. I could tell him what specifically was hurting, pinpointing what kind of pain it was—nerve, muscle, surgical, bone, or infection. We had great communication; I listened to my body, and he listened to me.

Unfortunately, there'd be complications with surgery number seven.

The plan was to open my right knee, then bend the knee as far back as possible, ending with my right heel pulled into my bum. Then, Dr. Sethi, my orthopedic trauma surgeon, stretched my iliotibial band, also known as the IT band in the thigh, to one side, gaining access to my tibia bone. He used an auger to manually pull bone marrow from my right shin. Pushing and straining the iliotibial band in order to reach the top of my tibia (shin bone) he worked and worked to retrieve the necessary bone marrow. He then combined my bone marrow with cadaver bone and a man-made bone composite to create a bone-based material to replace the bones that were crushed in the accident.

The plastic surgeon cut into the newly grafted skin to create a flap on my lower left leg, opening up the area along my shin that would receive the new bone graft.

Both surgical sites were stitched closed, and I went to post-operating recovery.

Sounds systematic, right? Wrong.

According to my orthopedic trauma surgeon, "You have the hardest bones of anybody I've worked on. My wrists still hurt," as he rubbed and moved both of his hands around.

Strong, hard bones sounded like a good thing to me. And they are. Unfortunately, for me, that made getting the bone marrow more difficult, causing extensive strain to the already damaged iliotibial band.

That explained the crazy pain in the right leg.

Here We Go Again…

Surgery number seven started with pre-op at 5:30 am. At 7:00 pm, I was in post-op recovery. A very long day.

It took seven surgeries for me to figure out one of my biggest problems regarding pain. Because I tolerate pain better than most, I wait too long before taking pain medications, or as the medical world says, "You're getting behind the pain. You've got to stay ahead of it."

In the wee hours of the morning after surgery, while most of the world was asleep, excruciating pain hit me. I pushed the morphine pain pump. Nothing. I looked at the nerve block pump—empty.

"Oh, crap! Not again."

It may have been the morphine side-effects. I don't know, but I panicked!

Immediately, I pushed the nurse call button. The nursing staff put in a request for orders for more IV pain meds. After two and a half hours of waiting, we called my surgeon directly. Within ten minutes, I had pain medication, and I started to get some relief. I'm not sure why a refill order wasn't automatically attached to my patient record. Maybe dispensing controlled substances doesn't work that way.

The morphine pain pump seemed to work pretty well for pain relief. Unfortunately, the side effects became too much for my body to handle. I understood that the intense itching and spiders-crawling-all-over-me feeling were morphine side effects, but the hallucination side effect—that was crazy! The serious issue was the continual drop in my blood pressure. Seventy-seven over forty-two is too low—even for a healthy body at rest. Especially if it's trying to heal.

My body did much better on the Dilaudid pain pump. That, combined with the right-leg nerve block, and oral pain meds every four hours, I'd get through another week's stay in the hospital.

After the week in the hospital for surgery number seven, I was more than ready to go home. If everything worked right with my rebuilt legs, I'd be done with surgeries. Woohoo!

Come on, rehab!

Because of my extremely high risk of infection, I wasn't a candidate for the rehabilitation facility. That's okay. I had my own personal rehab center at home.

Hurry up and wait was the theme. Hurry up and heal, legs. I couldn't wait to start the rest of my life.

Because surgery number seven was harder on my right leg than originally expected, it took weeks rather than days to use that leg again. My home physical therapist, Elisabeth, was a gem. She was patient yet persistent, gentle yet tough. Of course no one was tougher on me than I was.

One day, I asked her, "What can I do to get my bottom back on my bottom, all the while still sitting on my bottom?"

After she quit laughing hysterically, she replied, "Butt squeezes."

"Seriously? Are you kidding me? Butt Squeezes? Do you have any idea how many thousands of butt squeezes I've done over the past four months? I think I could crack peanuts with the number of butt squeezes I've done."

Apparently, when one sits on their bum constantly for months, gravity automatically pushes said bum out to the sides. Great. Thanks a lot, Mother Nature.

Two weeks post-op surgery seven—I was standing, with walker assistance, on my right leg.

Three weeks post-op surgery seven—I was making laps around the house on right leg, via the walker, every hour.

My midsection, aka "tummy," looked like a something out of *101 Dalmatians*. The daily Lovenox® blood thinner shots were making their mark on me— literally. My stomach was covered in dozens of dime-sized bruises. After nearly three weeks of daily injections, I was running out of pale white patches of skin.

My trauma surgeon told me that I was in the top one percent of successful re-attached amputation procedures. That's a lot of pressure—on both of us. My legs, especially the left one, was his prize-work. He should be proud. He'd gone above and beyond to find a way for me to not only keep my left leg but also he figured out a way to get it working again. For me, never a quitter, I wanted to succeed, to overcome, to triumph regardless. It was a team effort. Besides, we worked well together.

Together everyone achieves more.

Redecorating...

Little by little, things started disappearing from our home. The hospital bed was the first thing to leave. There was something so freeing, so encouraging, to see our home look more like a home than a hospital setting after all those months.

I was becoming quite proficient with the walker. That confidence urged me to try a regular potty—well, one with a handled, elevated riser attachment.

It was mid-February—my last night to have a babysitter. How appropriate that it was one of my TNT girlfriends. Tiffany had stayed with me before at the house so she knew the routine. I told her I needed to use the potty. So, we both proceeded to the bedside potty.

At the very last minute, with excitement in my voice I said, "Oh, hey! I can use the real potty."

Off we went, down the hall, in choo-choo train style—me and my walker, Tiffany, and our li'l caboose, Daisy. Once Tiffany was assured I'd be okay, she gave me some time alone to enjoy the moment. That may sound completely bonkers to some of y'all.

Let me explain. For nearly four and a half months I hadn't flushed a toilet. I hadn't pushed a lever and heard the 'swoosh' of swirling water. I'm sure most of you have never paid attention to the sound of a toilet when you flush it. For the previous four and a half months, someone—sometimes more than one someone, had witnessed my every processing moment. It's not that I'm extremely modest or bothered by bathroom functions. Hardly. It's a part of life.

In that moment, I felt like royalty...on my very own throne.

EVERYONE faces hardship in life... some become stronger because of it.

February 12, 2012, was a big day. Not only was I done with the daily blood thinner shots but also I spent my first night alone. As with anything that's new or different, I was a bit uneasy about being by myself all night long. I'd come to depend on the cocoon of safety I'd been in. It was time. I needed to prove to myself I could do it—that I'd be okay.

That first night all alone was a catapult glimpse into things to come.

What's Normal?
Life was tough, really tough. Nothing came easy. Most days were filled with a new normal. Unfortunately, that "normal" was always changing.

My body was slowly learning to move and flex again, and so was my mind. I found joy in the simplest of things. I had to. I started using crutches most of the time around the house, but still used a wheelchair out in the real world. The left leg remained elevated when sitting. I wasn't able to wear a shoe on the left foot. So, I got creative with foot coverings. Colorful stocking hats became a fun accessory. The more proficient I became with crutches, or crunches as my little niece called them, I started decorating them. There were dozens and dozens of creations and themes—holidays, seasons, sports, colors, etc. I could start a business with the multitude of crutch decor I designed.

Life was hard enough. I desperately needed to find and create a little "happy" anywhere I could.

Life on crutches provided so much more—more mobility, more strength, more freedom. It would take time for my physical stamina to return. After all, I'd been bedbound or in a wheelchair for the better part of four months.

Little by little, day by day, I got stronger. I finally mastered crutches on steps at home, giving me the strength and confidence I needed to venture out into the real world without a wheelchair. For months, my wheelchair would still be used on occasion—mostly for uncharted ground or longer times away from home.

March came in like a lion—roaring with success! The skin graft flap, from surgery number seven, had finally healed. Well, all but the graft over the left heel.

In order to take the next step, I needed a custom-fitted rigid walking boot. The first one didn't work. I wasn't too surprised. Rarely would things work the first time, even custom-fit stuff. Remember that top one percent category the trauma surgeon said I was in? It can have its drawbacks. The second custom fit walking boot was much better. It was a lot taller than the first one, going all the way up to my knee, cushioning and supporting both foot and leg.

Like my crutches, the newly appropriately named Honkin' Boot was blinged out—complete with scripture, cool crosses, and the stenciled words "Faith, Trust and Heaven-sent." The Honkin' Boot allowed me the freedom to slowly put weight on my left foot/leg. It also granted me access to first class. No more riding cargo transport in the back of the van for this girl!

The Honkin' Boot eventually provided an even greater gift than first class. I got to be in the driver's seat. Whoop-whoop! But first…oh, how I'd tire of all the "but firsts" along this journey. Back to the story. But first, I'd have to master getting in and out of my truck on the driver's side. Yikes!

We found this neat li'l gadget called a Handybar®. It looks like a handle with a heavy metal hook on one end. The hook part goes into the door loop. Obviously, that's not the technical term. The loop is the ring thingy that the door would lock into when the door was closed. Now that I have you completely confused on my description of auto anatomy, I'll try and explain how I used it: Hobbling on crutches, I opened the truck door, (which is a small step forward and two steps back, equaling one big swing backwards via crutches.) Then a bit of a balancing act to stabilize. Phew! Next, I backed my hind side up to the seat. Hobble, hobble. Wobble, wobble. Here comes the fun part. With the crutches leaned up against the inside of the door, so I could reach them once I made it to the seat, I pushed down on the Handybar® tool with my left hand, steadying myself with the right hand. The whole time pushing my body upward until my right foot reached the running board. Then, it was heave ho onto the seat. You'd think the story was over, right? Naa. I still had to figure out how to get my Honkin' Boot inside the truck, on the floorboard. Sliding the seat all the way back, I was able to hand lift the Honkin' Boot and place it on the floorboard.

Wait! Don't forget the crutches. With the seat still all the way back, I wrangled the crutches, one at a time, into the front passenger seat floorboard. I'd eventually get the hang of the process. Soon, it would become second nature just like driving after months of not being able to.

By the end of March, all my hard work was paying off. It had been nearly six months since the accident. Six months of constantly battling to survive and overcome massive, life-threatening, life-altering injuries.

The fight was worth it as I stood, full weight-bearing, on BOTH legs for the first time.

Hallelujah!! Thank You, Lord!

Faith is the first step, even if you can't see the staircase.

The next couple of months were filled with struggles and victories. Every day I gained strength and mobility. Albeit tiny improvements, I was improving.

The setbacks were tough. It was a constant battle in my mind. My legs felt, and pretty much worked like wet noodles—wobbly and uncertain. I started Big Girl PT, aka: outpatient physical therapy. My physical therapy team was awesome. Led by Semper Fi Mary. She's tiny, but she's mighty! I loved her approach—"Figure it out, work through it, and move on."

My life felt like a constant tug-of-war, on a high, tight rope. Every moment was a struggle to maintain some sort of balance. I had to think about every single move I made. Oh, the mental and emotional energy it took to get through the day. Even at home, in my known surroundings, I'd struggle. Progressing from using two crutches to one, then from one crutch to a cane was a huge victory. Walking around the house, mostly without a cane, but with the Honkin' Boot felt so good. That is, until I'd over-do it. Sometimes the setbacks would be a day or two. Sometimes it'd be weeks. I'd also battle more open wounds. Mostly on the left heel.

All that would change anytime I left the house. Depending on the environment, the terrain, elevation, duration, or steps I'd need to climb, I'd have to adapt. First in my mind, second with my body, I'd have to stop, think, and devise a logical, most of the time creative, way to accomplish the simplest of tasks. It sounds a bit extreme, and it was. Every movement required prior thought.

If I leaned this way, I could reach that, but if I leaned too far, I'd risk twisting a knee or ankle, which meant another setback. That bag only weighs five pounds. *If I carry it on my right side, my damaged right knee or severely-damaged IT band would have to bear the load. However, if I carry it on my left side, I could be putting too much weight on the weak foot and leg. Ugh!*

All. Day. Long. Questioning, thinking, creating, reconfiguring, overcoming. Repeat. Repeat. Repeat. Reentry into the real world was overwhelming, to say the least. I would keep telling myself:

Stars can't shine without darkness.

It took everything within me to maintain a will to survive. It took all the strength I had to keep fighting—fighting to not give in, to not give up. Nightly rest would come, but with huge costs. I'm not sure if it was from the side-effects of the medications I was taking, my mind never stopping, my body hurting from being still too long, or a combination of all three. Sleeping through the night no longer existed.

Outwardly, I tried desperately to "keep it together." The "suck it up buttercup" upbringing of my youth began to haunt me, as I was putting more and more pressure on myself. I have no doubt prescription drugs, albeit necessary at times, can and do, have significant side-effects.

Open up any magazine and you'll see an ad for a new medication along with pages of teeny printed side-effects. I was no longer on IV antibiotic multiple daily infusions, but the infectious disease doctor had me on oral doses of strong antibiotics—for years. I also took a Pregabalin drug. It's a nerve pain inhibitor. I was off the heavy narcotics, but uncertain of the residual side effects they'd caused. I won't list the pages and pages of potential side effects from the prescription drugs I've taken (some for years) as that'd be a waste of good paper. However, just a few (Can you detect my sarcasm?) include: nausea, insomnia, impaired thinking, dizziness, problems with memory or concentration, impaired or delayed reactions, confusion, unusual thoughts or behavior, memory loss, anxiety, depression, cognitive impairment, tendon weakness, etc. While I have no doubt I experienced all of the above, in some degree or another, I wasn't always aware that I was suffering from them. Guess that explains the cognitive impairment.

Some of the side effects I definitely knew I was suffering from. Insomnia was one. When you can't sleep, you know it. I'm not sure I understood the depth of damages the side effects were taking on my body, especially my cognitive and emotional capabilities. I knew I was fighting to keep it together on a daily basis. It was exhausting. It was as if my brain wasn't firing on all cylinders. Sometimes, I'd think I had it all together, and I would do pretty well. Suddenly, something would go awry and confusion or frustration would set in. The life lessons of my youth carried me through, many times on auto-pilot.

The constant battle was for the most part internal. It's a difficult place to be. Outwardly, my innate "you can do it, don't give up" would take over, but inwardly, I was fighting a whole different battle I didn't quite understand. I'm not sure if, in my situation, the never-ending physical fight to recover is what helped me not fall into despair, addiction, depression, or if it was God. I chose to believe it was God.

It took all the energy I had to survive physically. I didn't have much left in the tank to deal with the mental and emotional sides of life.

True, my wagon was beyond full.

It was about to get much fuller.

When we fail to acknowledge our weaknesses they can become infections to our soul.

Chapter Nine

My body was gaining mobility and strength, in spite of the constant pain, thanks to daily physical therapy. Physically, I was making great strides. Sadly, the real me, the inner me, was struggling more than I cared to admit. I'd spent every last waking moment focused on my physical recovery. Yes, it was the top priority, but not the only priority. Neglecting the other areas of me took its toll. I may have learned the importance of physical balance, but truly healthy balance in my life was far from center, let alone healthy. My life, yet again, took another drastic turn.

Earlier I shared the "hurting people hurt people" saying about my relationship with my husband. Unfortunately, that never stopped in our marriage. When the accident happened, our problems were put on the back burner.

Someone recently said to me, "I think your husband healed from your marital problems during those months you weren't really conscious. You, however, weren't given that luxury until years later."

I believe there's a lot of truth in those words.

~ ~ ~

Sadly, as my body began to heal and I once again became mobile, those previously buried marital issues surfaced—with a vengeance. All the crap Satan was telling each of us did nothing but fuel the fire. Because I chose to no longer argue and fight with my husband, he saw it as my giving up, or no longer caring. In one way, he was right. I didn't care. I had absolutely no energy left in me to fight. I didn't understand it at the time, but it took everything I had to physically survive. It took every ounce of strength I had to literally put one foot in front of the other. Yes, I was doing it—walking, taking care of my daily physical needs, trying to regain some sort of normalcy in life—all at a huge cost.

When I said "I didn't care," please don't misunderstand me. I didn't mean, "I didn't care about my husband." Far from it. I never stopped caring about him.

I could blame it on the countless narcotics, the strong nerve blocker drugs, the hours and hours of anesthesia, or the untold doses of heavy antibiotics. I could blame it on the crazy side effects of all those drugs combined, and while they all definitely contributed to my inability to care, I believe Satan used those to his advantage, in my weakened state of mind, to further wreak havoc on my marriage. How could I fight to save my marriage when it took all I had to fight to physically survive?

So, yes, in many ways, my husband was right…I no longer cared.

It took me by complete surprise when I came home from physical therapy one day finding divorce papers on the kitchen island. My surprise wasn't the fact that our marriage had come to that, but that my husband had filed. The week prior, he told me he'd never file for divorce. If I wanted it, I'd have to file. I may be wrong, but I don't recall ever saying I wanted a divorce. The Christian marriage counselor we'd been seeing highly recommended a separation period. We were seeking separate living arrangements, or so I thought, when I discovered the divorce papers.

In many ways, I don't really blame him. He was reacting to what was happening in that moment. I can't speak for him, but chances are, his choice to file for divorce was based on the manipulation, lies, and deception Satan was filling his mind with. That, and his "never give up" wife, by all indications to him, had given up.

It's imperative for you, the reader, to understand something else of great importance to me. I'm by no means faultless. There were many things I said, and did, that I take full responsibility for. It's taken years for me to learn from those mistakes, to confess them, to repeatedly ask forgiveness for, and to ultimately forgive myself. God's grace is sufficient.

Only the healing power of God can close the wounds of one's failures.

Less than ten months after the accident, my husband's attorney submitted signed documents to the court to end our twenty-one year marriage. The counselor-recommended separation turned into a ninety day marital dissolution waiting period.

However, for me, the nightmare was just getting started.

~ ~ ~

During the waiting period, we both continued to live in our home—he in the master bedroom, I in one of the guest rooms. We had a showering schedule as it was unsafe for me to use the guest tub/shower unit. Why wasn't I in the master suite that was specifically remodeled for my physical needs? Good question. Apparently, someone told my husband that if he moved out of the master bedroom, I could sue him for abandonment and take everything. Although I tried to convince him that wasn't true, again, I chose not to fight about it. He remained in the handicap accessible master suite, I in a guest room.

The next several weeks were filled to over-flowing. Between working part-time, outpatient physical therapy three days a week, and regular chiropractic care, there was little time to find a new place to live post-divorce. Our home was too big for me to financially take care of by myself. That, and I no longer had the physical ability to take care of the property. Besides, my husband made it very clear he was keeping the house.

~ ~ ~

My amazing physical therapy team had me learning what they called brain mapping. In layman terms: it's a technique that retrains the brain. Teaching my brain how to move my left foot and lower leg. The team was also teaching me how to walk, yet again. This time, without the Honkin' Boot. It was interesting to say the least. Many times, I'd be frustrated or confused as I couldn't feel a good bit of my lower left leg and foot. I knew in my head my left foot was there, but learning to walk on something that I had trouble feeling was mind blowing. I spent a lot of time looking down, which also messed with my psyche. I've never been one to look down. My personality is anything but shy and reserved. I missed looking people in the face, and I missed seeing the world around me. There were times it really bothered me. I would fight the emotional strain of yet another way the accident tried to once more take a part of me away from me.

Confidence is silent; insecurities are loud.

In time, with constant dedication, I was walking on my own two feet. I say "on my own" but that's far from the truth. God blessed me with countless medical professionals who took every single step with me.

My physical therapy team entered into my recovery with gusto. While Mary was my lead therapist, from time to time I'd have a fill-in therapist. Over the years, I'd come to know, personally, most of the staff members. They'd all cheer on my improvements and celebrate the small victories. I'd joke with them, "So, I see other patients get a t-shirt when they graduate from physical therapy after six, eight, twelve weeks of physical therapy. If they get a t-shirt after just weeks of therapy, I expect a full wardrobe when I finally graduate!"

~ ~ ~

My chiropractor and nutritionist, Dr. David Pence, was a Godsend. From the very beginning he went above and beyond to do everything he possibly could to help my body heal naturally. Yes, I had serious injuries that required medical and surgical specialists. Those massive injuries, all the drugs, and the ongoing trauma took major tolls on my entire body. What a gift it was to have Dr. Pence in my corner, providing natural healing, while my body continued to recover. I'm blessed to call him, his wife, and his precious staff my friends.

My physical rehabilitation also included acupuncture and massage. The acupuncture was beneficial in helping stimulate nerve function throughout my legs—specifically in the lower left leg. It's crazy how your entire body can get tense and strained from trauma. Regular therapeutic massage helped my body relax, giving me the opportunity to physically let go of some of the frustration I was carrying. I highly recommend board certified acupuncture and licensed therapeutic massage.

~ ~ ~

Initially, I wobbled like an infant learning to walk. Fortunately, I was a quick learner, and like a toddler, I was ready to conquer the world.

Conquering the world would have to wait a bit longer. The constant thorn in my side, my Achilles heel, reappeared with a vengeance. Initially, it was a small wound on the back of the heel. I immediately saw my trauma surgeon and the wound care specialist. X-rays ruled out any contributing factors such as soft tissue tears, bone breaks, or wide spread infection.

The trauma surgeon thought it was a pressure point ulcer. Possibly from the compression stockings. I was wearing them to help with post-surgery swelling while transitioning to walking from being idle. The wound care specialist thought it was due to the thin grafted skin drying out, causing a deep crack that eventually opened up. The deep crack was from where the heel pad was ripped off during the accident and re-attached in an earlier surgery.

The treatment plan was pretty cool. They packed the open wound with silver nitrate, dried it, then bandaged it. I was sent home with supplies, and instructions to continue the daily treatment. Bonus—they added a second oral antibiotic just in case there was any underlying infection. Yuck! I hate antibiotics. They taste nasty and upset my stomach. Being on one antibiotic was enough; add the second, and my gut was anything but happy.

As instructed, I cleaned and applied the silver nitrate treatment every day. The foot and ankle continued to swell regardless of our efforts to stop it. The battle was constant to maintain enough movement in order to keep circulation for healing, but oh, so cautious not to over-do and cause further swelling. Have you ever tried to elevate your foot, with an ice pack on it, all the while not putting any weight or pressure on the back of your heel and lower leg? It was a circus act most of the time. Did I mention, I didn't have any feeling in the Achilles heel?

For weeks we tried a variety of treatment options. Sadly, the spot on my heel continued to cave inward. One treatment would dry up the oozing and draining, but then it would be too dry and cause a deeper opening. A second treatment, the hydrogel treatment plan, was to act as a mini debridement—clearing out, at a cellular level, the infected tissue, allowing healthy cells to grow and heal. Being very familiar with debridement surgeries, it made perfect sense to me. Unfortunately, it backfired on us. The two and a half inch by two and a half inch square hydrogel pad gave my heel a perfect two and a half inch by two and a half inch square of countless blisters. Ugh! I was no longer just allergic to latex. My medical charts now included latex and adhesive allergies. (So now we were back to the silver nitrate treatment, a little slower, but less damaging to the skin.)

Real faith is refined in the fires and storms of life.

For the first time since before the accident, I could feel my left ankle. It was pain that I felt, but I felt it. Pain is a feeling, and when one feels something, it's still alive. There's still hope.

Interestingly, I also had a couple of green toes on my left foot. Weird. I had no idea why they were green. One morning, while doing my "before I can get out of bed stretches, so I don't fall flat on my face" exercises, I noticed the green toes. Remember when you were a kid and wore what I call bubblegum jewelry—the kind you'd get from a gum ball machine? The kind that turned your skin a yucky shade of green. That's what my toes looked like.

After a session of show and tell with my physical therapist Mary, she asked if I'd been stepped on, bumped into, or dropped something on my toes. Chances are, any or all of those things could have happened, and I'd have never known it. I couldn't feel my toes. On occasion, I could feel the big toe, but the little ones were super slow to catch on. She determined that most likely I'd had a small blood vessel burst. Apparently, because of my extensive injuries, I was predisposed to having broken blood vessels. As we worked harder and harder to gain full mobility, more and more vessels would burst.

My mind, once more, started playing games with me when the wound on my heel wouldn't heal. Satan used my ongoing fear of infection to mess with my thoughts.

Am I overdoing it?

Have I not kept the wounds clean enough?

Did I let someone work on my wounds without gloves?

Have I exposed myself to some toxic environment?

Am I using the wrong kind of soap?

I was doing everything the medical professionals asked me to do, and not to do. Results were slow, and I had to be a patient patient. Not my greatest gift, that's for sure.

Patience is not simply the ability to wait— it's how we behave while we're waiting. —Joyce Meyer

Peregrinating...

Peregri...what?

Many of you are thinking, she's lost her mind. She's making up words. True, I'm known for that. I'm also known for using the wrong word to explain something, and I can lose my words all together. I know the word I'm looking for. It's just that I can't find it. It's as if my brain is a giant warehouse of filing cabinets. Those thousands and thousands of filing cabinets are stuffed full of paper-filled files. My brain has to sort through every cabinet, every file, and every page to find the one word I'm looking for. Thank goodness it's not as bad as it used to be. However, if I'm tired, stressed, or hungry, all bets are off when it comes to what and how I use words.

So, what is peregrinating? Webster's Dictionary defines it as traveling on foot. I was finally cleared to walk for exercise. YES!!

Of course, there's always a "but." Ugh!

With a serious look on his face, my trauma surgeon said, "However…if ANYTHING hurts, you must stop. You are not like everyone else. Not anymore."

There was a part of me that knew I was no longer normal, until that very moment, when it was spoken out loud, with authority, I hadn't really believed it.

It had been eleven months since the accident, and I could cautiously walk for exercise. I was way ahead of schedule from what the medical specialists told me in the beginning. Originally, I was told I'd eventually be able to walk again. Although, I'd most likely walk with the assistance of a foot and leg brace, it'd take at least a year to walk again. Thanks be to God, not only was I walking without a brace, I wasn't just walking, I was walking for exercise. Yay, God!

You're either making progress or excuses.

Crud!

Not a week had passed since the peregrinating authorization and I awoke with yet another oddity. My left calf and top of my left foot were red and covered with raised spots.

Now what?

Will this roller-coaster ride EVER end?

My physical therapist thought it may have been the allergic reaction from the hydrogel treatment going systemic. The wound care specialist didn't believe it to be an allergic reaction. He believed it to be irritation from being hit. I didn't recall a hit, but again, I felt very little on my lower left leg, even less on my foot or ankle.

I was beginning to learn how not normal my life had become.

When God gives you a new beginning, don't repeat the same mistakes.

It had been about six weeks since my husband filed for divorce. Trying to live under the same roof was taking its toll on both of us. Physically, I was stable and completely self-sufficient. The wound on the left heel looked better than it'd ever looked, and I was off all narcotics. I remained on nerve blockers and antibiotics, but those had become a daily norm. Emotionally, I was drained. I'd spent the past six weeks frantically trying to find a place to move to after the divorce was final. Options were limited for a self-employed, part-time, independent contractor manicurist. Only by the Grace of God did I find a wonderful location at a fair price for me to purchase. It was a small townhouse. The bedrooms were upstairs, and that concerned me. I'd learned how to climb stairs, but I was far from mastering them. I remember my trauma surgeon saying to me, "If you don't use your legs every single day, they won't work for you." (The old use-it-or-lose-it analogy.) After consulting both my surgeon and my physical therapist, I proceeded with the townhouse purchase. Ironically, they both cautioned me with "Healthy balance, Sheila. Healthy balance."

~ ~ ~

With tensions rising in our home, we needed a change. Unfortunately, my options were limited. I couldn't afford to fly, rent a car, or pay for a hotel, so I called my dear friend DeeDee, who lived in Oklahoma. I could budget for gas and go spend a few days with her. With a post-divorce place to live secure, and a few extra days off, I made the road trip across a few states.

Along the way, I stopped at an old friend's home in North Little Rock, Arkansas, for a brief visit resting my legs a bit. We hadn't seen each other in years. Isn't it wonderful when you spend time with an old friend you haven't seen in years, and it's as if you were together only yesterday? What a blessing that visit turned out to be as she went to heaven weeks later. As I left her home, while walking to my truck parked in her inclined driveway, I felt a freaky "pop" in my lower left leg. I couldn't tell exactly where it popped, but I thought it was the Achilles heel tendon. Not wanting to frighten my elderly friend, I said nothing to her, quickly getting into my truck. A few blocks away, I pulled over and assessed the damages. It was weird. I have no doubt the "pop" happened. However, I felt no pain, and by all indications, the foot and ankle maintained its odd, yet new, normal mobility. I considered turning the truck around and heading back to Tennessee. With pain and mobility seemingly unchanged, I headed farther west, rural west Oklahoma to be exact. The atmosphere was completely different; the scenery, the pace, the simplicity, the quiet, the calm. I felt my level of angst I'd been living in nearly disappear. Ahh…

DeeDee and I had a relaxing evening packed with girl talk. We laughed and cried as we shared more than three decades of memories together.

When I laid my head on my pillow that night, a peaceful calm washed over me. I didn't know how I'd financially manage on my own after the divorce. I didn't know if anyone would ever love a girl like me with mangled legs. I didn't know what or how my future looked, but God did. I truly believed it.

For the first time in nearly a year, I slept like a baby.

Oh, God! What's Happening to Me?

I awoke with excruciating pain like I'd never experienced. My lower left leg felt like it was on fire! The pain was so deep.

For the life of me, I couldn't figure out why. It made no sense to me that it would have been a residual, delayed reaction to the "popping" of the day before. Through tears of pain, I'd convinced myself I must have kicked myself in my sleep.

DeeDee was scheduled to work a few hours at the church that morning. Before she left the house, she brought me a rolling chair, so I could get around. I was hopeful that the pain would subside once I moved about a bit.

I don't know how long DeeDee had been at work when I called her and said, "I have to get to Vandy! Something's really wrong. I've got to get to Vanderbilt now!"

Without hesitation she replied, "I'll be right there. I'm bringing crutches, and I'll make a couple of phone calls to see if I can get you something for the pain."

Within minutes, DeeDee rushed through the front door with crutches in hand. She'd also, somehow, had a couple of low-dose pain pills. After all the massive, heavy dose narcotics I'd been on over the previous year, what she gave me did very little to ease the pain. Either that, or the pain was so intense that the pills weren't strong enough to stop it.

Again, while hysterically crying, I told her, "I'm leaving. I've got to get to Vanderbilt, even if I have to crawl to my truck, I've got to get to Vandy hospital!"

A Proverbs 17:17 Moment...

Literally, within fifteen to twenty minutes, DeeDee dropped her life and without hesitation she took over for me. She packed and loaded my truck with all of our things, including me.

The longest ride of my life was just beginning...

DeeDee and I had a nine hour drive ahead of us, which didn't account for the numerous stops we made, so I could throw up. Sometimes I could give her enough warning that she could pull off on an exit ramp. Sometimes there was just enough time to pull over on the shoulder of the interstate, and sometimes, I was fortunate enough to get the window rolled down in time to hurl. The passenger side of my truck looked awful.

One of the times along the side of the road, while barfing my guts out, I said, "I have to pee."

DeeDee replied, "Okay, I'll pull over at the next exit we come to."

Having no idea where, or how long that might take, I said, "I've got to go now! There's no holding it."

I'd been violently throwing up since I arose that morning. Not because of an illness, but because my body was in so much pain it's all it knew to do in an attempt to rid itself of whatever was causing the pain. I was so extremely weak from hours and hours of barfing that I had no strength to use crutches, let alone stand. Somehow, someway, along a rural stretch of interstate, I had to find a way to relieve myself.

I'm not exactly sure how we made it work, but while standing on my right leg, leaning against the door frame and holding onto something—the seat I think, I was able to relieve myself.

Apparently during the process, in a delirium state of mind, I told DeeDee the following story.

"Oh, those poor critters." I started.

"I'm sorry. What did you say?" she asks.

"God's critters. Ya know, all the animals out here in the wild."

Thinking to herself, "She's losing it! She's not making any sense."

"I feel so sorry for them," I said.

Playing along, DeeDee asked, "Why's that?"

"Well, it's one thing for the critters to eat what I threw up, but now I've just peed on it. Some meal that'll be."

Bursting out laughing she said, "You're hilarious even in your current state of mind."

It's true, laughter increases the body's level of endorphins, which decrease pain.

Laughter is the BEST medicine.

That particular road stop proved to be a win-win; bladder and endorphins released; the pain let up at least a little, so I could rest a few minutes.

The next thing I remember was that it was late—really late. We stopped at my house and dropped off Daisy. Then DeeDee drove me to the Vanderbilt Emergency Room. I'd been in contact with my trauma surgeon earlier that day. He told me who was on-call for him that night; he wanted me to ask for her when I arrived in the emergency room. She was my favorite resident and very familiar with my case.

Throughout the long drive home, I could feel my body shutting down on me. I'd been there before. That state of "I don't care" was taking over yet again. Thank God there were random moments of clarity when I'd tell DeeDee what was happening, what needed to be done, and what medical help to ask for. That's a lot of responsibility. She handled it well.

I briefly remember the emergency room. DeeDee and I both asked for the orthopedic resident on call by name. To this day, I don't know why, but the emergency room doctor denied that specific request. His diagnosis: I should have never been walking on such a severely damaged leg to begin with. He sent us home with narcotics for pain and said to follow up with my orthopedic trauma surgeon on Monday.

By the way, this was the wee hours of a Friday morning.

I remember very little of the next few days. I don't remember leaving the emergency room or my sweet, childhood friend sitting in a chair bedside me 24/7. What I do remember is not caring at all.

Looking back now, God was protecting me. I may not have cared, but He did. I wasn't lucid enough to fight the emergency room doctor demanding to see the orthopedic resident or coherent enough the next few days to call my trauma surgeon. Even though my husband was no longer involved in my medical case as an advocate, God never left me. He provided me a dear friend who never left my side.

A friend is someone who helps you up when you're down and if they can't, they lay down beside you.—Winnie The Pooh

When Monday finally came, I knew I had to get out of bed. I had to get dressed, and I had to see my trauma surgeon. I remember wearing a soft cotton long skirt.

As I sat on the exam table, waiting for the doctor, I knew. I knew the left leg was seriously infected. It had been oozing yellow fluid over the weekend. How serious, I didn't know. I just knew it wasn't good.

When my trauma surgeon came in, his usual kind and friendly self, he pulled up a rolling stool next to me. With several staff in the room with us he said, "Let's take a look."

Gingerly, I pulled the long skirt up to reveal a swollen, purple, blood-red leg.

The room went silent.

There was no need for words as I saw the man I'd grown to admire and respect, slump like a rag doll. This amazing trauma surgeon, who stepped out in faith, rebuilt both my legs when others said 'take it off at the hip' had once again been defeated with infection. This time, it was serious. Really serious.

When Dr. Sethi slowly turned his stool around and faced me, I knew.

With tears in his eyes he said, "It doesn't look good. I've got to put you in the hospital. We're going to have to do surgery. The hardware must come out and then I'll see what all we're dealing with once I get in there."

I reached over and touched his arm, "It's okay. Whatever it is, whatever happens, I'll be okay."

We all cried…

If you accept defeat, then that's what you'll get.
—*Facing the Giants*

I was immediately sent to the hospital via wheelchair. Neither DeeDee or I had any clothing or hygiene supplies with us. Oddly, that didn't seem to matter. Once again, DeeDee never left my side.

The first hospital room was a basic standard room. All kinds of tests were done, I was given high doses of IV antibiotics, fluids, and narcotics. Late that first night, one of the blood test results came back. The infection I had was methicillin resistant staphylococcus aureus; aka MRSA. I'd never seen the hospital staff work so fast. Although most of us are carriers of MRSA, it usually remains dormant. Unfortunately, a hospital setting is the perfect environment for it to spread. The next thing we knew, I was moved to an isolated room away from the general population. It was so quiet.

The next week or two was a blur for me. Typically in my daily moments of lucidity, I'd journal, creating a written record of my journey. Sadly, I have very little written documentation during this time frame.

Even though I was in an isolated room and guests were seriously advised against visiting, there were a few who took the risk—a couple of girlfriends and my parents. It's strange, I only truly remember one of the people who visited me—a man from my Sunday school class. Maybe because he's a bit older than me, and because we weren't all that close is the reason that I recall only his visit among many. Or, it could have been that he looked memorable because it was so out of character for him to be dressed in hospital garb from head to toe.

When interviewed for the book, one of my girlfriends, Donna, shared this story about her visit:

> Sheila acknowledged me with a nod when I came in, but little else was said. She was lying in the hospital bed, hooked up to all kinds of monitors and tubes. I took a seat for a few minutes. I wasn't there long when Sheila slowly opened her eyes. I'm not sure she even knew I was still in the room.
>
> I watched, fascinated. I'll never forget what happened next. In super slow motion, while never looking away from her left foot and leg, she slowly pulled the hospital bed linens off her left leg. She sat there, fully focused on her left foot. When I looked at her face, she looked serious but calm. A peaceful concentration, never taking her eyes off her left foot.
>
> After a few minutes, an interesting peace washed over her

face. With a tender intent, she carefully covered her left leg and foot. Gently she closed her eyes, drifting off to sleep with the most content look on her face. It was as if she was visited by an angel—letting her know everything would be ok. It was beautiful.

The exploratory surgery was performed the day after I was admitted to the hospital. It was a Tuesday. All the hardware that was used to rebuild my lower left leg had to come out. My trauma surgeon also removed tissue and bone as the MRSA infection had spread from the blood to the bone.

According to my records, I was later told I had three options as to how I wanted to proceed. The first surgical option, for whatever reason, I wasn't a candidate for. The second option—start over; fight infection, rebuild, fight infection, more surgeries, fight infection, repeat...The third option—amputation. Since option one wasn't available, I had two choices—start over or amputate.

I'd been through hell for nearly a year. The idea of doing that again held very little appeal for me. I'd watched a friend who had been fighting for years and years to keep his leg after a similar accident. Dozens and dozens of surgeries, countless PICC lines, infection after infection all the time. I wasn't sure I could handle a life of constantly worrying about the next infection.

In the deepest part of my mind, I knew what my answer would be. I'd known for a very long time what my answer would be when and if I was ever faced with the question—"keep fighting or cut it loose."

I had no idea what life would look like if I were to choose amputation. I did, however, know what life was like constantly fighting to keep something that was dying—be it a horrifically mangled leg or a badly broken marriage.

I gave my trauma surgeon my answer. I think, in one way, he was a bit disappointed. After all, we were a team. We both fought hard for a year to rebuild a leg that by all accounts didn't have much hope of surviving. I remember telling him "Thank you. Thank you for trusting your God-given talent to do all you could to rebuild my legs. If you hadn't done that, I wouldn't have had the past year to heal my left hip and upper leg. Because of you, I can and will move on in life as an active amputee, rather than living life confined to a wheelchair because of an amputation at the hip. Thank you!"

If you recall, my left leg was extensively damaged in the accident. My hip and femur are filled with titanium rods. Spending a year rebuilding the lower left leg gave my upper left leg and hip the opportunity to heal and be as functional as possible, all things considered.

Chapter Ten

Thursday September 13, 2012...

A date I'll never forget.

Without hesitation or reservation, I made the hardest decision of my life. I chose amputation.

Later that day, when I awoke in my isolated glass room, in one of the isolated burn unit rooms, I saw my left leg for the first time post amputation, or should I say, what was left of it. It was kind of hard to tell what it really looked like as it was crazy swollen and covered in bandages. The next few days were rough. I was still on a pain pump and heavy IV antibiotics. Surprisingly, with the infected, dying limb no longer a part of me, my body healed quicker than ever before. Please, don't get me wrong, the battle was just beginning. However, this time, it'd be a whole different kind of battle.

It's not what they take away from you that matters, it's what you do with what's left that counts.

Because the divorce was yet to be final, my initial recovery was in our home. Back to the guest bedroom I went. Sweet li'l Daisy never left my side. Home health nurses would come by to take blood, flush and clean the PICC line, and check the surgical site of my short leg. I'd eventually have home physical therapy as well.

The first time someone used the "S" word to describe my short leg, I nearly threw up. I hate that word. Even now, I can hardly stand to write it. Stump. Creepy! I am not, and will never be, a tree. I understand it was once a commonly used medical term. The key word in the previous sentence: "was." That word was used decades ago. It's no longer acceptable. For me and my fellow amputees, please do not use that term. The appropriate medical term is "residual limb" or "compromised limb," or as I personally refer to mine—"Shortie."

Most lower limb amputees are blessed to have a good leg to stand on. For me, I don't have that luxury. Both of my legs were severely damaged in the accident. I have a short leg and a long leg. Hence the term "Shortie."

"Shortie" was healing nicely, though still really swollen. I remained on IV antibiotics via a PICC line, narcotics, daily blood thinner shots, and nerve blockers for a month or so in order to recover from the surgical trauma of the amputation, as well as to fight off any residual MRSA in my system.

Fortunately, I was still greatly skilled in the use of crutches. Unfortunately, with my long leg having compound issues of its own, using crutches all the time took its toll on my right leg—especially my right knee.

After a couple of weeks, my clients were kind enough to come to me at my home so I could do their nails. I love my clients! What a gift they've been to me and for me over the years. Their love, loyalty, support, encouragement, and prayer have carried me through many times when I knew not how to do so myself. God has blessed me with countless angels along this journey. Too many to list by name. From the depths of my heart, I thank each and every one of you.

Life is rich because of the people in it.

Recovery from amputation surgery wasn't too bad. Learning to function as an amputee was, and is, a whole different ball game. I was about two weeks postamputation when the crazy phantom pains began. I'd heard very little about them and had no idea how insane they could be.

Except for the one time during home physical therapy when my therapist briefly described phantom pain, I really didn't understand the magnitude of it. Phantom limb pain is a pain that feels like it's coming from a body part that's no longer there. For some people, the pain will go away. For others, like me, it can be long-lasting and severe. It was explained to me that when a limb is removed, the severed nerves try to "rewire" themselves to the missing limb, sending pain signals—a typical response from the body when something is wrong. Phantom pains can be as simple as sensations of electrical jolts, a squeezing feeling, or bee stings. For me, phantom pains mimic off the charts, insane pain.

I asked, "How long will it take to 'rewire' the nerves to Shortie?"

"That's hard to answer. The human body has about one hundred billion nerve cells."

I've experienced unimaginable phantom pain: two ball-peen hammers smashing each side of my ankle bones, a straight-edge razor blade slowly cutting through the skin, an ice pick being plunged into my Achilles tendon, any number of toes, foot, ankle, or leg being twisted so hard it snaps off, what feels like an elephant standing on my toe, toes, or foot, a burning so intense it feels like I'm being branded like cattle, a sharp potato peeler slicing off thick layers of skin, knife stabbings and crushing pain from being smashed with a baseball bat by a giant. What's insane to me, for the year prior to the amputation, I had a horrifically damaged leg that I rarely felt. Now that it's gone, the pain can knock the breath out of me or bring me to tears—so unfair.

Phantom Chiggers...

Speaking of phantom pains, I've experienced a couple of other unique phantom sensations—chiggers and kisses.

Are you kidding me? Phantom chiggers?

I've had more than my fair share of phantom pains and I have handled them with a great deal of dignity and grace thus far. I've been in mid-sentence, when BAMB!, it felt like someone shot me in the shin. I could suddenly, without warning, double over in pain by many of the phantom pains I've endured.

One night, a particular phantom sensation was beyond batty. I was abruptly struck with the most intense itching I'd ever had. I swear it was as if a family of chiggers had moved in on my lower left leg. I needed so badly to scratch—but there was nothing to scratch. Do you have any idea how insane it sounds to desperately feel the need to itch something that's not even there? Aagghh!! I tried everything I could think of. I scratched the other leg. I massaged every trigger point known to man. I repeatedly thumped my prosthetic on the floor. Poor Daisy. I think she thought I'd lost it when I started doing my own version of the jig, hopping and wobbling about, trying to get the itching to stop. I tried hot compresses and cold compresses. Nothing worked. I was later asked, "How'd you get it to stop?"

"Pure exhaustion" I replied, "Pure exhaustion!"

Phantom Kisses…

Oh, so sweet…though a little weird.

My little Daisy thinks it's her job to help dry me when I get out of the shower. She's done it since she was a puppy. She's tiny, so it's not like she's accomplishing much, but because she's my li'l sweet pea, I let her help.

On this particular morning, my shower routine was like any other. As I dried myself, Daisy stepped into the shower to help. Funny thing was, that morning, after she dried my right foot, she leaned toward Shortie. She was smacking her lips, licking off the excess water from her snout. I kid you not. It felt as if she was kissing on my left foot. (You know, the one that's no longer there.) I looked away, thinking the sensation would disappear. Goofy as it sounds, the sensation increased. I'll take phantom kisses any day!

Wag more, bark less.—Ancient Proverb

The month or so post-surgery number nine was hectic to say the least. I wasn't able to drive, leaving me home bound to the guest room. Nurses, physical therapists, and friends would come and go. I was left with an awful lot of alone time for my mind to go a bit nutty. I had a contract on a townhouse, and I was scheduled to move by the first of November. I had no idea how I was going to live in a townhouse where the bedrooms and full bath were upstairs.

A client and her contractor husband stepped in. They took over the entire remodel project. They'd send me photos and updates making it a priority to have everything ready in time for my scheduled move. However, the question remained—How on earth am I going to get upstairs? I'd resolved myself to doing the fanny scoot on the stairs if need be. God had way bigger plans. I was given contact information for a local chair lift company.

After researching the costs, fear stopped me from calling. There was no way I'd be able to afford one. A friend suggested I call anyway. "Maybe they have used ones." The chair lift company representative was so kind. He met me at the townhouse and gave me a quote—one I'd never be able to afford.

"By chance, do y'all ever have any used or refurbished models available?" I asked.

"No, it's been years since we've had any used models in the warehouse," he replied.

"Would you please look or ask? Maybe there's something that'll work for me." I said.

"I'll check, but don't get your hopes up," he answered.

I'm thinking, "Buddy, my hope is in someone WAY bigger than you."

The next day, Mr. Salesman called me.

"Miss Sheila, you won't believe this. There's one used model in the warehouse, AND it just happens to be the perfect fit for the layout of your townhouse!"

"Thank You, Jesus!" was all I could say.

The used, perfect-fit, chairlift cost me a fraction of a new one. Not only that, the installers were able to schedule around the band of generous friends who helped me move. Correct that—two different groups of friends moved me completely. I sat in a wheelchair with Daisy in my lap while more than a dozen friends pitched in and got me moved. Many of those sweet people had never met each other before. You'd have never known it. Even the spouses worked well together.

"Sheila, you have amazing friends who truly love you, and...your friends are awesome!" One of them said to me.

My countless village of friends and family have been a huge part of the journey. I thank God for each of you!

Find joy in the journey!

Once again, I went through DTs—narcotic detox. One would think having been down that road many times already I'd have it mastered. Not hardly. It's quite the opposite. Each time it became more and more difficult. The "cravings" got stronger and stronger. My mind would play crazy tricks on me. *For God's sake, you've had a leg cut off, you need the drugs. You don't have to be strong anymore, you've been through SO much.* I was beginning to understand how good people become addicts—and that scared the ba-gee-bees out of me!

I was told for every week I was on the narcotics that it'd take that many weeks to get off of them. Oh, hell no! I wasn't going to give Satan any more artillery to use against me. I was fighting enough already. I didn't need to try and fight through drug addiction on top of it all. Whether it was medically right or wrong, I chose days versus weeks.

The DTs effects were awful, and I knew they would be. Detoxifying from narcotics was insane. For days, my body went through some really mind-boggling experiences—delusions, what felt like thousands of spiders crawling all over me, psychotic nightmares, itching beyond control, insomnia, severe abdominal pain, and intense anxiety.

Having a determined spirit was a HUGE gift.

Wait! No Weight...

The stitches were removed from Shortie. Yes! That meant I could finally go see the prosthetist! I was excited to move forward. My long leg was more than tired of carrying the load—literally.

"No weight bearing for three more weeks" my trauma surgeon says to me.

"I'm sorry. No weight bearing? Ahh, Doc, Shortie doesn't even reach the floor. How can it be weight bearing?" I ask.

"The three more weeks isn't because of the amputation. It's because of the surgery before that. The one where I removed the hardware from in and around your bones. The bones need more time to heal before you can put weight or pressure on them via a prosthetic," he explained.

Before I left his clinic I was fitted for a custom, rigid brace to be worn at all times—even while sleeping. It would quickly become a nuisance. Although the delays made sense, I still didn't like it.

Hurry up and wait...ugh!

Legendary Visitor...

A mutual friend, Marshall, initially introduced us via email and phone. Our correspondence was rather short most of the time, but that's all we needed. It's what worked for us. Imagine my surprise when legendary basketball coach Don Meyer asked if he could stop by to visit when he came to town.

"Of course, I'd love it!" I responded.

He had a sweet, sweet spirit about himself. Yeah, yeah, I know that doesn't sound like an appropriate description for an award-winning coach, but I'm telling you, he radiated the Holy Spirit. The tough John Wayne attitude was apparent as well as his genuine love for mankind.

When we first met, he asked, "What do you remember about me

from the David Lipscomb University days?"

I wasn't sure if I should've been honest or not. With a little reservation, I replied, "I remember you yelling…A LOT!"

He busted out laughing, "Yea, that's probably true."

I'm not sure what Coach Meyer had in mind regarding our time together. I believe he wanted to encourage me. He too became an amputee later in life due to an accident. I'd like to believe we encouraged each other that day, as he was very complimentary of my attitude, mindset. and determination.

One piece of advice he gave me I've never forgotten. "Sheila, don't ever, ever, I mean ever, EVER, be without your phone farther than an arm's reach away. It's not a matter of if you fall, but when."

Best practical advice from one amputee to another. Before he left, he prayed over me. There's nothing sweeter to your ears than a prayer from one who's truly walked in your shoes.

Coach Meyer went to heaven not long after our visit. To this day, one of his encouraging voicemails is one I still replay.

Coach Meyer was right. It wasn't a matter of if, but when. For me, the when was two weeks after our visit—my first fall as an amputee. I was at the salon getting ready to start my day. The cleaning crew had been there the day before, leaving a huge pedestal bowl of mints on my station. They were in my way, so I proceeded to move them to a nearby table. *How hard could it be? It's only four or five feet,* I said to myself.

While on crutches, I slowly carried the bowl of mints. As I stretched out to put the bowl on a nearby table, I got off balance. My "off balance" went in one direction while my over compensation went the complete opposite. Both crutches went air born.

Instinctively, I lifted up Shortie to protect it from the fall, which caused me to spin on my right heel. That started the teetering effect, ultimately landing all my body weight on my badonkadonk. It took me a minute or two to gather myself together and assess for damages. A sweet, male client squatted down behind me and lifted me upright again. Man, was I sore. Complete with a black and blue hind side.

Cop a squat...

The custom brace to protect Shortie was quickly driving me bonkers. Its purpose was to protect and restrict movement of the left leg. Okay, fine. Makes sense. Unfortunately, the design was less than desirable. It was shaped similar to a rigid knee brace with a hard bottom on it. Kind of like an ice-cream waffle cone with a flat bottom instead of a pointed tip. There were several adjustable Velcro® straps to help keep it on.

Unfortunately, like a waffle cone, if you only hold onto the ice cream, the cone slides right off. The thing was constantly sliding off. I'd hobble along on crutches, and suddenly, without warning, the thing would fall off. I'd try my darnedest to balance on one leg and one crutch, to put it back on. The more serious issue—the restrictive brace—literally became a stumbling block. Just as I'd pick up a little speed via crutches, the goofy thing would slide off.

Constantly doing an acrobatic balancing act to put the thing back on, I came up with a completely different solution. I'd "cop a squat." Rather than the one leg, one crutch balancing act, I'd gently bend my long leg until Shortie was pushed back into the brace, all the while using both crutches to steady myself. Oh, the looks I'd get from folks in public when suddenly I'd stop and squat. It may not have been the most graceful approach for a lady but it was effective.

Character is tested when you're up against it.
—Dick Vermil

Really?...Orange?...

I'd like to know which pharmaceutical chemist was sitting around (presumably drinking adult beverages) when they decided to add an extra special side effect to the oral antibiotic Rifampin. For those readers who've had the misfortune of experiencing this bonus side effect, you'll know exactly what I'm talking about. For the rest of you, put on your imagination cap and consider this:

After the first dose, my urine was orange. Yes, orange! Hi C orange. Extra strength Tang® orange. For all my Colorado buddies—Denver Broncos Orange Crush orange. It was a bit of a shocker the first time I turned around to flush the toilet seeing a neon orange glow shining back at me.

It gets better. Do you remember the original sunless tanner QT? Ya know, the one where we all turned a special shade of orange. Yep, that was the other nutty side effect. Every pore, every orifice, released a lovely orange ick. By day two, I was glowing like a traffic cone. Something told me to look at the pharmacy label on the bottle. Paying special attention to the fine print. I kid you not, it actually stated "Caution—if you wear soft contact lenses, discoloration may occur." What? Really?

What's the necessity of that much orange? Even though I don't wear contacts, I wasn't so sure things didn't have a bit of an orange hue to them. As I read the label closer, it hit me. "Take two capsules, twice daily for fourteen days." I'm no Harvard grad, but I calculated it to be a total of four capsules per day. Four capsules per day for fourteen days would make for a combined total of fifty-six capsules. There were only twenty-eight capsules in the bottle to begin with. First thing the next morning I called the infectious disease doctor and explained the situation to the nurse. We both had a good laugh about the orange side effects. Regrettably, after she talked with the doctor, she said the pharmacist must have made a typo in the dosage label. I was to take ONE capsule twice daily. I'd had five double doses. After all the medications my body endured up to that point, the real concern with the double doses was liver damage. They added a liver enzyme panel to my weekly blood test just to be sure. Lesson learned—read those labels!

Legman...

I've always had a tough time saying the word "prosthetist." Most of the time, it came out sounding vulgar. I can't tell you the number of times I'd tell people I was going to see my prostitute! The laughter of friends was one thing, but the look of horror on an acquaintance's face—priceless.

The first time I met my prosthetist was riveting for me. I was over-the-top excited to move forward with a new leg. Being a naive rookie in the wonderful world of prosthetics, I had a lot to learn. In my mind, I expected to be fitted for a leg one week, pick it up the next week, and walk out the door.

Ignorance isn't always bliss. Sometimes, it's a royal kick in the shorts. The first meeting with my legman (aka prosthetist) we spent a couple of hours taking dozens of measurements and answering beaucoup medical-history questions. He was a kind young man who handled my barrage of questions like a pro.

Shortie was measured and fitted with a liner. A prosthetic liner is basically a girdle for Shortie. The purpose was two-fold: help shrink the swelling and protect the wobbly bits below my knee. I learned I had about six and a half inches of my tibia and fibular bones still remaining below my knee. Those are the bones that needed three more weeks to heal before I could put weight on them. The liner felt pretty good, making Shortie feel protected. The liner was made of a thick gel covered in cloth—similar to a wet suit. It was about eighteen to twenty inches long, coming up to my mid-thigh. My legman left the room and returned with a bucket of water and what appeared to be casting materials. With the liner on Shortie, he wrapped it with clear plastic wrap. Then, he used the casting materials and wrapped them snug around Shortie. The casting process went from wet and cold to pretty warm. The warmth felt good.

Once the cast was hard, he gently removed it from Shortie. It looked huge. I had no idea how swollen Shortie had become. I left the clinic after scheduling for my first prosthetic fitting the following week.

Wearing the heavy liner to protect Shortie meant I no longer had to wear the goofy rigid brace. Praise God! That thing drove me batty.

Sadly, my new liner and Shortie didn't play well together. Less than twenty-four hours of wear and Shortie was covered with blisters. I sent photos of the blisters to my legman. His reply, "No more liner."

Me—"Dang it!"

A few days later, I had a follow-up visit with my trauma surgeon. I had two very important questions for him. One, can I drive? Two, am I strong enough to bear weight on Shortie? I took a plate of homemade cookies just in case I needed to bribe him!

Dr. Sethi received the cookies with deep gratitude as he said that beautiful, three letter word—y.e.s. Woohoo! By the end of the week, I'd be walking and driving, and I could hardly wait!

I almost forgot: A precious amputee mentor from the legman's facility met me at the trauma surgeon's clinic. She brought a one hundred percent cotton liner-liner! My sensitive skin prefers all natural materials. The thin cotton liner was worn between my skin and the regular, thick gel, liner that caused the blistering in an effort to stop them.

It's one thing not being able to drive when you don't care about living at all. It's entirely different when you've been given another chance at a healthy life. Maybe it's a piece of my daddy in me, but I love to drive. Always have. Probably always will.

As I drove to the legman's clinic at the end of the week, I was beyond giddy. Talking to myself, "A new leg. Oh, my gosh! This beats Christmas morning."

For the first time in my entire life, I wanted to be a bigger size. Shortie had shrunk so much in the week since the casting that the socket, the upper part where Shortie slides into, was way too big. This hurry up and wait thing was becoming a real thorn in my side.

There was an upside to the temporary setback. I learned it's actually a good thing Shortie shrank more than expected. Every time the limb shrinks, a new socket must be made. I learned more than I had bargained for that day. Typically, it's common for lower limb clean amputees to go through multiple sockets in the first eighteen to twenty-four months, as that's the usual and customary time frame for a compromised limb to reach its majority of shrinkage (aka atrophy). However, in my case, my amputation doesn't qualify as clean in any way, shape or form.

In the medical world, a clean amputation is when the amputation is initially performed by a surgeon for disease, diabetes, cancer, circulatory, or other issues. Technically, my lower leg was amputated in an accident. It was later reconstructed through several surgeries using man-made materials. Then, when the MRSA infected my blood stream and bones, the rebuilt leg was amputated and reconstructed again.

Poor Shortie. Combined with various compound issues on the remainder of both legs, my amputation becomes anything but usual and customary. Several medical specialists have compared my damages to that of someone having stepped on an IED (Improvised Explosive Device).

No Laughing Matter...

I love to laugh! It's the greatest medicine. As much as I love to laugh, I'm not a fan of mean-spirited humor. We all know the kind—the kind at someone else's expense.

It was the week of Halloween. and I had several appointments and errands to do. Mind you, I was still maneuvering life as an amputee without a prosthetic, all while on crutches. If I heard one person suggest it, I heard ten people say it: "You should be a pirate for Halloween." One fella had the gall (I wanted to use a different term here, but this is a family friendly book) to say, "With your peg leg, you'd make a great pirate." It took all I had not to use one of my crutches upside his head for batting practice.

Really, did he actually just say that? People can be so insensitive sometimes. I gave him my best *I hope you trip on your shoe laces and knock some sense into that thick head of yours* smile as I walked away.

It's one thing to laugh at your own misfortunes—it's rude to laugh at another's.

Life with Leftie…

I appropriately named my first prosthetic "Leftie." Remember my plan of get a prosthetic and walk? Ha! It hurt something awful. I was allowed to wear Leftie one hour a day to start with. Then, one hour twice a day. If the skin on Shortie held up, I could slowly increase to two hours twice a day. My lands, it was such a slow process. I had no idea.

Something else "slow" was getting dressed. Putting on a prosthetic, or my "plastic leg" as my little niece called it, took forever. There's a specific order, and if things aren't done right, one must start all over again. The legman used all these fancy medical terms to describe the various pieces and components. I no more knew what he meant than what it takes to operate a space ship. I made up new names that made sense to me for the different components.

I was so proud of myself when I finally mastered the process of putting on Leftie. All in just under fifteen minutes. Whoop-whoop! That is until I realized I wasn't dressed. Oh, for Pete's sake. Not only did I have to start over, I had to figure out how and when to dress Leftie in the process. Talk about wardrobe malfunctions. I failed to mention, I wasn't able to put on or change shoes on Leftie if it was already attached to Shortie. The same thing applied if I intended to wear leggings, tights, jeans, or pants. To this day, I lay my clothes out for the next day, in dressing order, every night before I remove my prosthesis.

I never considered myself to have much upper body strength before the accident. Living life in a wheelchair or on crutches changed all that. My upper body strength was better than it'd ever been, which is why it puzzled me that I had the hardest time getting shoes on and off Leftie. Obviously I couldn't change shoes if Leftie was attached to

Shortie. I promise, there were times when I'd break a sweat getting shoes on Leftie.

I asked my legman about it and he said, "It's the same size as your right foot."

"Well, it's worse than wrestling a squirming toddler to get shoes on or off." I replied.

"Hmmm…let me see," he said as he checked my chart.

"Yea, it says size eight. Let me check the molded foot shell," as he looked at the bottom of the foot.

"It's a twenty-six." he said.

"Well, that explains it. Twenty-six is definitely bigger than eight." I replied.

Laughing, he said, "That's true, but with this particular foot manufacturer their sizing doesn't compute to regular shoe sizing. However, a twenty-six isn't an eight. You need a twenty-three."

The correct size foot shell made a huge difference. It still wasn't easy, nothing like putting on or taking off shoes on a live foot, but in this case—size mattered.

Two words for anyone who thinks shoes aren't important…Cinderella and Dorothy

The reality of finality becomes apparent in the smallest of acts. The hardware on Leftie was configured with a cool release button at the ankle. Manually pushing the button gave me the ability to adjust the ankle to offset varying heel heights up to about two inches. A very big deal to a girl who loves shoes.

A few days after the amputation surgery, a couple of people from the prosthetic clinic stopped by my hospital room to visit me. Most likely, this was standard procedure. In my opinion, it was poor timing. I believe their intentions were good. However, when a patient is three sheets to the wind on heavy narcotics, they'll likely never remember you were ever there. This is what I heard—"Blah, blah, blah, leg. Blah,

blah, blah, the clinic. Blah, blah, blah, weeks. Blah, blah, blah, something, something." Whether I remember it, or I remember being told about it, I raised my hand straight into the air.

With a quizzical look on their face, one of them said, "Do you have a question?"

"I only have one. Will I be able to wear cowboy boots?" I asked.

"Eventually, yes," they answered.

"That's all I need to know." I replied.

Not sure if it was my unique question or the fact they realized I was higher than a kite but they left soon afterward.

At the time of the accident, I had over a dozen pairs of boots— varying styles and heel heights. I quickly learned, there's only one way to get a cowboy boot on a prosthetic—a zipper from the inside sole to the top of the shaft.

At one time, my daddy was a wonderful cobbler who put zippers in all kinds of leather goods. Unfortunately, my daddy was battling dementia at that time and wouldn't be able to help me even if he had the equipment. Fortunately, his brother and former business partner, my Uncle Ike, came to the rescue. Initially I sent him six boots. Not six pair, but six left footed boots. He did a great job installing inside zippers on the shafts. For the clog style boot, he put adjustable straps on them.

There would come a time when walking with any heel, more than three quarters of an inch high, would no longer be an option. Another cobbler, Ty May, an old high school friend and former champion bull rider, rebuilt several pairs of boot heels for me. Maybe one day I'll be able to have him design and build a custom pair of boots for me and ol' Shortie. He's truly a gifted artist!

With the boot situation taken care of, I needed to remedy my rather large shoe collection. Oh, how I dreaded it. I didn't shed a single tear after the amputation surgery, but I bawled like a baby saying goodbye to my fun shoes. I'm not a tall girl—about five foot four-ish. I was also married for twenty-one years to a man who was over six feet tall. I could and did wear heels almost daily.

Cheryl, my organizer buddy, volunteered to help me go through my closets of shoes. She was lovingly patient with me. As I sat in the middle of my king-size bed, she slowly brought me each and every pair. I know it sounds insane, but as I held each pair, my heart grieved. I don't think either of us were prepared for the flood of tears. I know I wasn't. Those shoes, my shoes, symbolized a part of me that I'd had for forty-seven years. The reality of the finality hit hard.

The old me was gone…

~ ~ ~

My shoe meltdown lasted several days. On top of that, it was November and gloomy outside. As I lay in bed one morning feeling sorry for myself, I heard a noise at the window a couple of feet away. I sat up and dropped my legs over the edge of the bed. Then, I heard it again. This time the scratching was replaced by sweet chirping. A cute little bird had attached itself to the window screen to serenade me. Aww, so sweet. He didn't stay long as he quickly flew off when I got closer.

Then, I heard it again, only louder. The little thing was fluttering and trying as hard as he could to grip onto the screen again. That's when I saw it. He only had one leg! I was instantly filled with—"See? If I care enough about the birds of the air, how much more do I care about you?" What a precious, precious gift. Not only was the little fella keeping on—he was joy-filled in doing so!

Chapter Eleven

Yes, God gave me parents who instilled in me a strong work ethic, and He continues to bless me by surrounding me with amazing people who carry me through life's hardest battles, but only God, and by God, trusting in God, am I able to literally walk out this journey. I have no doubt I'd be addicted to narcotics, severely depressed, suffer with post-traumatic stress disorder, or worse. If it were not for His divine presence in my life—especially during the horrific storm and recovery from the accident that forever changed my life, not only physically, but mentally, emotionally, and spiritually—I would not be completely transformed. I'm a whole new me from the inside out.

The supernatural, miraculous encounter I had on September 29, 2011, was confirmation that God had called me. He chose me to "walk out" this story—His story through me. Only in time, learning to trust Him when I had no other option, did I become His.

I grew up knowing there was a God. Most of my life, I had what I'd call "my parents' faith walk." I mostly practiced (I use that term lightly) in church, checking the boxes as I saw my parents or others around me "do" church. Please don't misunderstand me. My parents, and many others around me, had their own personal relationship with God. It was I who didn't. I knew of God. I believed He existed, but I never knew Who He was.

~ ~ ~

This journey has been beyond scary, intimidating, trying, emotionally exhausting, mentally draining, horrifically painful, depressing, and downright unfair much of the time. In spite of it all, I wouldn't trade brand new Barbie doll legs, my home, or my failed marriage for the beautiful spiritual journey I've been on, for the life-changing encounter

I've had, and continue to have, with God.

I live every day as a miracle, because for me…it is.

Day after day, week after week, the battles continued. Adjusting to life as an amputee was tough. The grafted skin on Shortie, as a result of the de-gloving of the skin in the accident, was always breaking down. Soft grafted skin against a rigid prosthetic socket, that doesn't give, wreaked havoc on efforts to heal and move forward.

Add to the thin grafted skin what I refer to as wobbly-bits and you've got a combination for disaster. Days and weeks turned into months and months of continuous blisters, bruises, welts, hickies, and skin erosion on Shortie from the constant changes taking place. Shortie atrophied so fast we could hardly keep up with new prosthetic sockets. Some sockets would last but a week, others maybe two weeks. Rarely would a socket last more than thirty days.

In the beginning, I'd name each new socket. My hope was if I'd name them, we'd somehow create a positive, working relationship. The first was Leftie, followed by L2, Trey, T2, Houston, Ocho, Sven and Bo to name a few. Just when I thought we'd have a decent, almost tolerable fit, Shortie would shift or shrink, and many times both at the same time.

Walking (I use that term very loosely—as I had yet to walk without assistance), became a painful dance, of sorts. Wearing a prosthetic that's too big is similar to wearing someone else's hiking boots that are several sizes too big. You can add several pairs of thick socks to make up for an extra wide, extra-long boot, but even after lacing the boot tightly around your ankle, it's a sloppy, unstable mess when you try to walk. Add to that a limb that has significantly loose skin, which constantly shifts and changes, and you have an equation for disaster.

I continued to live life on crutches. On occasion, we'd have a better fitting socket, and I'd advance to a single crutch, or even a cane, for a short period of time. Unfortunately, that would never last. Life on crutches took its toll on me. My body was constantly trying to adapt to the never-ending changes of life of 24/7 pain.

My long leg, the right one, was taking a beating all day, every day. Have you ever tried standing on one leg for more than ten minutes? I double-dog-dare you to try it right now. Go ahead, stand up, preferably near a counter or firm piece of furniture. Now, lift one foot off the floor. Hold it up for at least ten minutes. You're welcome to rest a hand on the counter if need be, but don't let your lifted foot fall to the floor, not even for a toe tap. Envision if, or should I say, when, you let your foot come down, you've now fallen. For those of you who are flexible, limber athletes, consider yourself among the elite. Most folks can't hold one foot off the floor for five minutes, let alone ten. I've yet to meet anyone who can hold it longer than thirty minutes at a time without their body writhing in pain. Multiply that times hours, days, weeks, and months, and you'll begin to understand the painful rebellion my body was going through.

A friend once said to me, "It never ends, does it?"

"You've hit the nail on the head...It NEVER ends."

It's how we rise to the challenge that defines us.

My team of medical specialists were awesome. Every single one on my team felt my frustrations. For a year it was one step forward, two steps back. Often times Shortie would have such large, open wounds, I could no longer wear a prosthetic. Unfortunately, my insurance company couldn't (or wouldn't) see the medical necessity of a wheelchair. Mary, my fabulous physical therapist suggested, "Hey, what about a knee roller?" I'd used a rolling stool to get around my home when my body couldn't take one more hop on crutches. We found a used knee roller I could borrow, with the intention of giving my legs a chance to rest and recover a bit.

Meet Christine...

Y'all, that knee roller gizmo was possessed! Most of the time, I sat on it, using my long leg to peddle about like Barney Rubble. After I reached my desired destination, I'd dismount via one leg, then put the roller in lock position. I kid you not, out of the blue, the goofy thing would start rolling away. Creepy!

Routinely, when I'd load or unload it in the backseat of my truck, it would nearly undress me. It never failed. If it wasn't a handle bar down my shirt, it was a wheel up my backside. Then, as soon as I would get the crazy thing situated, it'd roll itself right back out the door. Quite a sight to see as I would twist and grunt, sometimes fussing, all on crutches with only one leg! Who needs physical therapy or Zumba class when one can get a great workout with Christine, the rollator?

~ ~ ~

Phrases from my childhood haunted me. "Suck it up! Don't quit! Don't give in!" I continued to push myself. Sometimes I didn't know where the strength would come from. Other times, it was pure selfish, stubborn determination.

I'd already spent a full year after the accident rehabilitating and rebuilding my legs, including—eight reconstructive surgeries, physical therapy seven days a week, on and off narcotics more times than I like to count, daily blood thinner shots, numerous PICC lines, enough antibiotics to kill a grown person, various other drugs for residual accident related medical issues, typically no more than a few hours of sleep each night, and pain that never ended. That was all before the amputation.

My mind was fighting for a new normal. My body was nowhere near that possibility.

I was told that typically after an amputation surgery, one would be on crutches six to eight weeks. Because my compound injuries were anything but typical, I should expect six to eight months, even up to a year. That was tough to swallow, even for me. I could wrap my mind around a couple of extra months of transitioning my body into life as an amputee, but another year? I was fit to be tied...outraged... hopping mad!

"Really, God?"

"Will this EVER end?"

The constant pain, combined with anger created an emotional roller coaster. I'd spent all my time, since the accident, rehabbing my legs. Focusing on the physical, I had no time left for anything else, especially the emotional side of it all.

Prior to the accident, I'd get outside and power walk for an hour or so every day to de-stress. That option no longer existed with the legs I now had which added fuel to my fire of angst.

Years ago, I'd taken a self-defense course, and we spent a good bit of time working out with punching bags. That's what I needed. I needed to hit something! Because my townhouse didn't have space for a hanging punching bag, I settled for the next best thing: a kids blow up Bop Bag. I beat the fool out of that thing! It was bright orange with a bullseye target on it. Man, what great therapy!

Indy 500...

This journey has had some crazy twists, turns, potholes, and speed bumps. I could fill an entire book with the entertaining experiences I go through almost daily as a girl with *one foot in heaven*.

What began as a routine trip to a local big-box department store turned into an episode of Candid Camera. I'd become quite accustomed to the battery operated, motorized buggies. (For all you non-southern folks, that's what y'all refer to as a shopping cart.) No two battery-operated buggies are the same. However, I'd been using them all over town for a while and became quite proficient with various models. One could say, I was the Mario Andretti of the motorized scooter world. If you've never driven one you don't know; they're pretty simple to operate—except for this particular day.

As I hobbled into the store on crutches, I was thrilled to get the last remaining scooter. It had even been plugged in and fully charged. Score! I can't tell you how many times I've been stranded in the back of a store on a scooter whose battery has died. Believe it or not, I've actually called Home Depot from the back of the store for them to send someone to rescue me.

It takes me a few minutes to get settled. Crutches are secured in the basket—check. Cell phone is with grocery list—check. Reader glasses are out—check. Handbag is secured at my feet, (make that "foot")—check. Skirt tucked in so it doesn't drag the floor or get caught in the wheels—check. Ready for departure, I ease off through the store entrance thinking, *Finally! A buggy that has some gumption to it—yes!* All that gumption was about to backfire on me. I approached the produce section and let off the accelerator to make a turn. It didn't slow down.

This dumb thing.

What the heck?

You've got to be kidding me!

I looked down to make sure my crutches hadn't slid and pinned the throttle handle. Nope, all good there. I tried another option—push the throttle handle to the reverse position. Aagghh!…Wrong again! The thing is still moving, full speed ahead. I start to panic. The goofy side of my brain takes over. *What if I can't get the thing to stop and I hit something—or worse, someone?* My mind also had a quick image of a headline: "Woman survives horrific near death motorcycle accident, only to die in a runaway electric buggy."

Typically, these motorized buggies are designed to stop automatically when you take your hand off the throttle. I tried that. Nope. The "look Mom, no hands" approach didn't work either. I'm not sure if it was my hands in the air and the buggy running full speed ahead, or the loud thumping of my heart that drew the attention of a couple of fellas working in the produce department.

I'm trying to stay calm as I yell to them from a distance, "It won't stop!" They look at me like I'm the idiot that doesn't know how to operate an idiot-proof electric buggy. One actually waves at me. Apparently he mistook the "hands flailing about in the air" as my waving hello.

Both their demeanor and reactions abruptly changed when I yelled

"IT WON'T STOP!" while waving both my arms in the air. Suddenly, everything went into s-l-o-w motion. One of the fellas comes running towards me, trying desperately to catch me as I zoom away. At that moment, with all the excitement, one would think I'd have found the kill switch and turned the thing off. In that moment, it never occurred to me. All I could see was the glass freezer case ahead of me or an elderly couple, neither I wanted to hit.

Superman, aka; "Mr. Produce," swooped in, jumped on the back of the scooter, reached around me and hit the main kill switch. Just like that, Clark Kent saved the damsel in distress. My hero.

Once we all caught our breath, we busted out laughing. Both these fellas had been in retail a long time and neither had even heard of such a thing happening. Unfortunately, there were no other electric buggies available, which meant I couldn't shop that day.

I returned the following day for a second attempt. I kid you not, one of the fellas actually followed me around the store to be sure I was okay.

I asked him, "How'd y'all get the psycho scooter to the stock area for repair?"

"You were right. That thing was possessed. It took me forever to get it to the back," he replied.

"If it had to happen, I'm grateful it was me on it rather than a frail elderly person. It'd have scared them to death!"

If you climb into the saddle,
be ready for the ride!

After more than eighteen months of being on some form of antibiotics—oral, IV, or both, I was finally off of them. Praise God! Those things had messed with my tummy for far too long. They also messed with my sleep, or should I say, lack of sleep.

Speaking of medication side effects, I'm not sure what, or what combination of prescription drugs, caused my new vocabulary, but something sure did. I continued having the hardest time finding words. I'm grateful God has blessed me with a wonderful sense of humor and creativity. However, there are times it can get me into trouble. Calling makeup concealer "camouflage" is one thing. They, at least, basically do the same thing, but some words are definitely not the same.

I'd been out with a few friends to hear a fun local eighties band. I used to love to dance. I still do. Sadly, there wouldn't be any dancing for this girl. While my friends were out on the dance floor most of the night, I sat tableside tapping my toe and singing to the music. Sometimes it can be really tough to watch others do something you no longer can do. That night was a good night. I truly enjoyed the evening.

A few days later, while relating the story to a client, I said "We had a blast. The music was great. Unfortunately, I only got to table dance."

She busted out laughing!

I'm thinking, *That's not very nice—laughing at my inability to dance.*

She quickly noticed the hurt expression on my face and once she caught her breath from laughing so hard she explained. "When you said table dancing, I pictured you up on the table—dancing. Like in those girlie bars!"

"NEVER gonna happen!" I responded.

Play Doh® to the Rescue...

Who'd have thought a small ball, of what was originally designed in the 1930s as wallpaper cleaner, would play such a significant part of my prosthesis process. Modeling clay from the mid-1950s became my new best friend.

My legman determined that one of the constant skin breakdown spots on Shortie was caused by what he termed hammock (or traction) pressure rather than direct (or distal) pressure. Think about it this way: If you were to put a peach in a nylon stocking, letting it hang freely suspended, it would be okay. However, if the same peach is in a suspended stocking, but you put a brick on top of the peach, the weight of the brick on the peach would push the peach against the end of the stocking causing a hammock-pressure effect on the soft skin around the peach. The tender peach skin would pull away from the bottom causing it to pull apart. This process is what was happening to my skin. Because I didn't (and don't) feel much in that area, I had no idea what I was supposed to be feeling. We all assumed the skin breakdown was because of too much direct (distal) pressure. We thought the bottom of Shortie was being pushed into the prosthetic too far. We'd add more socks to "lift" Shortie away from the bottom of the inside of the socket. This attempt only made things worse, causing more hammock strain on my skin.

Play Doh® to the rescue! I'd drop a ball of Play Doh®, about the size of a quarter, into the socket—the upper part of a prosthetic that looks like a vase. Next, I'd put Shortie in the socket, I'd stand, and apply as much weight as I could tolerate. I'd sit down and slide Shortie out of the socket. The ball of Play-Doh® was never even touched. What was the conclusion? The hammock (aka traction) pressure was causing many of my issues and I never knew it because I feel so little of that part of Shortie. I'd been doing what I thought was right based on the amputee norm. In reality, thinking and definitely doing without proper research doesn't necessarily make for ideal solutions. Thanks to the McVickers and their world-famous invention, Play-Doh®, things were looking up.

The past is for learnin'—not for livin'.

Nemo...

Growing up as a daughter of a Navy man, I was taught at a very young age how to swim. Daddy had a huge respect for water and made sure us kids did as well. I enjoy being on the water, but I'm not a big fan of being in open waters. Like Jethro and Elly May, I prefer a concrete pond. I'll pass on getting into lakes, rivers, ponds, creeks, or oceans. God made me a girl, not a sea urchin. Besides, there's no risk of losing another limb if I stay out of the shark's house. All kidding aside, because of the abundance of hardware in my legs and my history of

MRSA, I've been repeatedly advised to avoid all open waters. Works for me!

I was struggling to find some kind of physical exercise I could do without further injury to my body. Mary, my physical therapist, suggested water rehab. Eager to try anything that might work, I gave it a go. Oh, y'all! My first attempt was a hoot! I didn't know one couldn't use every prosthetic in the water. How was I to know? I was a rookie at all this one-legged stuff. Fortunately, before I entered the water, I called my legman.

"Can I get this thing wet?" I asked.

"Well, sure, it'll withstand rain and water splashing on it from time to time," he replied.

"What about swimming?" I asked.

"Aaa…no. You can't do that with the kind of prosthetic you have. You'll need a water leg for that," he said.

Like EVERYTHING, when it comes to the shattering world of amputation, it's always a process. What they really mean to say is, "That'll take a lot more time and a whole lot more money."

My legman said he would use some parts from one of my old prosthetics to build a water leg. However, it'd take several weeks to have a new water leg completed. Not wanting to wait for weeks before getting into the pool, I created a (somewhat) safe way of getting myself into the water. With the use of crutches and strategically placed chairs near the handrail and pool entrance steps, I was able to gingerly lower myself to the top step. Once that was completed, I would do the bump-scoot, down each step, until I was in the water.

I can't tell you how amazing it felt to be immersed in the pool without wearing a prosthetic. For the first time since the amputation surgery, I felt whole in my body. I'm not sure how to describe it; perhaps as a weightless sensation encapsulated in physical freedom, similar to skinny dipping. Yes, I used to skinny dip. It's very relaxing when done in the privacy of your own pool, behind private fencing. I rather miss it.

I puttered about the pool for a bit, getting used to how my body responded to water depth, positions, etc. With a surge of excited energy, I proceeded to swim, freestyle, from one end of the pool to the other. This was a small community pool so I felt confident I could complete the task. Imagine my surprise when I completed the lap in record time. Not until I grabbed hold of the pool edge and opened my eyes did I realize why I set a pool record. I hadn't made it to the other end of the pool. Hardly. I'd barely made it half way!

What the...? How'd I end up at the side of the pool instead of at the other end? Weird!

Not being one to give up easily, I doggy-paddled and floated my way back to the starting line again.

This time, I'll keep my eyes open and my head above water to see what I'm doing wrong.

I tried again. I ended up in the same spot about midway of the pool. My third and final attempt revealed the answer. I grabbed a swim noodle from the edge of the pool. Tucking it under my arms, I used it as a simulated kick board device. With each attempt down the pool, I'd kick both my legs. In my mind I was performing the swim stroke correctly. What I didn't realize, "Shortie can't do what my real leg used to do." My rudder was messed up. With one leg doing the majority of the work, and the other failing miserably, my body slowly turned to the left even though I thought I was swimming straight ahead. Treading water in the deep end for extended lengths of time turned out to be a better solution.

Eventually my new water leg was ready. Like most of my other legs, it needed an appropriate name. "Nemo" was a great name for a water leg. It was heavy, bulky, and rigid, but it allowed me to do water workouts. It's so much easier on my joints to use water resistance.

One day after working out in the pool, I took Nemo off and set it on the side of the pool so I could relax a bit in the water. A neighbor, who also happens to be an amputee, showed up. His situation is way different from mine. He's super mobile even without his prosthetic. Picture this, a small community pool with only a few people in the water. Myself and my amputee neighbor being two of them. An older couple enters the pool area with their visiting grandchildren. I'd guess they were four and six years old. They were so excited! Carrying their toys, they made their way to the pool entrance. As they anxiously waited for their grandparents, the boys noticed Nemo lying on the side of the pool. Their eyes got as big as saucers. As I made my way out of the pool, exposing Shortie to these little fellas, my amputee neighbor monkey-crawls via two hands and one leg from his lounge chair to the edge of the pool. Those poor kids. They slowly backed away from the pool, never taking their eyes off me or my neighbor. You could almost see their thoughts—*Ain't gettin' in there!*

Fortunately, their grandparents saw the opportunity to educate the boys rather than encourage their fear of physical differences or physical limitations that many people have.

Disability is a matter of perception.
—Martina Navratilova

I've always done my best to encourage questions others may have regarding my situation; especially from children. They ask some of the greatest, albeit simple, questions. It's adorable when a five-year-old boy says, "Do you sleep with that thing on?" It's quite another thing when a fifty-five year old man asks the same question. I'm far from stupid and blessed by God who gave me a mind of discernment.

By the way, my typical response to the dirty-minded, grown man who asks that question—"Don't make me take this leg off and kick you're a--!" The response is usually bellowing laughter, but…at least they know, I know, they're acting like an idiot!

Chapter Twelve

Professor Sheila...

Over the years I've done a good bit of public education. I have a rolling suitcase, filled with treasures kids find fascinating. I created "Theodora," my therapy teddy bear. I cut off one of her legs, and I designed a special little prosthetic for her. She carries a crutch and wears a big pink bow on her head. I also take an old prosthetic for the kids to see, feel, carry and ask questions about. I've yet to write a children's book, so I use a couple of other books and modify the stories to fit mine. The kids love it!

Young kids aren't my only audience. I've been blessed to share my story with groups—small and large, organizations, clubs, church groups, civic organizations, and nonprofits. However and wherever God wants me to encourage, motivate, educate, inspire and give hope—I'm willing. Everyone needs to know there's hope. Even in the darkest times...there's still hope.

Toughest audience? Hands down—troubled teenagers. Once, at a teen detention center, I thought I'd met my match. These kids were walled off. Not literally, but they might as well have been. I was having a slow, rough start getting these kids to engage. Silently, I said a quick prayer. "Lord, I need Your help." With that, I was given the key to unlock these kids. "Choice."

All day long we're given the opportunity to make choices. I needed to break it down into the simplest form. Once I did, we connected. They came alive, engaging and asking great questions—so much so that when the bell rang, the kids didn't want to leave!

On another occasion, I had the opportunity to share my story with a group of Vanderbilt University medical students. A very different scenario than speaking with troubled high schoolers. My awesome trauma surgeon, Dr. Sethi, set it all up. Technically, all the arrangements were made through his assistant, Jordan, who was amazing. He took care of everything, right down to (literally) delivering me to the class, via wheelchair escort. For those who aren't familiar, the Vanderbilt University campus is massive. Jordan was precious when he asked if I could manage half a mile walk.

"Honey, I can barely do half a block." I replied.

"Not a problem," he responded.

On the day of the class, I met Jordan in the one place I knew well—the parking garage below the orthopedic trauma clinic. Jordan had a clinic wheelchair that he loaded into the bed of my truck. He jumped into the passenger seat and pulled out his phone. I kid you not, he used a special app on his phone to navigate around campus to get us to the building we needed to be in. That's how big and spread out the campus is. Once parked, we still had a bit of a trek to get to the correct building. With me in the wheelchair and Jordan pushing, we had a myriad of mishaps before reaching our final destination.

Dr. Sethi and his colleagues were addressing the class when we arrived. They greeted me warmly; I got a hug from Dr. Sethi (we've been through WAY too much together to settle for a handshake). Dr. Sethi presented my medical case with the assistance of a PowerPoint presentation. He began, sounding a bit like what one's medical chart/records would sound like if they could talk. There's something very real and heart wrenching when you see X-rays of your mangled bones on a larger than life, giant screen. Listening to Dr. Sethi tell my medical story in his voice was tough. Listening to a room, filled with shocked gasps from the students, when they saw my X-rays, takes on a much deeper reality. As I listened to Dr. Sethi, it was a statement that started with the sentence "I had only been in practice two months on my own when Sheila was flown in via Life Flight."

A chill ran through my entire body.

"Wait! What? Two months?!" I thought to myself. "How could that be?" This God-gifted surgeon had been rebuilding my legs for over a year. How did I not know this? By the way he'd taken care of me from day one I'd have thought he'd had at least a decade of solo experience under his medical belt.

Dr. Sethi looked my way. By my expression, he knew I never knew. I'm sure the look of pure shock on my face said it all. His look to me said "It's true." Y'all, at that very moment, I knew God had hand-picked this man to be my surgeon, to guide his hands, and rebuild my legs. From the very moment I consciously met Dr. Sethi, we had a unique bond—a bond that comes only from above.

~ ~ ~

Next, it was my turn to share my side of the story. Generally, I cater my speaking topic to meet the need of the audience. In this situation it was medical students. Great young people with eager minds are like sponges ready and willing to soak it all in. I tried to keep to the medical side of things for their benefit. Dr. Sethi wanted to be sure we had plenty of time for questions and answers. I LOVE that about him! He's never been intimidated or bothered by my multitude of questions throughout my journey. I believe that our willingness to listen and learn from each other has been one of the greatest blessings for both of us.

The students had great questions like: "What's your biggest fear? What's been the hardest part of recovery? Why are you not bitter, angry? What's the hardest thing to do now?"

My second surprise came a few minutes later. As we were having an open conversation, complete with random questions for me, Dr. Sethi laid out a bit of the history regarding the MRSA and the timeline of the amputation surgery. What he remembered most was how I consoled him. He was so touched that I was more concerned about him than I was about my own leg. Chances are, when the MRSA was taking over my body, I may not have realized the full extent of the implications. Whether I knew it or not, it's reassuring to know my response left a positive impact on him.

In his book, *The American Dream in Tennessee: Stories of Faith, Struggle, and Survival*, Dr. Sethi shares part of my journey as his final chapter:

"I knew something was wrong, and the moment I saw her leg, my heart sank. I looked up into her eyes. I could tell by her face that she already knew what I was going to say. She smiled and held my hand, 'Whatever it is, it's going to be okay.' This moment was another demonstration of the strength that emanated from her. I was invested, and my heart was broken for her, and she could tell. In this moment she could have done anything, yelled in anger or cried in frustration. Instead, she took my hand in hers, looked into my eyes and said, 'You did everything you could and everything right. This is God's will, and it's time for me to move forward.'"

"'It's okay,' she reassured me again, smiling brightly as a single tear fell down her cheek. "We'll make it through this.'"

"In a moment of such profound loss, she wasn't even thinking about herself."

The third and final surprise that day was a definite aha moment—without a doubt, a God thing. The students were still asking questions and something was said about my determination—my spit and grit spirit. Dr. Sethi got real quiet. He slowly rotated his chair in my direction. As he did, I could tell his next question was going to be a doozy. He briefly hesitated. The room fell silent. I swallowed hard and sent up a quick prayer, *Whatever it is, please give me the right words to respond.*

Slowly and deliberately, in a genuinely kind and sincere tone he asked, "How do you do it? Where does that strength come from?"

I glanced up at him and looked around the room. With a smile on my face, tears in my eyes, and a warmth flowing from the inside out, I pointed heavenward. The Holy Spirit spoke these words through me…"God put that spirit within me, and that's the only reason I can endure."

Keep your heart open for God to show up.

Months were ticking off the calendar, yet skin breakdown issues with Shortie remained. My entire medical team worked together to come up with productive solutions. Unfortunately, our efforts continued to fail.

Difficult as it was, I tried my best to have as much of a normal life as possible. Whatever "normal" looked like.

Faithful Friendships...

My thirtieth high school class reunion was coming up and I really wanted to attend. I knew it wouldn't be easy traveling in my physical condition. I rarely let difficulties stop me, and this trip was no exception. I enlisted the help and assistance from a couple of my dearest childhood girlfriends. Their excitement fueled my excitement. Each of us were coming in from different states: Melanie from Texas, DeeDee from Oklahoma, and me from Tennessee. I could hardly wait!

I'm not sure Melanie and DeeDee realized just how much I needed time together, away from the never-ending frustrations my life had become. Between the life-altering accident, the divorce, the amputation, and moving from my home of nearly twenty years, I needed a break. Taking a trip to my childhood home, beautiful Colorado, was the perfect location.

I'd also recently learned I'd soon be going back in for more surgery. The titanium plate and screws in my right femur, my long leg, needed to come out. After nearly two years, the hardware had done its job. My body was rejecting it. I'd had nine surgeries the first year after the accident and was in no mood to have any more. I intended to put off the hardware removal surgery as long as I possibly could.

It was truly a joy to see former high school classmates! Most I'd not seen in thirty years. Maneuvering about on beat up legs via crutches presented constant challenges. Thank God for Melanie and DeeDee— my trusty faithful sidekicks. We had a blast together!

The Bridge...

There was one place I had to go while in Colorado—Cherokee Christian Camp. I'd done some research ahead of time, and found it was no longer a camp but a private event dude ranch. There's something about reminiscing through one's past that helps with the "nows" in life. As we made our drive through the foothills, up into the mountains, anticipation bubbled up within me. I had a feeling of excitement, energy, and anxiousness all rolled into one. My tummy filled with butterflies. As we pulled up to the entrance to the dude ranch, one of the girls pointed out a sign. "Sheila, it says private property—no trespassing."

I'm typically a rule-follower by nature, but something in my spirit said, "Keep going. I've something here you need to encounter."

As we drove through the long and winding dirt road, I could sense the concern from Melanie and DeeDee—I knew they were thinking, *Are we gonna get into trouble for trespassing?* For me, there was no fear. I couldn't turn the bend fast enough to see that which I'd come so far to see. Just as we entered the final stretch, the main lodge and mess hall came into view. This feast for the eyes included: the pond where I was baptized…all the cabins scattered about…the hillside that was once an outdoor rustic chapel…the open meadow between the mountains that led to the large bonfire pit where we'd sing sweet praise and worship songs every night…and the bridge—oh, the bridge!

Before we reached the main lodge and parking area, we were stopped by a big, burly rancher dude. He had an air of authority and toughness about him when he walked up to my window. Without saying a word, he looked into the vehicle only to find three girls not dressed in dude ranch attire. I had the forethought to take a couple of old photos from my camp days, decades ago, with me before I departed Tennessee.

"Ma'am, this is private property. I'm going to have to ask you to leave," Mr. Dude said.

"Yessir. I understand." Handing him the old photos, I continued my plea. "We won't stay long. We won't bother anyone or anything, and, we won't go inside the lodge or cabins. Sir, this was my childhood camp decades ago. I'd sure appreciate it if you'd let us stay. We've come a really long way. Please sir?"

I'm not sure if it was what or how I said it, if it was the faded old photos of the main lodge, or if God moved on his heart, but the gruff ol' dude rancher softened.

"Thank You, Lord. We're in!"

I parked where he directed us to park. As we got out of the car, me taking much longer due to a prosthetic and crutches, I noticed the old fella watching us from a distance. As he looked down and saw my physical situation, his entire countenance changed. Those big, burly shoulders relaxed. He lightly shook and dropped his head. I see that same reaction in folks all the time. He never checked on us again. It's as if he knew. He now understood.

Melanie and DeeDee headed toward the main lodge. Instinctively, I was drawn to the sound—the pure, peaceful noise of God's great sound machine. Tears filled my eyes as I hobbled toward the bridge that covers a beautiful wide mountain stream. It was on that bridge, nearly four decades earlier, where God planted a seed of writing in my soul. As a kid, I had trouble sitting still, especially when outside. Every day, like clockwork, we'd have a session of quiet time. Quiet time for this first-time camper, at the age of nine, quickly became time to throw stuff into the river as I sat with my legs dangling over the edge of the bridge.

For ten years, every summer during my weeks at camp, I had 'my spot' on the bridge during quiet time. The first summer or two was mostly a time of tossing. I'd throw whatever I could into the water and watch it float away. Sometimes it would float away so fast I couldn't see it anymore. Other times, it would get stuck on a rock or plant life. Eventually, after time and beating by the water, it would move on again. Then there were those random times, even in the rushing waters, it would get stuck and never move.

Eventually, the tossing led to reflection. This ultimately led to creative writing and/or journaling. Back then, we didn't have social media, so whatever we shared about our thoughts, ideas, etc., we put into our (locked) diaries. Rarely would we share our diaries. Not even with our closest friends.

Over the years, I looked more and more eagerly to my quiet time on the bridge while at camp. The bridge was special as well. Like most camps, Cherokee Christian Camp had rules we had to follow. Breaking rules had consequences. Some were more severe than others. The bridge—my bridge—was a boundary marker. As campers, we were allowed to be on the bridge, but if we crossed over the bridge to the other side, our parents would be called and we'd be sent home.

When sharing this story with my dear friend Larry, he asked me, "Did you cross over to the other side when you were there visiting?"

"Ya know, I thought about it. I walked to the opposite edge of the bridge and looked both ways, but I never stepped off the bridge. I chose to honor and respect the rule...the tradition."

I go to that bridge, my bridge, a lot in my thoughts. That beautiful location, where God planted a wonderful gift in me, holds volumes of symbolism. Isn't life a lot like the objects thrown into the water? There are seasons in our lives where life floats merrily along while there are other times we hit obstacles that not only hurt, they can set us back and ultimately change our path. Then there are situations in life that hit and hurt so hard we're stuck. Satan tries to tell us "It's no use. You're doomed. Your life is over. Just give up!"

Like the water, God continues to move in our lives if we let Him. Yes, we get stuck. Sometimes for long, hard, nearly impossible seasons in our lives. I've found that many times the longer we're stuck, especially when it feels like we just keep getting beaten down over and over again, those are the seasons when God is refining us. A diamond is an ugly hunk of coal until heat and constant pressure re-create it into a priceless gem.

You, my friend, may be a diamond in the rough.

Pressure Changes Everything...
My trip to Colorado taught me something else about my new designer

legs. In general, my body temp runs lower than the norm of ninety-eight point six. Mine usually runs about a degree lower, around ninety-seven point six. I'd never thought much of it as my brother and my mom both share the same thing. I chalk it up to genetics.

While having lunch at Melanie's mom's home, we all went outside. It was a gorgeous sunny day. Not a cloud in the bright, blue Colorado sky. Taking advantage of every opportunity to soak up God's all-natural vitamin D, I sat on a bench in the sunshine. It wasn't long before I heard Melanie's family saying how hot they were. I'm thinking to myself, "Huh? How can they be hot when they're in the shade? I'm shivering—sitting in the sun."

I'd later learn that, most likely, I can endure heat longer because I have titanium rods where others have bone marrow, which ultimately can lower one's over-all body temp. So, if you find me snuggling up to you, it may or may not be affection I'm seeking. It may simply be that I'm freezing and need to borrow some of your body heat.

Another painful side effect of rebuilt crushed legs filled with hardware are barometric pressure changes. Oh, y'all—when the weather patterns change, be it from low to high or vice-versa, these legs let me know it. I feel a deep aching in my joints, which is bad enough. Add to that what I call "Paul Bunyan wrenching" and it's a combination that often brings me to tears. Day or night, awake or asleep, at work or at play, when the sudden wrenching hits there's nothing to do but try to breathe through it. It's as if giant hands are squeezing and twisting my bones from deep inside my legs. Sounds crazy, right? I've been told that some atmospheric scientists don't believe there's a correlation between the human body and barometric pressure changes. If they had my legs, they'd say otherwise.

Speaking of pressure changes: flying has become a whole new "game" for me. On most flights, when the cabin pressure is adjusted for variations in elevation, my legs feel it. Typically, the ascent isn't too bad. It can be uncomfortable, but nothing like the descent. I've had several flights over the years where the bone-wrenching pain is so severe I can't help but cry. Have you ever experienced excruciating pain in your ears when you fly? Imagine that same pain throughout both of your legs.

Because it's nearly impossible for me to bend my legs, especially Shortie with all its hardware, I sit in the first row, usually with Shortie to the aisle as it's difficult for me to promenade side saddle in tight spaces. This routine seat leaves me sitting across from the forward-cabin flight attendants. Many have been precious to me.

"Are you okay?"

"Can we get you anything?"

"How can I help?"

My common reply, "I'll be okay. Unless you can have the pilot land this plane faster or trade legs with me...please tell me about you."

I've discovered, if I can successfully distract myself from the pain, it'll eventually pass. Yes, there are a number of prescription drugs on the market I could take. However, I choose not to rely on drugs any longer. It's not easy. I pray every day for a pain-free, healthy body. And while the 24/7 pain remains, I'm so, so grateful God gives me the strength to endure it all.

TSA Jail...

One time, on a return flight, I had a bit of a run-in with a TSA agent. When I fly, it can be like traveling with a young toddler. Instead of a stroller, car seat and diaper bag, it's a wheelchair, crutches, and a huge carry-on bag. I also have a companion or assistant with me. On this particular trip, I reserved an airline assistant. I received a wonderfully, kind young man from Sudan who worked for the airport. He was gentle and attentive to my needs as we made our way to the security check point. I make a point to travel with my prosthetic appendage clearly exposed. For various reasons, it's proven to be the best option. My assistant pushes the wheelchair through a side lane, up to the TSA agent. I slid my right boot off, handed it, along with my crutches and carry-on bag to my assistant, to place on the scanner belt.

The TSA agent asked, "Can you stand?"

"Yes, I can stand on one leg, but am unable to bear any weight on my prosthetic. I can't walk without crutches," I reply.

Looking down at my prosthetic, he says, "Can you take your leg off?"

Without thinking, I snapped back at him, "Can YOU take your leg off?!"

Thinking to myself, *How rude!*

Quickly, my hand flies up to cover my mouth. "Oh, crap! I'm going to TSA jail. I don't know if such a place exists, but if it does, I'm going."

My response to his question wasn't received well. His swollen attitude just stepped up a notch.

Calmly, but with a firm tone I told him, "Sir, I apologize for my response. However, unless you can show me, in writing, where the TSA has made changes requiring me to remove a durable, medical piece of equipment that allows me greater mobility, no sir, I will not take it off."

My wheelchair was shaking. It was as if time stood still.

The agent never said another word to me.

Maybe he was new and didn't know better. Maybe he thought he was being funny, and I didn't get his humor. Maybe he was just being a smarty-pants, know-it-all with a TSA badge. Regardless, he met his match that day. I thank God for that good ol' southern spit and grit in my soul.

My assistant and I proceeded through security. After a TSA full-body pat down, which is standard procedure for me, he retrieved my items, and we continued to the elevator. No sooner had the elevator doors closed behind us when my assistant bursts out laughing. In his broken English he says,

"Bahahaha, THAT SO funny! Those guys think they so tough. You, little one, showed him. I can't wait to tell guys at lunch. Little girl gets in big man face! Ha-ha ha-ha!"

"Easy for you to laugh, my friend. For a moment, when the wheelchair was shaking, I thought I was headed to TSA jail!" I said.

My assistant confessed, it was he who was shaking the wheelchair, from holding in his laughter. Poor fella, chances are, if he'd have laughed in the moment, he'd be looking for a new job.

Never a dull moment, I tell you. Never!

~ ~ ~

We tried for over a year to create a winning, long-term solution for Shortie and a proper fitting prosthetic. I'd been through at least a dozen different sockets, several hardware configurations, every physical therapy regimen known to man, and prayer beyond measure. It was a hard year of constant failures and setbacks for both of my legs. Regardless of Shortie's lack of progress, I had a more pressing (literally) issue. The hardware on my long leg had to come out. We couldn't wait any longer.

With the hardware removal and knee scope surgery scheduled, my mind began to wander back in time. For two years, I'd gone through unbelievable circumstances. My legs were crushed, I'd all but died on at least two occasions, I'd lost my twenty-one year marriage, I'd lost my home, I'd lost a number of clients because of my erratic schedule, and I'd lost a leg.

I spent hours and hours, night after night, week after week and month after month, talking to God.

"How am I gonna do all this?"

"How am I gonna financially afford it?"

"What if I can't work?"

"Who's gonna help me?"

"Will any man ever love me with these legs?"

"Will the pain ever go away?"

"God, why did you save me?"

When a Part of You Dies...

Many have asked me, "How does 'it' feel?" The 'it' they're referring to is my leg, or more specific, the part that's no longer there. That 'it' can be described in many ways—painful, unstable, lacking, less of a person, limited, fearful, scary, grotesque, different, slow, etc.

Add two words to the question above. How does it make you feel?

Surprisingly, the answers remain the same. Yet they become deeper, harder to bear.

How does one describe losing a limb to folks who've never experienced such a thing? Was it tragic? Absolutely! However, I couldn't continue to live my life in a state of tragedy. That's exhausting. Believe me, I've been there.

Why are you trying so hard to fit in, when you're born to stand out?—*What a Girl Wants*

When I was interviewed for a book on survivors, one of the questions asked of me was, "How has your life changed since the accident?" I sat in silence as heartache, and tears bubbled up inside of me. One word kept repeating itself...EVERYTHING. Absolutely, positively everything has changed in my life. From the tiniest mundane task to routine chores such as: sleeping, thinking, working, eating, entertaining, exercising, reading, writing, sharing, caring, teaching, cooking, cleaning, bathing, giving, believing, worshiping, singing, dancing, dating, talking, not to mention walking, let alone loving. Even breathing has changed since the accident.

I've compared the loss of a limb to that of a severed relationship. When there's heartbreak after a broken relationship, a part of you dies. However, in time, the heart heals and is able to love again. When one loses a limb, it doesn't grow back. It's gone...forever. A great-fitting prosthetic helps, but it's not the real thing. It's artificial, fake, and pretend.

Hmmm...sounds like some relationships I've had. Just as a less-than-real relationship fills a temporary desire, a poor fitting prosthetic fills a temporary need as well. Both are far from the real thing.

Do I feel less of a person because I'm an amputee? NOT AT ALL. Shortie doesn't define me. Yes, being an amputee is a part of me, but it's not who I am.

Those yucky parts of your life, things you've done or things that have happened to you, don't define you. They're part of you, but they're not who you are. Satan does his best to manipulate and tell us that the yuck—the sin—in our lives is who we are, but he's a liar!

Ten and Two Times Two...

It was early fall in Tennessee and change was in the air. I'd been a full-fledged amputee for about a year when I received prosthetic socket number ten. For some goofy reason I named it Bo. Maybe in a far off place in my mind, I thought it would be the one that would not only allow me to finally walk without crutches but also I hoped that I'd one day run along the beach like Bo Derek in her breakthrough hit movie in the late '70s. My dream was a long shot, but hey, you gotta dream before you can achieve!

Bo, with its cool, new vacuum system, was a perfect fit...for two days. For the first time since the surgical amputation a year earlier, I walked without crutches all day long both days. It was awesome! Kind of weird, too. I felt several inches taller. Physically, standing upright, rather than leaning into crutches, I was actually standing a bit taller. However, it was the renewed confidence that truly had me walking tall.

Ironically, the wonderful two days with Bo came to a crashing halt with surgery number ten, two days later. Surgery ten was another twofer—first, remove the hardware that held my right femur together for the past two years, and second—right knee scope surgery and removal of some of the screws in the same knee.

While surgery number ten was successful, the recovery was yet another uphill climb that included more narcotics, blood thinners, open incisions, nerve blockers, and new pain. I understood the nerve pain and surgical pain. What I had trouble figuring out was the new bone pain. I thought the removal of most of the hardware in my long leg would alleviate the constant bone pain. It did, but now I had a new and different kind of bone pain.

Not sure why, but I asked the surgeon if I could have the hardware after they took it out of my long leg. After surgery, I asked him about the new and different bone pain. He said, "Remember the bag of hardware you were given?" I nodded yes, as my girlfriend handed him the bag of hardware. He pointed to what looked like a wrench one would find at a hardware store, "This plate was partially embedded into your bone. Removing it from your femur bone took quite a bit of effort which explains your new and different bone pain."

"Will the pain ever go away?" I asked.

"Eventually, as the femoral bone heals itself," he replied.

As I held the plate in my hand, or "wrench" as I call it, I could visualize the surgical titanium hardware sinking into my bone and the crevice it left behind once removed. No wonder it hurt.

Surgery ten held its fair share of poopy post-op side effects. I expected the tired, beat-up feeling that always comes after the general anesthesia and IV narcotics wore off. It was all the bonus side effects I grew tired of: all over itching from medications, baseball-size bruising on my tummy from blood thinner injections, blown veins from IV needles, a dry bloody nose, and Shortie feeling beat up, although that last symptom wasn't a part of this particular surgery.

Constant nausea prevailed. I couldn't find physical comfort, and my entire body was swollen. I couldn't sleep because of the intense bone pain. One would think, after ten surgeries in just under two years, my body would have figured out how to respond better. Chances are my body, although struggling to endure, was beat.

Let Jesus turn your impossible into I'm possible.

Do Nots...

Because I moved to a neighboring city after the divorce, I wasn't able to retain my previous home physical therapist, Elisabeth. I was disappointed not to have someone I already knew, loved, and trusted, but I was even more concerned about training with someone new. There's absolutely nothing routine, customary, or normal when it comes to my case.

In the past two years I'd been surrounded by an amazing team of highly-competent medical specialists who knew my unique and special case very well. I trusted them and they trusted me. Anytime new personnel were added to the team, it required of me a rather large dose of "due diligence."

A home health care nurse arrived at my home on a Friday morning. She was kind, courteous, and professional. Our first session consisted mostly of case history, assessment, and her initial documentation. We got off to a roaring start when she asked me, "Please briefly share with me your story."

Briefly? How does one "briefly" share all I've been through in the last two years? I thought to myself.

I couldn't help it…I burst out laughing!

I did my best to be "brief." She asked a boatload of questions, and she somehow muddled through the massive library of electronic records Vanderbilt had on me. Then, she proceeded to go over their Home Healthcare Booklet. (Little side note—I've seen this written handbook—many times.)

After several "um-hums" and "yes ma'am's" on my part, she realized she was wasting both our time going through it page by page. She was, however, quick to say, "I see you're more than familiar with this. However, in reading through your records and now meeting you in person, there is one page in the booklet I MUST point out. As I believe this was written just for you."

With a smile on her face, she flipped to page 35—the DON'T's page. (She actually ear marked the page.) She made a point in emphasizing the Don't Over Do It caution. In doing so, I could cause more harm as the inside of my leg and knee had yet to heal from the latest surgery.

Hmm…where would she ever get the idea I would overdo anything?

She was right, though. Sometimes we need to be reminded we can't do it all at once. All in God's timing.

All in all, surgery number ten—the hardware removal party, was a huge success. I was progressing nicely with physical therapy. With my long leg in recovery, and Shortie unable to support me on its own, I remained on crutches. My life of two steps back, one step forward continued.

A word of caution to my friends who don't like pictures of surgeries.
Be careful looking at the next few pages.
I don't want you to be sick!

Community fundraiser prior to the accident

*Heroes in Recovery Race,
12 days before the accident*

Pre-accident race day

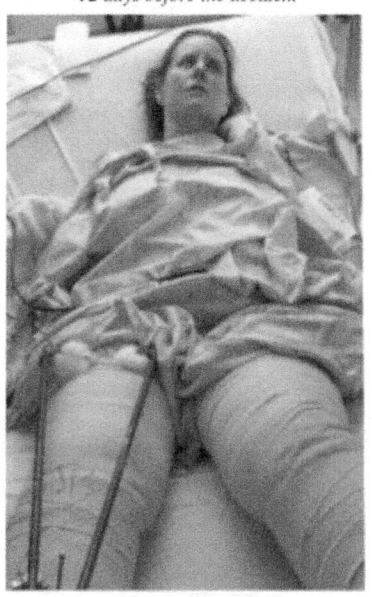

Swollen Mummy

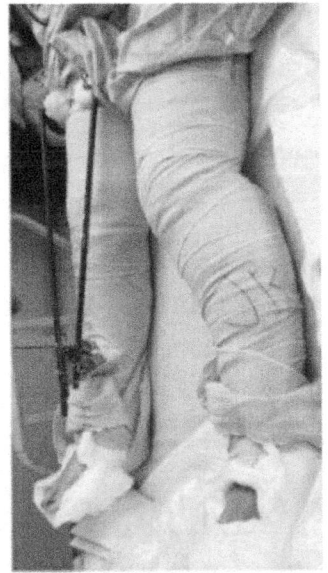

Immobilized legs

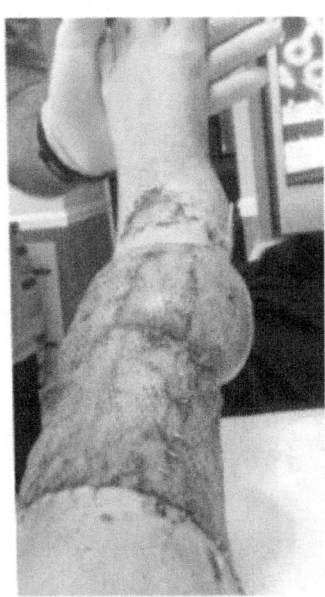

Skin and muscle grafts to rebuild left leg

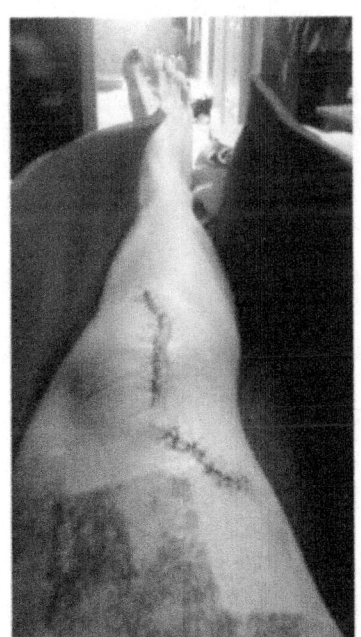

Skin donor and bone graft sites

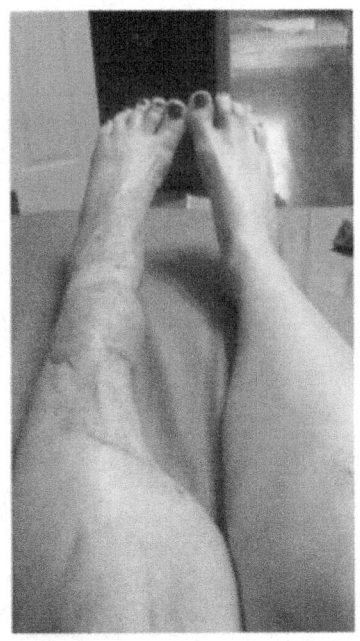

A re-attached amputation healing

Home-bound hospital bed

100 days later...finally standing!

Honkin' Boot

My hero and younger brother Jake and I

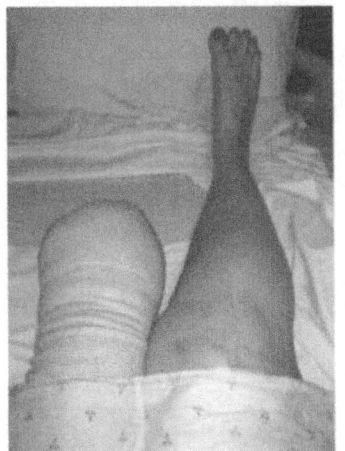

It's gone...

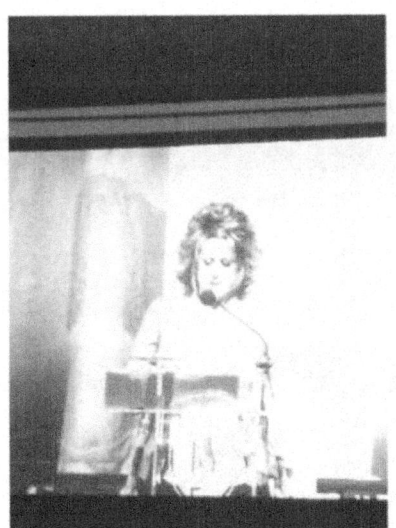

Public speaking--inspiring others

Legendary visitor Coach Don Meyer

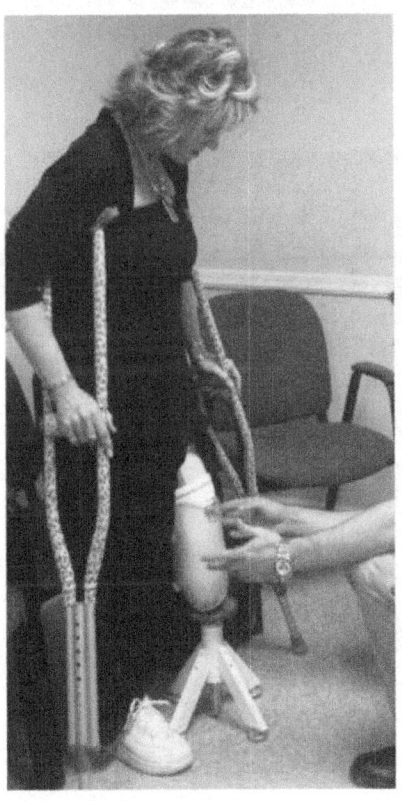

First time trying on a socket

Pub Ed with young students

Meet Theodora

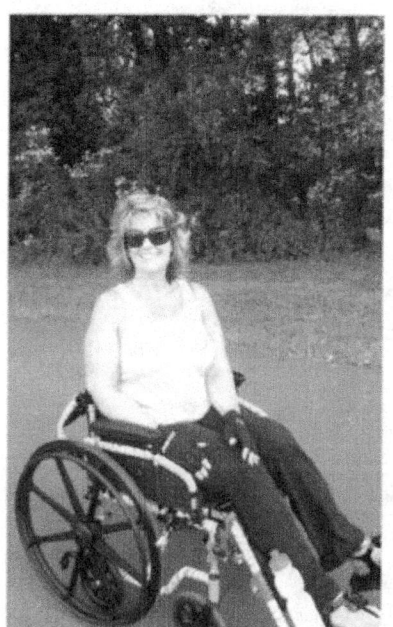

Me and Herbie

First 'chair' race

The incredible Dr. Sethi

Philippians 4:6 Pray about EVERYTHING!

Me and the Hot Wheels racer

Melanie, me, and DeeDee on 'The Bridge'

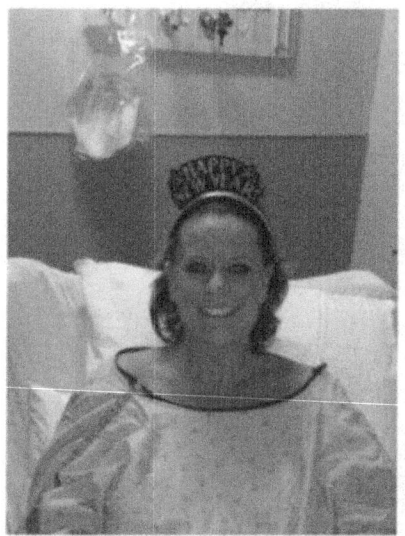

New Year's Eve surgery #11

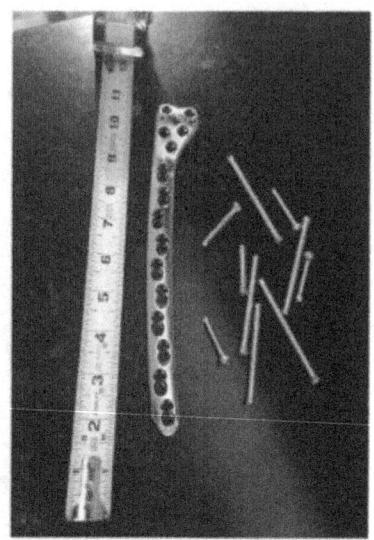

Hardware removed from my right femur

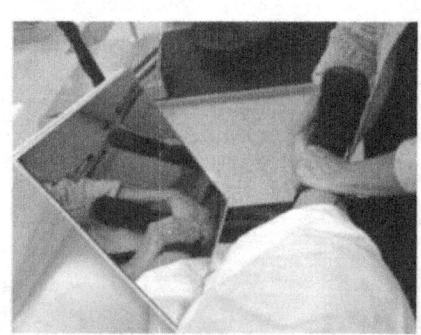

Mirror Image Therapy

I danced! Stryker and I at the Heritage Ball

Five years later...completed a one mile walk

Tammy and me

Tiffany and me

My li'l sweet pea, Daisy

Chapter Thirteen

Partial Amputation?

The woman driving the car that crashed into me the night of the accident chose not to be accountable for her actions, which meant we—my auto insurance carrier and its policy holders (myself and my ex-husband) at the time of the accident—had to file suit against her and her insurance carrier. Sadly, the driver at fault had state minimum insurance coverage. (For all you mathematicians out there, her insurance policy covered about two percent of my medical expenses.) Over time, that percentage gets less and less because an amputee's medical expenses never end.

Once again, God had my back—or in this case, my back pocket. The legal world is not my forte. I had no clue how to proceed. Similar to the recent divorce proceedings, I had no strength, energy, or wits about myself to really know that I needed to protect myself financially. Due to the various prescription drug side-effects, I didn't know that I didn't know. At that time, I was simply functioning on my internal default settings.

I don't remember exactly when, but sometime within the first couple of weeks after the accident, I remember opening my eyes to find a beautiful blonde-haired woman, sitting silently with a note pad in her hands at the foot of my hospital bed. She gently smiled at me. Then she asked me several questions, although I don't remember it. What I do remember is her response to a male lead nurse who spoke boldly to her saying she couldn't video tape me in their hospital. He tried to threaten her with their legal department. She replied "Okay, here's my card. Have them contact me if they need to." All the while her video kept rolling.

Full disclosure—this amazing woman, Rebecca Byrd, Attorney at Law, wasn't filming the medical staff or hospital procedures. She was filming my horrific, life-altering injuries, complete with blood curdling screams from writhing pain upon any and all movement. Rebecca may be little, but she's mighty! Little did I know how important and invaluable my very own Erin Brokovich-style attorney would become.

Fast forward to a couple of years post-accident. The legal suit was in process and depositions were being taken. I'm not sure I can fully describe the emotional and mental stress of reliving the accident and my life since then—all while under oath. Facing the hardcore reality of the pain, suffering, and loss as a result of the accident was beyond intense. God has blessed me with an incredible spirit and I rarely, openly, share the depth of difficulties I endure every single moment as an amputee. I can and will say that there is nothing, NOTHING, easy about being a high trauma amputee with bilateral compound issues.

As the opposing attorney drilled me with questions, my emotional and mental energy diminished as I recounted the night of the accident and the years that followed. Hard as it was, I admit, I collapsed when it came to describing the point in the journey when the amputation occurred. Thank God, my wise attorney, Rebecca, called for a break so I could collect myself.

It was when we reconvened that I lost it. Let me explain. The opposing attorney asked, "So, where was the partial amputation?"

I thought to myself, *Huh? What the heck is a partial amputation?* I'm thinking, *Lady, you have NO IDEA!* It was then that I did something I've never done before. I swung Shortie, boot and all, up on the long conference room table. I unzipped my boot, not only showing her a prosthesis, but telling her boldly, "There is no such thing as a partial amputation. It's gone! It's not gonna grow back!"

It may not have been the most ladylike technique, but I guarantee it was definitely effective. Her tone improved immensely. She apologized, kind of, and restated her question. Her blunt, bullying, heartless demeanor chilled. When the interrogations were over, my attorney and I reviewed the session. I apologized to Rebecca for my response to what I believed was not only ignorant, but hurtful when the opposing attorney tried her best to minimize my amputation. My attorney is awesome! She fully supported my unique technique.

Later that night, I couldn't sleep with the constant loop of the day's earlier events playing in my mind. I was so disturbed by the partial amputation comment, I had to see what Mr. Webster had to say about each of those words.

Partial—incomplete.

Amputation—removal of an extremity.

I believe my show-and-tell technique cleared up any confusion for the opposing attorney. At least I hoped so.

Empty—Hollow—Void…

A few weeks later, I was asked to attend the defendants' depositions. Not that I would be called on to speak, but more for the other driver to see me—the new me—for the very first time.

As I made my way up the sidewalk toward the building, I noticed a couple strolling towards me. They appeared to be window shopping and had stopped. As I approached the double doors, the woman looked at me scanning down Shortie and my crutches.

It was then that she did something I'll never forget. With a blank look on her face, she turned away turning her back to me. A sick feeling, deep in my gut, washed over me. I took a deep breath, and as a gentleman passing by observed my struggle with the door, he kindly offered assistance. Once inside, as I waited for the elevator, I thought, I've NEVER had someone turn their back on me as an amputee. Sure, there've been a handful of folks who, for whatever reason, look away, but never physically turn their back to me. Then it dawned on me, *Oh, my gosh! Could she be the driver who crashed into me?*

A few minutes later, as I sat in the conference room, the couple from the sidewalk came in. I gave a polite smile and nod of the head to each of them. He returned the same. She, however, expressed absolutely nothing.

As the next few hours passed, I sat in (almost) silence. You may recall, I was there primarily for visual. I say almost silence, because though I couldn't say a word, I sobbed through most of it. At one point, my attorney had to take a break. Not for herself, or for them…but for me.

I've never seen another human being show such blatant lack of compassion, remorse, accountability, or responsibility for their actions toward another, especially while sitting across the table one from another. It felt as if she had no regard for my life, or any life, for that matter. This can be explained if her insurance company advised her to say as such. However, when asked, "When did you speak to your insurance company?"

Her reply, "The following week." Neither she nor her husband ever called to see if I lived or died. So sad.

Up to this point in their depositions, I had been looking away, keeping my head bowed, listening, and taking notes. Not until I glanced up, across the long table, did I see it. There sat a body…but not a spirit. Her soul wasn't remotely alive. My heart ached. With notepad in my lap and pen in my hand, I silently pleaded with God to breathe life into her. Please awaken her spirit, fill her soul with (at least) human kindness. That simple prayer filled me with peace, even though it hasn't, that I'm aware of, made an impact on her.

Not until their depositions were over did I realize what I'd written at the top of my notepad—"God grant me peace." He did.

I can't, and won't, share the details and specifics of their offer to settle. I can tell you this: it was deplorable, unthinkable, and unfathomable. I pray no one ever has to go through what I endured. Sadly, there are empty souls in this world.

The other driver never took or admitted responsibility even though she was ticketed "at fault." Numerous witnesses, at the scene of the accident, confirmed her at fault. When repeatedly asked by my attorney if she was at fault, she denied it. My attorney asked, "If it's not your fault, then whose fault is it?"

Without hesitation and void of emotion, she replied, "Hers," pointing to me. I nearly threw up.

It would take years before the case would finally be settled. The defendants offered me less than one, one hundredth of a percent of my medical expenses to drop the law suit. It was a slap in the face. We could have continued the legal fight but the defendants made it clear they'd be filing bankruptcy in order to be able to walk away from any financial obligation. I chose to be the bigger person and walk (or in my case—hobble) away from their shameful offer.

Four and a half years after the accident, I finally received a small check from my auto insurance carrier for a claim against my own underinsured motorist policy coverage. In the grand scheme of things, it was a very tiny pie that was divided into many slices—medical bills, legal expenses, my ex-husband, past due bills and a car I could get in and out of without pain. It wasn't much, but it helped.

Rolling Victory…

With the mental and emotional ongoing stresses of my physical limitations combined with the legal battle, I needed an outlet to release some pent-up frustrations.

Thanks to the church I attended, its Caring Ministry helped me secure a decent wheelchair. I dubbed it Herbie. Herbie wasn't fancy, nor was it designed for outdoor, off-road use (which I later found out).

I missed the daily, three, four, five, or more miles I'd power walked prior to the accident. One would think with the daily physical therapy workouts I'd not need another option to release frustrations. I'd load up Herbie and go to local paved walking trails. A half a mile was all it took pushing Herbie's wheels, to grasp just a bit of the old workout high I so deeply missed.

I had a dear friend who, in spite of his battle with ALS, was a huge inspiration to all who knew him. There was a one mile ALS Walk in Nashville coming up. I knew I wouldn't be able to walk it, but by golly if James could endure all he endured, I could use my arms and push myself through the course. I enlisted my precious neighbor Jen, who is always up for field trips with Sheila, to be my back-up pusher if need be.

I had my doubts as to the likelihood of me being able to complete the course without help. God must have known how desperately I needed to accomplish the goal. I'm not gonna lie. Pushing one's self in a regular wheelchair for a mile, on uneven terrain, is no simple task.

I thought my arms were in decent shape. Shoot, I'd been using crutches almost daily for years. About a third of the way into the race, I whispered a little prayer—"Lord, please help me." Philippians 4:13, NIV—"I can do all this through him who gives me strength"—came to life and poured into my upper body. Jen actually got to run a bit. I, on the other hand, loved yelling out, "Comin' round on your left." Y'all, we were passing folks! Jen never once had to push me. When we crossed the finish line, tears puddled up. It may have been only a mile, but it felt like I'd completed a marathon. I was hooked!

Herbie and I continued our training together when time and weather allowed. We eventually completed a 5K. The "K-Love Run For Love 5K" required a back-up pusher. I love my neighbors—both Jen and Shelbie—two beautiful young ladies, who technically could be my daughters, jumped at the idea when I asked for help.

Jen and Shelbie were amazing! They thought they were going for a morning "stroll." Ha! They each took a turn at helping me push uphill. As far as I know, I was the only participant competing via wheelchair. Tears of joy filled my heart as hundreds of folks cheered me on as I rolled through the finish line.

Whatever your struggle…don't give up!

I was quickly learning that competing via wheelchair, even at the minimal level, was causing significant physical strain on my shoulder joints. Ignorance isn't always bliss. Sometimes ignorance can be quite damaging.

I couldn't understand how so many other athletes could do what they love via wheelchair, but I couldn't. After a visit to a couple of local wheelchair distributors, I quickly learned of my ignorance. Herbie was simply a transfer-only chair. It was designed to transfer a patient from one place to another, indoors, and basically on smooth, level ground (i.e. grocery store, around the home, church, social events, etc.). It was not created to be used outside with any regularity. Its wheel placement and design was for limited use. I was told I'd put more miles on Herbie in a few months than most people do in a lifetime of use with a transfer-style wheelchair. Oops!

Never one to give up easily, my online research for a sports wheelchair began. I was fascinated and intrigued by a sports racer-style chair from a manufacturer in a neighboring southern state.

After much correspondence with the company, I made the initial trip to their fabrication warehouse for custom measuring, specifications, and model options to fit my special needs. The company was well known for its paraplegic sports racing chairs. My case was unique in that, unlike a paraplegic, I still have feeling below my waist. Modifications to their usual design was, without a doubt, necessary.

A couple of months later, my girlfriend, DonneLynn and I made the road trip once again to pick up my new custom-made racer. What a gift it turned out to be to have her with me. She was a second set of ears and eyes as we went through the training. I'd also been suffering with regular phantom pains—not a good combination when driving at interstate speeds. What a fun trip!

It was so cool! The three wheel, dragster-style racer, with inverted back wheels and one smaller front wheel weighed less than fifteen pounds. Guess what color I picked for them to paint it? Metallic hot pink! I couldn't wait to start training.

The Hot Wheels racer was financially possible because of the kind, generosity of friends.

No man is a failure who has friends.
—Clarence, *It's a Wonderful Life*

Turtle Tumbling...

The reality of not using my legs to do what the athlete in me so desperately wanted to do hurt deeply. Admitting it wasn't easy. Accepting it was even tougher. The new Hot Wheels racer helped fill the void I'd been missing. The learning curve was harder than I expected.

Little by little, I gained strength and skill. Like everything else in life, balance was key. I quickly learned if I got too zealous with my speed, I'd relax my body, causing my core body weight to be too far back in the seat. No big deal, right? On the contrary. The fella who designed the racer called it "turtle tumbling." It's what happens when your center gets off balance and the entire racer flips backwards with you still in it. Because my feet and legs were securely strapped in, if I was to turtle tumble, I'd land backwards on my upper back, shoulders and neck, with the racer up in the air (aka backasswards).

My training started at a snail's pace, quickly advancing to granny speed. A nearby high school gave me permission to train on their track. The racer's sleek design, my ability to pull it with one finger and lift the entire trike with one hand, fascinated folks young and old alike. The ease of manually pushing it was the greatest benefit for me. I'd done a few small wheelies, but fortunately, no turtle tumbling.

It was completely different from using Herbie. With Herbie, I was sitting upright—almost like sitting in a straight-back kitchen chair with my hips and knees at ninety degree angles. With Hot Wheels—my sleek racer's name—my legs, hips, and knees were like an accordion, as tight as they would go. My knees were at my chest and my hips were at my heels. Not quite like that of a paraplegic athlete, but almost. A paraplegic racer has their feet up under their hips with their toes facing backwards.

I was more than eager to step-up my game plan with the Hot

Wheels racer training. Up until then, I focused on the track with a couple of parking lot sessions here and there. It was approaching late afternoon—near the end of the school day, which meant track practice would be starting soon. Since I wasn't allowed on the track during practice, I thought, *What the heck, it's about time I branch out and expand my training.* There was a great park near the school with a nice paved trail. Perfect.

I unloaded Hot Wheels and got myself all strapped in and ready to roll. Feeling confident and eager to get in a good work out, I took off. Within seconds, I knew my bright idea had turned into a really dumb decision.

In one way it all happened so fast, in another, it was all in s-l-o-w motion. Before I knew it, the combination of downhill speed, a curve, and a dip in the road had me doing a full-on turtle tumble. As I and the racer went straight back, my bum went upwards. Fortunately, I was only doing about five to six miles per hour. The racer was designed to travel at speeds up to thirty-five miles per hour. The front end hit a dip about the same time that I tried leaning back to slow things down. The combination of the two caused the front wheel to shoot straight up in the air, my upper back and elbows took the brunt of the pavement in order to keep from hitting my head. As I lay on my back, with the front wheel sticking straight up, I heard a faint voice getting louder and louder as it got closer, "oh…Oh…Oh!…OH!…OH NO!"

A racer like mine was designed for both feet and legs to remain strapped in at all times—even during a crash. I couldn't move a thing from the waist down, even if I tried.

All those years of working my core in physical therapy came in handy. As the faint voice got louder (I couldn't see her from my angle), I was able to rely on my core strength to lift the racer, with my lower body still strapped in, and rotate the racer to one side. By then, the sweet faint voice was upon me, offering assistance. Bless this Good Samaritan on my path. I'm certain she was freaked out by what she'd just witnessed. She tried to help, but not knowing how the straps released created a huge problem.

The racer and I remained on our sides. I needed to get my hands and arms beneath me, so I could do a side push-up and hold it there all the while trying to explain to a stranger how to release the straps. It was not an easy task. However necessary, the side push-up caused extreme rotation in my legs, knees, ankle and foot. My body was about to give up when I sent up a silent prayer, *Please God, help us.*

Just then, my sweet Samaritan pulled the right strap, and all but my feet were free. I could breathe. Wiggling and straining a bit more, I was able to reach the straps on and around my feet.

From start to finish, I could sense the fear in the kind stranger. I owe her an apology. In an effort to calm her, I lied to her. As she approached me, not knowing what to do, or how to help, she expressed verbal stress over the situation. I told her, nonchalantly, "Oh, it's okay. It's not the first time. I'm sure it won't be the last." That statement wasn't true. It was the first time I'd crashed in the racer. I was trying to lighten the moment for her.

Once I was free from the racer, she asked what else she could do to help. I told her I'd be fine and sincerely thanked her for her help. Not until she walked away and I remained on the ground did it dawn on me, *How am I gonna get up off the ground?* I sat there a few minutes, assessing the damages, when I noticed a couple of raised concrete culvert braces across the road. *Sure wish there was one of those on this side.* The crash must have jumbled my mind a bit because it took me a minute or two to look around and see that there was a concrete brace not far behind me. *Yes, thank You, Lord!*

I did the crab walk—on my hands, my bum, and one foot. I reached the concrete brace, did a back push-up, sitting on the concrete, giving me space under my legs to stand up. It was then that I realized my turtle tumbling wreaked havoc on my body more than I initially thought. My upper back was sore, which made sense since I hit it pretty hard with the initial impact. Both elbows suffered road rash, and my left wrist was throbbing. My knees and right ankle were wrenched. What didn't make sense was the thumping in my left ankle.

Weird! I don't have a left ankle. Apparently the wrenching impact of Shortie, inside the prosthetic, aggravated nerve endings and they mimicked ankle sprain/strain.

The trek back to my truck was a slow, humble one.

Even if you're on the right track, you'll get run over if you just sit there.—Will Rogers

Over time, Hot Wheels and I fell into a rhythm. So long as our training sessions were under thirty minutes, we got along well. Anything more created problems for my legs. Once again, I recruited a neighbor to accompany me for a 5K race.

Shelbie was a huge help as I hadn't yet mastered uphill climbs. The race went well. Unfortunately, when the race was over and I proceeded to get out of the racer, I couldn't feel my legs. It scared me. With help, I was able to stand. Eventually, blood flow returned to my legs, but it was a slow process.

As much as I loved exercising with the Hot Wheels racer, my medical team and I learned how counterproductive a good thing can become. I heard Dean, my friend and former preacher, ask, "Is water good or bad? How about fire?" He went on to say, "Water is life. We need it to live. However, too much water can be deadly. Just ask those who've lost loved ones in a flood."

I've referred back to that analogy many, many times along my journey of recovery. As an amputee, a healthy balance is vital.

Sadly, I found that if I was in the contorted racing position for more than fifteen or twenty minutes, I lost all feeling in both my legs. After everything I'd been through to save my legs, the option of deliberately causing potentially long term damages wasn't worth it.

My efforts in seeking design options with the manufacturer failed miserably. They either wouldn't or couldn't help me. Once again, being a unique high-trauma amputee set me back.

What crushed my spirit even more was having to look at the racer, sitting in my guest room, every single day. Not only was it a constant reminder of yet another loss, but it screamed out—a huge financial waste just sitting there collecting dust. Someone, somewhere could use this, I thought to myself. But who? Lord, please help me find a good home for it.

A friend of mine, whom I went to church with, is a paraplegic. I rarely saw Rick because we went to different service times. Maybe two or three times a year we'd cross paths. The following Sunday, I saw him. We briefly spoke and I asked him if he had any suggestions for the racer. Until that day, I never knew what he did for work. Oh, y'all. God is SO good! My friend Rick was the Founder of ABLE Youth, a nonprofit that brings physically disabled kids together with ways and specialty equipment, allowing the kids to participate in sports. Score! The Hot Wheels racer had a new home, and I got the happy ending I needed for a very frustrating situation.

Chapter Fourteen

Déjà Vu...

I found myself in the same parking spot, in the orthopedic trauma parking garage, almost at the same time of day, with my head hung low. Tears poured down my face. I'd been there before. As a matter of fact, not too long before. I'd just come from my post-op visit with the head of orthopedic trauma. He did the knee scope clean-up portion of surgery number ten.

While there, he assessed the ongoing skin breakdown issues with Shortie. With his many years of experience, he recommended a revised amputation surgery—basically, a major facelift for Shortie. There was a section of grafted skin that was attached to what little shin bone I had left.

Not good. The grafted skin in itself was a significant issue. Combine that with the remainder of loose skin and soft tissue that had atrophied tremendously, and you have some major saggy, baggy skin.

The biggest problem that presented was the abdominal muscle that was placed at the distal bone end of Shortie, to act as a padded cushion, wouldn't stay in place. I was trying to walk, full weight-bearing, with bone against a hard, rigid carbon prosthetic. Again, not good. Hence the constant open pressure-point ulcers, not to mention the intense shooting nerve pain with every step.

If left untreated, the skin would never heal. My other option—life on crutches or in a wheelchair. In my head, there was no option. I got it. I understood the need for yet another surgery. It was my heart and spirit that had grown weary. I was constantly telling myself, "Sheila, you can do this. You've been through worse." I'd had Philippians 4:13 on a continual loop in my mind for years. I'd be lying if I told you there wasn't a part of me that fought those words.

How many times am I going to have to learn to walk again? Four, five, six? How many times am I going to have to start ALL over again with the prosthetic process?

My cup was no longer half full. It wasn't even half empty. It was nearly bone dry.

While I respected the head orthopedic trauma surgeon, I needed to see my trauma surgeon, Dr. Sethi. I didn't really expect him to disagree with his superior, but I needed his reassurance, his explanation and his step-by-step plan of attack for this latest battle. Knowing and understanding the why, what, when, where and hows are huge for this girl. As he always did, Dr. Sethi answered every question and laid out what needed to be done—all while exuding a professional confidence that only he can give.

Because the skin on Shortie was so fragile, surgery eleven required the expertise of a young, progressive thinking evaluation with a plastic surgeon. Dr. Sethi referred me to a colleague of his on the Vanderbilt Medical Center University Campus.

Fat's Your Friend...

A few days later, I met with the plastic surgeon for the first time. Nice young man. I liked his demeanor. I could see why he and Dr. Sethi worked well together. He'd researched my case and offered an interesting approach. Progressive, yet less invasive.

"Am I a guinea pig for this procedure?" I asked.

"No." He replied.

Phew, I thought.

After chewing on his plan a bit and asking him various questions, I liked his idea. If all went according to plan, it'd be a win-win.

Imagine the look on my face when he said, "The excess cushioning on your thighs is a huge blessing!"

I'm thinking, *Oh, sure, dude. That's just what every woman thinks when she looks in the mirror. I'm so blessed to have fat thighs.* I must admit, it was gentlemanly of him to use the terminology he chose—"excessive cushioning."

"So fat's my friend, huh?" I asked.

He grinned at my goofy sense of humor then we both laughed. A connection was formed. I knew God had blessed me with the right surgeon for the job. Make that two right surgeons, as surgery eleven was another tag team procedure.

In layman's lingo, the plastic surgeon would liposuction fat from my thighs and put it into Shortie, filling up and cushioning around the end of what remained of my tibia and fibular, creating an all-natural padding. Benefits—my fat combined with my body equals a happy combination, or in medical terms, less chance of rejection. Another benefit was thinner thighs. Woohoo! Sorry, Granny Burns. I didn't mean to disrespect your "excessively cushioned thighs" DNA!

Dr. Sethi's part involved bone revision. In order to repair the damaged tissue areas caused by pressure-point ulcers, and to break loose the skin that was attached to my shin bone, Dr Sethi would need to remove more of my tibia and fibular bones. Otherwise, I'd not have enough skin to cover Shortie once they fixed all the skin issues. I could have had more skin grafts, but the past year of fighting to heal grafted skin on Shortie wasn't working. This was our best option.

Happy New Year...

Not sure why, but surgery eleven was scheduled for the morning of New Year's Eve. It probably had something to do with insurance deductibles and co-pays. I prefer to think it was God's great sense of humor. He knew that particular date would give me something other than another surgery to focus on. Boy, did it ever!

No matter how many surgeries I'd have, they'd never cut my spirit.

I recruited a dear girlfriend with, "Hey, how would you like to attend a once-in-a-lifetime New Year's Eve party with me?" Donna knew me well, and based on previous excursions together, she was always a willing participant. Regardless of the event, location, or people involved, we made the best of things. New Year's Eve 2013 turned out the same, although I don't remember most of it.

One of my love languages is gift giving. That, and words of encouragement. I recently took *The Five Love Languages* survey again to see if anything has changed. Not really. Gift giving and words of encouragement still rank at the top for love that I like to express. In receiving love, I rank highest in time and touch, followed closely by words of affirmation. No surprise to me. I hold hands and wash feet for a living. As a professional manicurist, time and touch with my clients fill an innate need for me. I love what I do!

As a gift giver, I was prepared for the New Year's Eve party at Vanderbilt Hospital. Because of my severe latex allergy, my scheduled surgeries are always the very first surgery of the day, before any latex spores fill the air in a sterilized operating room.

We arrived before dawn with a tote bag filled with a few personal items and loads of New Year's Eve party supplies. I also had special gift bags for both of my surgeons. I knew one of Dr. Sethi's weaknesses. His gift bag contained his favorite chocolate. After a little recon work, I found out my plastic surgeon liked a nice bourbon on occasion. When off-duty, of course. Prior to the anesthesiologist pre-op visit that morning, I gave both of my surgeons their goody bags.

"Thank you so much for taking such good care of me, and thank you for doing this on New Year's Eve," I said, as I handed each of them their gift bag. "However, under NO circumstances are you allowed to consume any of the contents until after you've completed my surgery. Deal?"

Laughter filled the room, as the increased endorphin side effect kept me calm, going into surgery.

I awoke later that day to a beautiful, sunny beach. Some of you are thinking, "Wow, she had some good drugs." While that may be true, think how confused I was.

Wait. Where am I?

I don't feel so good.

Why are there tubes and wires in me?

What has happened to me?

Coming out from under anesthesia has never been my greatest talent. Fortunately, I've never panicked as some folks do. For me, it's rather entertaining, so I'm told. From this particular surgery, I awoke with the munchies.

"I'm starving!" I blurted out from a sound sleep.

"Hey there. How ya feeling?" I heard as Donna got up from the chair and came to my hospital bed.

"I'm ravished. I could eat a cow!" I replied.

Donna giggled as she realized I was still out of it. That, and I didn't eat beef because I'm allergic to it! (She knows this about me.)

"Honey, what are you hungry for?" she asked.

In a drunken, slow motion slur, "Funyuns®!"

"Funyuns®? You sure?"

Nodding like a bobble head, I add, "And M & M's®!"

Ever the trusty sidekick, Donna set out to complete my totally random request for nourishment. While she was gone, I dozed in and out, as I cherished my time at the beach. I later learned, my beach time was all in my head. Thanks to the television monitor set on an ocean beach shoreline…my happy place.

Donna returned a hero with Funyuns® and M & M's®. It had been years since my raiding of the vending machines in college when I'd had the sweet and salty combo.

Prior to surgery, I'd asked Donna to please make sure each and every nurse whose care I was in, received a New Year's Eve party favor. She was in charge of my tote, which contained party hats, blow horns and "Happy 2014" glasses. By second shift change that evening, we had nursing staff from other areas of the hospital stopping by my room to wish us Happy New Year and get a party favor of their own.

"Oh, my gosh. Did you see him?" I nearly fell out of bed looking through the open doorway.

Donna looked out the door opening, "Who?"

"That guy. He was beautiful!" A few minutes passed. "Him, that's him! He's SO cute!"

Getting up this time, going to the open door, stepping

out…looking both ways, Donna came back in and said, "Honey, there's no one there. Maybe you should get some rest."

A little while later, I startled Donna, as I yelled, "Hey, handsome! What's your name?" as I once again nearly fell out of bed.

This time, Donna not only stepped out into the hall, she went around the corner and down the hall. She came back into my room laughing so hard she was crying. Not having a clue what was going on, I asked, "What's SO funny?"

With a roaring belly laugh, she pointed to me and said, "YOU!"

Apparently, the handsome fella I kept seeing wasn't a figment of my imagination after all. He was, however, young enough to be my son. Not to mention, he had long passed my doorway before my delayed reaction kicked in. Oh, the joys of prescribed medication's side effects. No wonder I never had trouble getting girlfriends to stay with me. The entertainment alone was worth it.

The next few days in the hospital were tough. Once again, pain was my constant struggle. Shortie hurt like crazy, which I expected. My right thigh felt like it'd been hit repeatedly with a baseball bat. I didn't understand why only one thigh was hurting. Apparently I misunderstood when the plastic surgeon said he'd use fat from my thigh—singular. It made sense to me that he'd take equal amounts of fat from each thigh to fill the void in Shortie. Nope. The only reason he'd go to my left thigh was if he couldn't get enough from my right thigh. You guessed it. Thanks Granny Burns! He had all he needed without going to the left side. I also found out that it was medically safer not to liposuction my left thigh because Shortie needed no further potential complications. Great. I now have what I refer to as my very own mail slot. I've a large crevice in my right thigh thanks to liposuction.

As I understand it, liposuction is designed to remove fat pockets but only looks smooth and contoured if and when the recipient maintains an exercise regimen that keeps the surrounding muscle toned. Needless to say, my "mail slot thigh," along with countless other scars across my lower body, are medals of honor from numerous battles won.

The way I see it, the man God has for me is going to have a grand fondness for patchwork quilts.

Scars are reminders that you survived the battle.

I tried to look at my right thigh. I was still hospital bed bound and it hurt something awful to put any pressure on my legs or to stretch them. Donna used my phone to take pictures so I could see it. As she did, she said, "Oh, wow! It's a heart."

"What's a heart?" I asked.

"Your bruise is shaped like a heart. Only you Sheila. Only you," she replied with a smile on her face.

My "heart" turned out to be nearly the size of a dinner plate. No wonder it hurt.

One night during my hospital stay while another girlfriend Jackie, was keeping vigil over me, the fire alarm sounded. Jackie stepped out into the hallway, seeking direction from the hospital staff. What she discovered was "business as usual." Ever the dedicated, diligent comrade, she went to the nurse's station and inquired, "What are we to do?"

"Nothing to be concerned about," the nurse replied.

"I AM concerned. I'm responsible for the well-being of my friend, and I need to know how to get her to safety," Jackie said.

"It's not our floor, but a floor below us," the nurse responded.

Realizing she was on her own with the mission at hand, Jackie made her way back to my hospital room as the alarm continued. As she reached my room, the alarm shut off. But, not before my gallant girlfriend set her mind to making sure she'd do all she could to save us if need be.

I, on the other hand, in my drug-induced stupor, slept through the entire ordeal. What a gift to have such precious friends!

We can't always fix others' problems, but we can promise they won't have to face them alone.

Recovery from surgery eleven was slow. My body had endured horrific struggle for the past twenty-seven months. It was also my least favorite time of year—winter. I was doing everything right: home physical therapy, clinic physical therapy, rest, proper nutrition, regular chiropractic care, and massage. Still, my body was having a hard time bouncing back from this one.

Two of a Kind...

In between NFL play-off games, I let Daisy outside to potty. Little did I know, the neighbor's cat was outside as well. Daisy's always on a leash, whereas the cat, obviously, was not. Daisy spied Nate, the cat. (Yeah, I know, I too thought it was a funny name for a cat when I first heard it.) Daisy somehow morphed into a catlike goofball. She crouched low and proceeded super slow, one paw at a time in slow motion towards the cat. Nate is what we used to call husky. He's at least double the weight of my little sweet pea. Ol' Nate wasn't budging.

The stare down began. Based on his expression, the caption above his head could have easily read, REALLY? I've coughed up hairballs bigger than you!

About that time, Nate's owner came out to rescue his cat. Like most of us, he's very protective of his pet. With Daisy on a leash, and out of fear for her safety, I wasn't about to let her experience cat scratch fever. I'm balancing on one leg, with crutches, all while trying to reel her back in. It's incredible how strong seven pounds of canine can become when they have their eyes set on a feline!

The neighbor scurried his cat out of my yard, which set Daisy into action. In her haste to reach the cat, she nearly knocked me to the ground when her leash wrapped around one of my crutches. My heart was beating out of my chest as I got Daisy under control and she and I untangled. That's when I saw it. Blood. Oh, no! Where's it coming from? WHO's it coming from? There was a lot of it, and I couldn't see any sign of it on Daisy. I'm not stupid. I never let Daisy get near Nate. One swipe of his paw and Daisy'd be split wide open.

The blood was all around my crutches. Big, red drops everywhere. Panic! Please Lord, not Shortie, "please."

After what seemed like an eternity, I finally got Daisy settled enough so that I could get her leash off. Then I saw it. Her front paw was bleeding. Why is it, that at the very moment you need your pet (or child) to sit still, they have ants in their pants? The more I tried to access her injury, the more she'd run around the house—leaving a red trail of blood everywhere she went. Hardwood floors, leather sofa, pillows, throw blankets, bull hide rug, etc. I needed to stop the bleeding, or at the very least, stop my beloved pet from bleeding on everything. Hard as I tried, I was still really slow maneuvering about on crutches because of the latest surgery. I'm thinking, if I sit still, she might come sit next to me.

First, I gathered supplies to clean and bandage her foot. Once I sat still, she finally came to me. She wouldn't let me investigate close enough to see what caused the bleeding but at least she let me wrap and bandage her paw. Phew…bleeding stopped. I was exhausted!

As the adrenaline rush from all the excitement died down and I caught my breath, I looked around. I've got to get all this blood cleaned up before it permanently stains everything. What would have taken y'all five minutes to clean up turned into nearly an hour's workout. With her sweet, dark eyes, following my every move, Daisy laid on the sofa looking pitiful. When I finally sat down, she moved about a bit, waiting for me to get situated. Then I saw it. She struggled, wobbled, and bobbled with her balance, trying to figure out how to get around without the use of all her limbs. Lifting her bandaged paw, she looked up at me…her little face said it all…We're two of a kind, aren't we, Mom?

I later discovered the cause of her injury. She'd somehow ripped a toenail completely off. Like Shortie, it'll never grow back.

Girl Down…

I'd been home from the hospital less than three weeks when my left crutch hit something on the hardwood floor sliding out from under me. I fell straight down. The bottom of Shortie hit the floor with a hard whack! I then fell forward, landing on my right knee while trying to catch myself with my left hand. (For a girl who's filled with Grace, I sure don't fall gracefully.) I won't lie. It hurt! Hardwood flooring over a concrete slab is not forgiving…at all.

I sat on the floor for a few minutes as I begged God for there to be no serious damage. Once I stopped shaking, I called my neighbor Jen. I was afraid to move and thought it best to have someone there when I tried. Jen and her mom, Marilyn, were there in a blink.

They brought me several ice packs as I remained on the floor. So soon after surgery, this particular fall was a rough one. My body and my mind needed time to adjust and settle before I tried getting up. They were so sweet to me. Jen knew me well and knew that talking about something, other than the current struggle, was usually the greatest benefit for me.

About thirty minutes had passed when I scooted on my bottom, reached the sofa, and rested my back against it. With my arms and elbows pointing behind me, I did a backward push-up, lifting myself up and onto the sofa. You work-out folks probably have an official term for that kind of a push-up. Obviously, I'm not familiar with it.

I'm sure some of you are asking, "Why didn't your neighbors help you up?" It's simple, really. As a single girl, I need to be able to get up off the floor, on my own, if at all possible. Not having done that in a year or so, I thought it best not to try it solo, if I didn't have to, especially since I still had open surgical wounds.

Shortie ached, my right knee had a goose egg on it, my left hip was jarred in the throw down, and my left hand and elbow felt the effects of hand-to-floor combat. I talked to and sent photos to my surgeon and physical therapist. Injuries appeared to be superficial on soft tissue. Following doctor's orders, I used ice every hour, elevated most of me, rested, and used slow, easy movements for several days until my body could heal.

True Grit, Western Style…

The morning started out early with my second post-op visit to the plastic surgeon. The re-amputation flap was looking really good, healing nicely. Unfortunately concerns remained with some of the skin grafts. Two years prior, some of the graphed skin adhered to my shin bone. Some of it never let loose, even with my working on it every single day. A big part of the plastic surgeon's job during the last surgery was to remove skin from the shin bone. Sound simple? Not so much. Think about it like this: Have you ever removed wallpaper? The REALLY glued on tight stuff that ain't budging for nothing? Well, that's kind of what my plastic surgeon did. He had to get underneath the very thin, fragile grafted skin and remove it from the bone…without tearing it. Considering what he had to work with, he did a fantastic job. Sadly, some of the thin, fragile skin tore in the process—and the open wound was now about the size of a fifty cent piece.

I'd followed doctor's orders to a tee with my home-care regimen. The surface wound had shrunk in circumference, but the wound was tunneling inward. The surface scab had fallen off a couple of nights before. Based on what I saw, I had a feeling it would need further physician's treatment. I wasn't exactly prepared for what treatment that would be.

After climbing up on the exam table with one leg (that in itself is entertaining), I unwrapped Shortie for the surgeon. It didn't take but a second of "show and tell" for him to say, "We gotta de-bride that thing. Get it cleaned out, and then I'll sew it back up."

I'm thinking, "he'll give it a few shots to numb it up, give it a few minutes for the numbing agent to settle in, then he'll come back and work on it."

Um…none of that happened! He prodded around a bit, pushing on Shortie as his nurse rounded up supplies and instruments. It was tender, but I could tolerate it. He said it wouldn't take long and he didn't expect me to feel a thing.

He started by flushing the wound. Then he took several really long, cotton tipped dowel rods and proceed to shovel out the wound. Some REALLY gross looking stuff came out of it. At this point, I'm thinking to myself, *You got this, girl!*

Little did I know, the dude was just getting started. I tried to make small talk with the nurse to keep my mind, and eyes, off what he was doing. No use. It's like a train wreck. You can't look away, no matter how hard you try. This is when I thought my mind was playing tricks on me.

He started cutting my skin. As I watched him, with a scalpel going through my skin, my mind said, "Do I feel it? Na, you don't feel anything. Oh, wait, he didn't numb ANYTHING, so you MUST feel it." Y'all, it was so weird! Downright creepy. I knew it was real when I saw the bright red blood, my blood. He packed and dabbed, to get the bleeding to slow down. All of a sudden, my brain finally got the message—AAHH!!!

The surgeon told me, "We're almost done. Just need to tie it up."

Shortie continued to bleed as he put in one stitch, then another and another…okay, I'm gonna make it. On second thought, maybe not!

"Say, doc, remember that New Year's Eve bottle I gave you? By chance, is it anywhere in the building? I don't drink brown liquor, but right about now I could use a good stiff drink!"

My mind flashed to the days of the Old West when all folks had was a strap of leather and some moonshine. Those folks were tough!

One end of the wound was left slightly open for draining purposes. I was instructed to change the packing twice a day for two to three weeks until the hole healed properly from the inside out. The packing was kind of cool looking. I kid you not, it looked like saturated, flat shoe strings. I didn't realize how deep the wound had tunneled until I pulled out the antibiotic saturated packing. It was nearly a foot long!

Labor and Delivery...

It had been more than six weeks since the re-amputation and facelift surgery for Shortie. I couldn't wait to see Dr. Sethi for his approval to start back with my legman. I so desperately wanted to begin the new prosthetic process.

As I got ready for bed, I noticed a dark dot on Shortie. Odd, I don't remember that being there. It's probably nothing a good night's rest won't cure. When I awoke the next morning, the dark dot was the size of a dime! It was also warm to the touch and swelling. Blood was pooling, but why? Thank God I was scheduled to see the plastic surgeon that very day.

Before I left the house, Shortie started to openly bleed. Strange, it wasn't bleeding at the dark area but rather about an inch away from it. Anxiety kicked in.

As I prayed my way to Vanderbilt it dawned on me: It's a long walk from the parking garage to the surgeon's clinic. Crap! I sure don't need to let Shortie "hang" that long, especially since it's bleeding.

A reflection in the rear view mirror caught my eye. It was the sunshine, or SON-shine, reflecting off Herbie. I had forgotten Herbie was in the back seat. I got parked, hobbling, wobbling, and balancing on one leg while unloading and assembling Herbie. With me in the chair, Shortie elevated and crutches propped between my legs, I was off to the plastic surgeon's clinic.

A few minutes later as I sat in a treatment room waiting on the doc, I continued to fill God's "in box." *Can ya cut this girl some slack? Can ya give me a break?* Before my plea turned into *Oh, Lord, give me strength, help me endure,* the plastic surgeon walked in.

He took a look at Shortie's newest addition and said, "It's probably a...blah-blah-blah." I'm thinking, "a what?" Then he said, "I'm gonna have to open it to see for sure."

Me—"Of course he does. Here we go again."

These in-office surgical procedures really did not need to be a routine thing. He rounded up a nurse and supplies. I was still trying to understand what it was that was in there. The best I understood his description, chances were it was an oil pocket that had become infected. Blood had pooled in it, so the body could rid itself of the oil. "Huh? So, it's a Paul Bunyan-sized zit?"

No, not exactly. Apparently, when you take fat from one area of the body and transfer it to another, there are oil glands that are part of the liposuction. Part of the refining process is to separate the fat and oil glands using only fat when re-depositing. Unfortunately, not all oil glands are completely removed. Typically the body adjusts. Though in rare instances the body can reject the newly placed oil glands. Yep, bingo! I was one of those rare gems.

The surgeon had everything set up and ready to go. He flipped on the bright surgical spot light. As I watched, he gently cleaned the area with Betadine. Next came the mega syringe. He lanced one area, just on the edge of the dark blob. Pulling the syringe and squeezing Shortie, he said, "Oh, it's nothing but pus." He squeezed things a bit harder.

Okay, doc. It wasn't hurting, but if ya do much more of that I might have to hit you with a crutch! Did I forget to mention we're doing this without local anesthesia?

He told me to hold real still as he opened up the area right above the dark blob. Y'all, I would not have believed it had I not seen it myself. Shortie gave birth to a big ol' dark looking lima bean! The whole thing plopped out in one piece. We were expecting it to bust open and the blood drain out of it. The doc rubbed and dug all around Shortie with great umpf, making sure any residual would work through. *Dude, I'm not a jersey cow. Ease up there, fella!* The nurse took over, cleaned and packed the newly opened wound. I was sent home with yet another prescription for antibiotics. The hardest pill to swallow that day…it'd be at least another four weeks before I could think about seeing my legman.

Be stronger than the storm.

Chapter Fifteen

MAJOR Meltdown...

If I heard it once, I heard it a thousand times, "Sheila you're doing great! You're pushing through the pain and doing everything that's being asked of you. Your recovery is going well, all things considered." Every time I heard those encouraging words, I wanted to throw up! Please don't misunderstand me. I appreciated the folks behind the words, but I was tired. Beat. Whooped. Exhausted. Drained. Empty. I was done!

I'd been in recovery going on three years and I was sick of it! All I dreamed of was two simple letters...E D. I longed to be recover-ED. I was emotionally, physically, mentally, and spiritually sick of being in recovery.

I'm a doer, an organizer. When I take on a task, I see it through to completion. I was raised to be reliable, responsible, and dependable. Nowadays, some (lazy) folks call it "anal." Regardless, I'd pushed and pushed myself for two and a half years. Surgery after surgery after surgery, a horrible divorce, the loss of my home, and then, to top it all off, the loss of my leg. The harder I tried, the harder the climb. That suck it up buttercup, git 'er done, spit and grit spirit was gone. I'd had previous moments when I'd get down. Usually a good cry and a dose of alone time with the Lord would quickly pull me through. This one was BIG. It was beyond real, and it scared me. My "come to Jesus" moment turned into an extended vacation of checking out of life.

I'd never really questioned God about why. I prayed hard and often for answers to *How am I supposed to do this? How do I keep fighting? How do I endure? How do I get through this? How many more setbacks? How much longer until I'm recovered? How will I ever live again?* In that moment, the why didn't matter. It all happened and there was nothing I could do to change it.

I've heard it said, God meets us where we are. I have NO DOUBT, whatsoever, that God has been with me every single step of this journey. He has been there at every edge of the cliff...ready to catch me if I fall, or give me wings to fly. His construction plans for our lives can be mind boggling. Some of us simply need a new coat of paint, while others need a room or two remodeled. Then, there's those of us that get torn down to the foundation and completely rebuilt.

Dang! The demolition season is tough—really tough—and it hurts! It was no longer just my physical body that was crushed. My mental and emotional well-being was anything but well. Oh, I put on the best happy-face I could muster up, but inside I was slowly dying. For months, I'd pretended to have it all together if I was outside the walls of my townhouse. When I was home alone, I'd close the blinds, curl up like a baby and cry for hours upon hours, all through the night. I'd cry so hard, I'd make myself sick. Oh, and the headaches—my head would pound from constant crying. No matter what I did, I couldn't stop the tears.

Looking back now, that was a season of great change in my life.

Things change...and they change you.

Winter Olympics—Sheila Style...

It was a morning like many mornings—up early and at 'em for another doctor's appointment at Vandy. Like every other snowy, iced-over morning, I used my remote start so the truck would be nice and warm once I got in it. (Love that invention!) It took a couple of ten minute rounds with the remote starter before the snow on the windshield and windows were melted. Thanks to some friends who popped by earlier that day to check on me; they cleaned my sidewalk and made a path around my truck. I headed outside. Feeling super confident, I maneuvered safely through the small icy patches, only to be brought down once I reached the truck. No, I didn't fall. Thank God! It was WAY more entertaining than that.

The door was frozen! Not just a little! It wasn't budging. I pulled and pulled. All that did was shake the truck. You've got to be kidding me! Keep in mind, I'm doing this while balancing on one leg, not really able to hold the crutches since both my hands are pulling on the door handle.

I confess, I tried the ol' Fonzie approach—I hit it with my fist. No luck. *Crud!* I am NOT missing this appointment. Just as I was about to let frustration get the best of me, I hung my head and prayed...*Lord, not sure how, but I need to get this door open.* I took a deep breath.

Then it hit me—try the other side. Leaving my bags on the ground at the driver's side, I hobbled via crutches around to the passenger's side.

Yikes! A lot more ice on the ground past the driver's door and around the back end of the truck. Thanks to the sunlight, there wasn't near as much ice on the passenger's side—yes!

Saying another quick prayer for good measure, I pulled on the passenger door handle. Nothing. Ugh! Something said, press on, and don't give up. I tried one more time. It was like it was never stuck. It opened right up.

Here's where the one-woman (Laurel and Hardy) show began. My truck is a bit too high for me to get into, since the accident, without a boost. That 'boost' is actually a clever little tool called a Handybar®. Anyway, my Handybar® was kept just inside the door...on the driver's side. Naturally, I couldn't reach it from the passenger's side. With absolutely no grace at all, I strained, struggled, twisted, wiggled, and finagled my way up and onto the passenger's seat. If one could do the splits, in the air, with one and a half legs, I was doing it. For a brief moment I thought, *Hmm...wonder if I'll see this on YouTube later?*

It was way below freezing, but I'd broken out in a sweat. Did I forget to mention I was wearing an above the knee sweater dress during this early morning routine? Thank goodness for tights. At one point the dress looked more like a top, it was so contorted. Stay with me. It gets better.

Once I was in the passenger's seat and I caught my breath, I realized I had to get over the console. Though not pretty, I was finally in the driver's seat. Great! Only problem…my bags were on the ground, outside the truck. For Pete's sake! I did the ol' heave-ho a few times with my shoulder trying to get the driver's side door to open from the inside. No such luck. *Crap! Now what?*

Looking back now, I can't believe I did this. That's not entirely true. I can be pretty creative, especially when determination kicks in. I rotated in the driver's seat, keeping my bottom on the seat. I put my right hand on the door handle, my knees were at my chest so my right foot (oh yea, duh, I only have a right foot) was on the door. I pulled the handle while kicking the door. Suddenly there was huge movement. No, not the door, but rather me.

Remember the sweater dress? It slides real slick-like on leather seats. Are ya kidding me?! Where am I going to get leverage, or should I say traction, for my backside? Bingo! The console. I lifted the arm of the console and put my hind side down in it (Be nice—I didn't say it fit). With a twist and a kick, all the while pulling the handle, the door finally opened. Hallelujah!

No matter how hard I strained, I couldn't quite reach my bags on the ground without getting out again. I'll just grab my crutches. Ah, man! The crutches are outside the passenger's side door! I had to laugh to keep from crying.

Back over the console, slide out the passenger's side, crutches in place, gingerly make my way over the ice patches and around the truck to the driver's side, bags loaded, and finally, me loaded. Who needs PT?!

You are not your limitations.

I called the doctor's office to let them know I'd be a few minutes late. The receptionist was precious, "You okay?"

"Um, yea. Long story. Let's just say I had a little car trouble."

The doctor appointment, which I was NOT going to miss because I was certain I'd finally be given the approval to see my legman, was another disappointment. A small surface wound, about the size of a pencil eraser, needed to be completely healed before they'd let me see my legman and start the prosthetic process. This hurry-up-and-wait was getting old.

Falling Down, Falling Down, My Fair Lady...

A week or so later, I took a doozie of a fall. Unless you're an amputee, you may not understand my next sentence. All it takes is one tiny drop of water, in just the right spot, and I can suffer a hard fall. Actually, from all the falls I've taken over the years, only two were my own fault. My very first fall after becoming an amputee, happened when I over did a stretch and got myself off balance. The other, I'm not real proud of, but this is an open book about my journey—the good, the bad and in this case, the desperate. So, here it goes.

It was Christmas time and I'd volunteered to drive from Tennessee with my parents to see my brothers in Kansas. I'd been an amputee for less than ninety days and lived life the best I could on crutches as I didn't have a prosthetic yet.

Mom and I knew the road trip would be interesting, to say the least. Daddy was in the early stages of Alzheimer's which was tough on everyone. He still had random moments of normal frame of mind, though they were quickly diminishing. He was a tough, stubborn man, and when he set his mind to something, he'd do it, come heaven, hell, or high water.

I like to think I got a dose of his stubbornness, deeply blended with my mama's sweet nurturing spirit, creating a healthy balance of strong determination. Nothing would do, but for daddy to drive the first leg of the trip.

Oh, y'all. It was SO hard watching that horrible disease take over. The man I knew and loved, who my whole life knew the interstates, routes, and many side paths across this entire country, was trying desperately to decipher life with scrambled up brains. Prior to Alzheimer's, he could tell you every detail of rest areas, truck stops, big towns, small cities, and great little roadside dives. Sadly, when he got behind the wheel, it wasn't long before all his memories were jumbled together and mixed up. In his frustration, and both mom's and my effort to give him direction, he shut down…literally. On a main state highway, in the middle of the road, Daddy slammed on the brakes, put it in park, and said, "Who's driving, you or me?"

At the time, I was sitting in the backseat, side saddle, with my legs elevated on the seat. I admit, I was not wearing a seat belt. (My legs were hurting and I'd just put my legs up to rest them for a few minutes when he chose to slam on the brakes.) The sudden impact threw me into the floorboard.

Now I REALLY hurt. I tried not to make a fuss as Mom was already upset. I climbed my way onto the backseat, as Mom and I both tried our best to talk Daddy out of the driver's seat. He put the car in drive and off we went. I had a sick feeling in my gut—if he stayed behind the wheel, we'd either die from a crash or we'd end up in North Dakota. I had to get those keys!

"I've got to go to the bathroom and there's NO WAY I can hold it," I said. It took a little convincing, but it worked. Thank God! Daddy was known for leaving the keys behind, and this time was no exception. Mom got the keys, and I immediately asked her for them. I had a set, and she had a set. No one else needed them. From then on, no one but me got behind the wheel. Mom and I chose to keep Daddy well fed with snacks. We both knew, a full belly combined with a long car ride, like a baby, would put him to sleep. It worked.

Please know, there's no way my father would have deliberately hurt anyone. Yes, he was a tough man, but he loved his family. That day, I knew my daddy was no longer here. It was a hard one to swallow.

We finally made it to Kansas and spent some time with my

brothers and their families. One early morning, I awoke and needed to use the restroom. I didn't think anyone was up yet as I hobbled via crutches to the hall bathroom. The door was closed. I tapped lightly. I heard Daddy's voice—I'm in here, he replied. I waited patiently. A few minutes passed and nothing. "I really need to go, you almost done in there?" No reply.

Here's another fun amputee fact, it's impossible to do the potty-dance if you're an amputee—especially if you don't have a prosthetic. For a brief moment, I considered going outside but my younger brother lives in a city neighborhood with very few trees, none of them big enough to hide behind. Here I was, desperate to use the potty, and my dad, the man who grew up using the outdoors most of his life had taken up residence in the bathroom. I need a pee-can. (Not to be confused with pecan.) I hobbled to the kitchen, and finding an old big gulp plastic cup I relieved myself. Phew!

As I reached to pour the yellow liquid down the drain, Daddy snuck around the corner like a kid, scaring me half to death and yelled, "I'm done!" I dropped the cup, the yellow liquid creating a huge puddle on the floor, seeping under one of my crutches. This caused the crutch to slide out beside me, and I fell to the hard tile floor, the end of Shortie took the full brunt of the fall.

Dad looked at me like I meant to fall. I could see the confusion on his face. I told him I was okay and to go back to bed. Like a kid, he did what I said. I laid there with tears rolling down my face, Shortie throbbing. I didn't know if I'd messed up the recent amputation; all the while sitting in the soft glow of the kitchen stove light, in my own urine. *Can it get any worse, Lord?*

Eventually, I gathered a couple of dish towels that I could reach from where I sat on the floor, and along with my nightgown I cleaned up my mess. Using the kitchen sink counter area, I pulled myself up from the floor. I found an ice pack and hobbled back to bed. Time would tell if I'd done any real damage to Shortie or not.

Several hours later, as I shared the story with my younger brother, he was beyond supportive. That is, after he finished laughing his head off! Once he confirmed that I was okay, he let loose with the jokes. "I give it to ya—definitely creative," my brother said as he choked down another belly laugh.

When you share life with another, the happy times are twice as good, and the sad times are half as painful.

Not long after surgery number eleven, I took another bad fall. While in the kitchen, at home, my crutch hit a wet spot on the hardwood floor. I had no idea there was water on the floor. I later figured out that it was a tiny ice chip that had bounced out from the ice-in-the-door on the refrigerator. Shortie, again, took the first bounce. I landed on my left wrist, only to top it off with a nice knot on the head. I'm not sure if the head-butt was from the kitchen table or from the table leg. It really didn't matter. I sat on the floor for a few minutes as my li'l Daisy came to the rescue. She's such a sweet pea! She gingerly made her way towards the pile of "Mommy and her sticks" all spread out on the floor. I sat and cried as she did her best to comfort me. Most of the time, the crying after a fall isn't from the pain, but rather from frustration—the frustration of the reality of my new normal as an amputee.

It took a bit of creative thinking to figure out how to get up off the floor from that particular fall. I'm not a hundred percent certain how I did it without the use of my left hand or my left leg. By the Grace of God, I managed to get into a chair.

My left wrist was sore, as was my head and Shortie. I spent the night with ice packs once again. The next morning I was scheduled to see Dr. Sethi regarding the progress of Shortie. While I was at his clinic, he suggested we X-ray my hand and wrist to be sure everything was okay. My photo shoot in the cold X-ray lab confirmed a hairline fracture in my wrist. NO! How am I going to use crutches with only one hand? Fortunately, he wasn't prescribing a hard cast as it would create extra unnecessary difficulties—which I did not need.

He opted for a rigid immobilizer brace for four to six weeks and no pulling, pushing, or lifting. Ugh! Now, I really looked like a goofball on crutches. My right crutch I used with my hand and forearm as I always did. The left one? Without the use of my hand, I had to rely on my armpit and upper arm to get around.

The follow-up visit to Dr. Sethi's clinic wasn't all bad. He finally cleared me to see my legman IF the plastic surgeon gave his blessing as well.

A week later…he said YES!

Let the Games Begin—Again…

It was the end of March, three months post Shortie's re-amputation surgery, and I was finally getting started with the process for a new prosthetic. After having tried for over a year to get a good fit with Shortie and a prosthetic the last time, I was convinced I'd need everything custom made. While most amputees can use off-the-shelf supplies, I'd need to go a different route. This meant a lot more time and, of course, more money.

The first step: a new liner. The liner is what goes directly over the skin on Shortie. Most liners look like they're made from what looks like scuba suit material—a thick gel or silicone covered in smooth, strong fabric. A plaster-cast mold was made of Shortie, complete with all the divots, bumps, lumps, and dimples. Not to mention all the wobbly bits. Countless measurements were documented as well.

The mold itself reminded me of grade school art class. Remember those fun piñatas made with a balloon and paper maché? Shortie was the "balloon," as my young legman layered warm casting strips all around it.

The completed cast was sent off to the custom liner company. It would take several weeks for the new liner to arrive. In the meantime, I was to wear a compression sleeve 24/7 to give and hold Shortie's shape and for support.

Lead Weight Lucy...

Three weeks later the custom liner arrived. It fit pretty well, but it would take time to get used to it because it weighed a ton. Okay, well, not really a ton, but compared to the others I'd used it felt like there was lead weight in the end of it.

The "weight" was actually a much thicker gel cushion built into the end, to give Shortie distal padding once inside a hard, rigid socket. Made sense, but man was it heavy. When Lead Weight Lucy was on Shortie, it felt like there was an extra eight to ten inches added to Shortie. Of course there wasn't that added length, Lead Weight Lucy only added an inch or two. Crazy how nerve endings and the brain play tricks on you.

Six More Weeks...

For the next several months the cycle continued: new liner, new socket, new liner, new socket. Shortie would shrink, and we'd have to start over again. With each change of liner or socket, it'd be a minimum of six more weeks. I understood the process, but struggled to get a good fit. Life on crutches, even fun decorated crutches, was wearing me down.

Drive-through Heartache...

I'm often asked, "Sheila, don't you ever just lose it? Doesn't it all get to you? Do you EVER break down?" If you want a yes or no answer...YES.

In reality though, it's not that simple. Sometimes I can schedule the heartaches. Unfortunately, schedules can be disrupted, sometimes without warning.

As I was leaving to run errands, I noticed a neighbor and his girlfriend walking up to his place. At first the sight of them made me smile. "Aww, how sweet." Then, I noticed her cute, flowing dress. Adorable! It was strike three that knocked me down. Her legs. They were perfect.

As I drove to the bank, my mind was working overtime. "Don't

compare yourself to another. You have amazing traits, etc., etc., etc."
By the time I pulled up to the drive-through at the bank, the tears were
spilling forth. No matter how hard I tried, they wouldn't stop. My
thoughts threw out horrible punches, straight to the heart! *I'll never have
pretty legs again. What kind of man will want me? I'll be alone the rest of my life.
The woman that hit me has no idea what my life has become,* and so on, and so
forth. It's awful how hard we can be on ourselves, isn't it?

How did I get through it, you ask? Like most things—a lot of tears
and even more prayer.

Dating Dilemmas...

Speaking of heartaches, dating as an amputee brought about its own
bushel full of heartaches. I could fill a whole other book on middle-age
dating in the modern world. Wow! Apparently, the last time I dated it
was the middle ages. At least it felt like it compared to the modern
dating of today's era. I'm not a bar-hopping girl, and I tend not to
cruise the gym looking for a fella. My top priority at church is not to
scope out potential single men in the crowd. My mom asked me one
time, "Honey, you go to that great big church. Aren't there any nice
eligible men there?"

With roaring enthusiasm I responded, "Well Mom, I sit in the
second row, and unlike you, I do not have eyes in the back of my head.
Ha-ha!"

She rolled her eyes at me as she replied, "Smarty-pants!"

I tried online dating. Oh, my! I had NO IDEA what all I was
getting myself into. I heard that folks met their soulmates that way and
thought I'd give it a go. I "gave it a go" alright. I tried Christian dating
sites, I tried secular dating sites. I tried expensive dating sites and free
dating sites. In my experience, they were all the same. The few fellas
that I had any real connection with disappeared after two or three dates
because I wasn't willing to put out aka: fornicate. I confess, I've failed

miserably in the past when it came to sexual relations. Only by God's mercy and grace I'm no longer that person. It amazed me how many men said how much they respected and admired (a woman my age) who chose not to have premarital sex. In reality, they thought I'd make an exception for them. Sadly, this scenario was just as common with professed Christian men as it was with non-Christians.

In the beginning, I had a hard time deciding whether I should inform potential dates of my amputation or not. After countless, wonderful back and forth online messaging, I'd finally feel confident enough to tell them I'm an amputee. Many, I'd never hear from again. Some, would be sympathetic, but quickly stop all correspondence. Some, would be real cowards and simply block any further communication. Sad but true.

My dear friend Tammy gave me the greatest piece of advice. I'd gone to her crying and broken hearted over a fella who cowardly crawled away from me after he learned of my amputation. She said, "Honey, you've got something most women don't have. You have a tool that lets you know, right up front, if they're man enough for you. If they can't handle Shortie, then they're not man enough for you, Darlin'!"

She's so right. Unfortunately, it still hurts to have someone walk away from you because of something that's not your fault. It's been some of the greatest advice I've ever been given when it comes to dating.

One evening after having dinner with a nice fella, we went to a local place to hear some great live jazz music. We were seated at a four seat table. My date chose to sit next to me to see the band. My legs were a bit sore, so I propped them on the opposite bench. My date and I had had nice conversation throughout the evening about various topics. As the band played, all of a sudden my date starts laughing. I look around, thinking I'd missed something. "What'd I miss?" As he continued to laugh he said, "I've been playing footsies with you for the past ten minutes. It just hit me…you can't feel it!"

We both laughed as I said, "Shortie is NOT that kind of girl!"

Chances are, I've heard them all. Here are a few of the common responses I get from men when they find out I'm an amputee:

"Really?!"

"Cool! Do you have a machine gun in it?"

"That's so sexy!"

"Are you pullin' my leg?"

"Is your name Ilene?"

"That's perfect cuz I have a foot fetish, not a feet fetish."

"Do you sleep with it on?"

One fella knew I was an amputee on crutches. I kid you not, he planned our first date for the Opryland Hotel. To walk around inside the entire hotel. I definitely earned extra credit physical therapy points that night. I slept like a baby after that date. Of course, I could hardly move the next day. Needless to say…that fella didn't work out.

Another loosing date…It was a first time dinner date, and we met at a nice restaurant. My date knew I'd been in a motorcycle accident, and he knew I was on crutches. He didn't know I was an amputee. I wore boots and a long skirt to dinner, which hid the prosthetic. As we got up to leave, my prosthetic, which wasn't fitting well, caught the table leg and rotated inward. It was the first time I was grateful my date was anything but a gentleman. He'd gotten up from the table before me and walked away before I had a chance to slide out of the booth. I looked down and Shortie's boot was doing a ninety degree right turn. I quickly twisted it back enough so I wouldn't trip myself as I hobbled outside. Obviously, I never returned his phone calls again.

Eventually, I did end up having a long-term dating relationship with a nice fella. On one of my beach trips, he flew in to join me for a long weekend. He'd never been to the Gulf of Mexico. It was fun sharing my happy place with a special someone who, like me, fell in love with the beautiful white sand and the calm, serene shoreline.

One morning, I had the strongest desire come over me.

Walk the beach Sheila…today.

Aaa…ya sure?

Yes, today. You can do this. I AM your biggest cheerleader.

Who am I to argue with the Holy Spirit? I rigged up a hot-looking orthopedic stocking for my prosthetic. Sand and salt are big no-no's for most components of a prosthetic. Feeling a little self-conscience about my attire, we headed down to the beach.

My gentleman friend asked, "Honey, do you want me to hold your hand or arm, or do you want to hold onto me?" We'd known each other long enough, and he'd learned that it's better for me to hold or lean on him if I needed help, rather than his holding me. A little side note bonus for you: As an amputee, I don't always know which way I'm going to wobble or weave, but one thing I know for sure, I definitely don't know which way you're going to bobble or weave. If I'm holding onto you and you lean forward, backward, left or right and I don't know it, I'm quickly off balance.

With renewed confidence, my inner two year old came out in me as I answered him, "Neither. I've got it." I looked over to see his eyes open wide with a no doubt, she's gonna face plant in the sand on the first step or two. Little did he know. I'd been on the sand before. I'd just not walked along the beach yet.

Think about it like this: It's tough for everyone to walk across loose sand, right? Everyone looks like they've been on a three day drinking binge. Well, for me…that's my everyday normal. Truth be told, it's much more comfortable on my joints to walk in the sand. No hard impact. Besides, if I happened to fall you couldn't ask for a softer landing!

We managed to find the happy medium sand. Not too close to the shoreline that water would get into my prosthetic, yet not too far into the loose, unstable sand.

At first, I didn't expect to make it much farther down the beach than to the end of the resort. With God, not only is everything possible, but when He shows up, He shows off! Y'all we walked close to a mile round trip!!!

We—okay me—collapsed on the beach chair once we made it back to the resort. While soaking up the victory, not to mention the sand, surf and sunshine, we enjoyed the calm serenity of the waves crashing into the shore.

If you don't step forward... you'll forever be in reverse.

As we soaked up the sunshine, listening to the waves gently crash into the shore, I thought I heard someone behind me. In my sun-drenched stupor, I slowly turned around to see who it was. Not a who, but a what. I gasped. There, all by its lonesome, was a one-legged, small seagull staring back at me. Tears puddled as I thanked God for this amazing sign. When I gasped, my friend turned to see what I was looking at.

"Oh my gosh! Had you not just told me the story an hour ago, I'd not have believed it" he said with wonder.

This wasn't the first time one of God's flying creatures with a Shortie like mine had visited me on the beach. The awesome timing of these sweet feathery friends can only be explained as "God winks." I'm convinced He knows the encouragement and joy these li'l creatures bring me. Watching others experience the one-legged feathered friends doubles the joy!

My friend, the day he departed while taking his final look at the gulf, said to me, "Thank you so much for sharing some of your special time with me here. I understand now why you light up when you talk about it."

Sunshine is Son-shine to my soul.

After seriously dating more than a year, he was suddenly gone from my life in a matter of two hours. At the time, his breakup made absolutely no sense to me.

"I don't understand. How can you love and adore me one day and without warning or notice walk away?" I asked.

"I'll always love you for who you are," he replied, "but I believe God is leading me in a different direction."

Something in my gut knew there was more to his story. He couldn't look at me, which for him, spoke volumes. Within days of his breakup, I had the real story. Basically, he spelled it wrong. It wasn't God leading him in a different direction, it was his groin.

My sweet friend Hope had the best piece of encouragement—"If you were happy with the wrong fella, think how happy you'll be when the right one comes along." Thanks, Hope! I love you.

Ironically…I still pray for him, as well as other fellas from my past.

A healed heart can love deeper and more than ever before.

A Tie That Binds…

Years ago, I heard a story. This is my version:

There was a young lady who desired more than anything to be a wife and a mother. She longed to share the love in her heart with one special man. By all standards, she was considered an amazing catch—faithful Christian, beautiful, kind, generous, intelligent, great cook, etc. Any man would be fortunate to win her heart.

As the years rolled by, this young woman watched friend, after friend, after friend, fall in love, marry and start a family. Sadly, she remained single.

One day, while at a ladies' event, the young lady was asked by one of the older ladies, "Are you married? Children?"

With a tear in her eye, the young lady replied, "No, ma'am." The wise, older woman sensed her pain. Gently patting the young lady's hand, and reaching up with the other hand to wipe her tear, the young lady began to sob. It was a beautiful scene of true compassion and kindness. Through her quiet tears, the young lady shared her heartache with the older woman. The older woman listened to every word—taking it all in—never interrupting.

When the young lady asked, "What's wrong with me? Why won't God give me a husband and a family?"

The older woman replied, "Have you asked God? Have you shared with Him the desires of your heart?"

The young lady, a bit frustrated, responded "Of course!"

"When was the last time you prayed to God specifically about it?" the older woman asked.

"I don't know, probably a few weeks ago. When I think about it, I pray about it. I figure He knows the desires of my heart, so why should I keep praying about it?" replied the young lady.

With a gentle compassion that only comes through a lifetime of experience, the older woman said, "Honey, if it's not a priority to you, and you're not willing to make it a priority in your request to God, why should it be a priority for Him?"

It was as if a light came on for the first time in this young lady's heart. "Wow, that makes sense, but sometimes I forget to pray about it specifically in my daily prayer time."

"Oh, honey, at my age, I forget a lot of things! I used to tie a string on my finger. These days, I seem to have reminders around the house for just about everything. If I don't write it down, it may not get done."

The young lady hugged the older lady, kissed her on the cheek, and thanked her for her compassion, wisdom and guidance. On her way home from the event, the young lady stopped at a men's clothing store to buy a man's neck tie. She hung it on her bedroom door knob to remind her to pray earnestly for her heart's desire.

A beautiful blue silk man's neck tie hangs today on my nightstand lamp.

Chapter Sixteen

Six-Week Cycle...

For months and months my life consisted of "six more weeks." Because of the amputation revision surgery, I had to start the prosthetic process all over again from the very beginning. That meant constant shrinkage, atrophy, soft tissue shifting, skin toughening-up to be done, and of course, skin breakdown issues. While I understood the process, because of the "been there, done that" from the prior year, that didn't make things any easier.

Most of the time knowledge is powerful, but for me, in this case, knowing how long, and how hard, and how painful adapting to a prosthetic would be was a constant reminder of the struggle. Nearly three years had passed since the accident, and I wasn't yet walking on my own.

The hardest climbs result in the greatest views.

Sorry, Charlie...

I love fish! Eating them, that is. They don't really appeal to me as a pet. I prefer the warm, fuzzy pets that give sloppy, wet kisses. Although, come to think of it, I did have a fella kiss me one time, and all I could think of was a guppy. Ew!

However, I'm referring to the four-legged mammal—the horse. Sadly, this was one horse I wanted to put down. For several weeks I'd endured some of the most intense Charlie horses ever! I'd had Charlie horses in the past and learned some pretty neat, albeit quirky, effective remedies. Lately, not even the ol' mustard trick made a dent in the pain. This go-round was different. The intense muscle spasms hit suddenly and without warning in Shortie, only to quickly radiate to parts (literally) unknown. Y'all have any idea how hard it is to "walk it out" when IT ain't there? So weird! I don't think I'll ever get used to the body's craziness after horrific physical trauma. If I had an ad to get rid of my Charlie horses, it would have read:

Horse For Sale

Name: Charlie

Temperament: Stubborn

Breed: Definitely Hot Blood

Strength: Off the charts

Relative: Donkey

Asking Price: Free

Family Tradition...

I didn't realize how frustrated I'd become about some things until a friend, okay more than one friend, made reference to my recent lack of patience around them. Apparently, my punching Bop bag wasn't compensating well enough. I needed another outlet to relieve a little pent-up stress.

I'd had a valid handgun carry permit for years. Unfortunately, there was a mix up with my renewal paperwork. I tried to get a medical waiver, etc. but the state wouldn't allow it.

Starting over from scratch was my only option. Starting over, as I've learned (repeatedly), isn't always a bad thing. I called an old friend who's an excellent marksman and an even better firearms trainer. Leroy was kind enough to walk me through the course again, one-on-one this time. He's amazing! We completed the classroom portion and proceeded to the range for the practical (the fun part).

Most folks put their prized artwork on the fridge. I've got a side-by-side refrigerator. There's no way my completed target sheet was gonna fit on it. I confess, I hung it on the mantle for the pure enjoyment I received every time I glanced at it. Carrying on an old family tradition of marksmanship, I'm proud to say, I scored one hundred percent. After I hung the target sheet from the mantle, I noticed my granddaddy's saddle scabbard hanging below it. That, for those who don't know, is a rifle holster that's hung on a saddle. I was an infant when my granddaddy passed. I like to think he's got a big ol' Texas grin on his face, full of pride, that his granddaughter has a touch of Annie Oakley in her blood.

Now, y'all know there's a funnier story I have yet to share about my time at the armory, right?

After I completed the required practical, Leroy thought it'd be good (I almost wrote "fun," but I'm not so sure that's what he had in mind) to practice some more "real life" scenarios. Years ago, we learned the "shoot from the hip" technique. Umm…I'm not sure what the official term of the technique we did was called (I'm giggling as I try to type this). I guess there's no other way to say it. If what we learned years ago was tagged, "from the hip"…this would be tagged, "from the girls" (aka: the chest).

I was facing the target, with both hands on the gun, elbows tucked in tight to my waist and my wrists were locked. (You're trying to do it, aren't you?) For me, that meant the gun was just below "the girls." So here I am, locked, loaded, and in position when I see a fella's hand gingerly block the girls. "Hmm…sure am glad I trust this fella, or does Leroy trust me?" I'm the one with a loaded weapon. It briefly crossed my mind to lay the gun down, turn, and shout (we both had double hearing protection on) "Excuse Me?!" Fortunately, I have great respect for my trainer, so logic kicked in—"There's a reason he's doing this."

I don't remember how many rounds I shot in that stance, but at one point, Leroy removed his hand. It happened in a flash. *Holy Moses! What the…?* The girls were on fire!

One of the bullet casings made a perfect shot, straight up, then straight down, landing in between the girls. While I'm no Dolly Parton, that hot metal casing was lodged dead center. I hadn't moved that fast in years!

Poor Leroy. Bless his heart! Not sure if he was more embarrassed or apologetic. I assured him… "If it's gonna happen, it's gonna happen to me." Note to self: Next time…wear a turtle neck!

Tower of Terror…

While I wouldn't call it terror, the result was basically the same as if I'd have been riding Disney's Tower of Terror.

I started the morning early at Vanderbilt Orthopedics for evaluation of my right knee. Although it was rebuilt after being crushed in the accident, I continued to have recurring pain. The concern was, because I was using primarily my right leg (my long leg) all the time, I'd worn it out. Physical therapy and strength training hadn't conquered the never-ending pain.

Once I completed the entertaining photo shoot (poor tech—I had her laughing hysterically at me trying to do acrobats in order to get the unique X-rays for the specialist—we both needed a potty break). I had a nice long chat with the resident. He was a nice fella with a great bedside manner. He's gonna make an awesome surgeon.

Not long after that, the knee guru came in. I won't bore you with all the details, but he had great news. I did NOT need a full knee replacement. Hopefully not for many more years to come. Thank God!

I was doing the "happy dance" (on the inside). This specialist was new to me, and while he had an excellent reputation, he's not all that chipper, if you get my drift, so I refrained from any public display of happy dancing in his presence.

As I continued to sit back on the clinic table—praising God for this awesome news and grateful for second and third opinions, combined with much less invasive options—he quietly, but firmly, said, "The radiologists have found something on your X-rays. You need to have a full-body nuclear scan and follow up with an oncologist as soon as possible."

In an instant my joyous high became a tower of fear. I pulled up my boot straps and held it together long enough to ask a few questions, schedule the four-to-five hour nuclear test and the follow-up appointment with the oncologist.

Once I reached the elevators to leave, the tower of terror, or in my case the tower of fear took over. My Jackie O sunglasses came out to hide my eyes.

I finally reached my truck in the parking garage. Once the truck door was closed with me safely inside, I collapsed. My body slumped over as my head hung low. I cried my heart out. *I'm trying SO hard Lord. IT'S NOT FAIR!* I was hurt and I was angry. I was mad at the lady who crashed into me. I was mad at my ex-husband. I was mad at the insurance companies. I was mad that I was all alone. I was fit-raging MAD!

As I sat there, all alone in my truck, having a massive come-apart, I noticed my lap was wet. Great, now I've wet myself and didn't even know it. *Can it get any worse?*

After further investigation, I hadn't wet myself. Not really. I'd hung my head so low and cried so hard that my lap was soaking wet. There wasn't a tear on my face. Oh, sure, my eyes were bloodshot red from crying, but my makeup was entirely intact.

As hard as my head was saying, *No need to worry. It's probably nothing,* my heart was saying, *God? Really? We've come this far and fought all these battles together, this is how I'm gonna lose the war?*

What was my gut saying? *I think I'm gonna throw up!*

Once I regurgitated, I had a chance to process it all. You know what? God never fails. He's ALWAYS with us. He'll get me through this as well, whatever it turns out to be.

Later that day I received a precious, heart-felt call from Dr. Sethi. Little did I know, he'd been monitoring my Vandy portal-record system. As soon as he read the report, he called me. (I love that man!)

He reassured me that he felt certain that the lesions the radiologist saw on my tibia bone were residual scarring from the bone marrow donor surgery that he did three years prior. Of course, he too made sure I followed through with the nuclear scan and oncologist. I couldn't thank Dr. Sethi enough for his sweet, sweet phone call! Isn't it cool when God uses us to encourage another?

I'm not gonna lie and tell y'all I was "walking on sunshine." I am human, after all, but because of Dr. Sethi, I had hope.

Earful of Tears...

"Earful of Tears" sounds like a country song, doesn't it? Whether it's been sung or not, it was a first for me.

The prior week was more stressful than usual for me as we worked through the latest hurdle: Did I have bone cancer? I endured a contrast MRI and then spent most of the day at Vanderbilt Hospital for the nuclear, full-body scans. Neither test was painful, other than the injections in the beginning. The IV staff have always had their work cut out for them when it comes to my veins. Even the best medical vampires have trouble getting needles in me.

For those of you who've had the good fortune to experience an MRI, you know how loud and annoying they can be.

After I left the knee specialist, the previous week, I understood the only test they wanted was the nuclear body scan. Well, the Orthopedic Oncologists' nurse called me and said they had me scheduled for an MRI.

I questioned the nurse: "I'm to have a nuclear scan, not an MRI?"

"The specialist wants a contrast MRI series as well," she replied.

"Umm...y'all realize I'm filled with metal, right? So, I have no intention of getting anywhere near a giant MAGNETIC machine."

"Oh...well...let me find out about that and call you back," said the nurse.

Several really goofy phone calls later, from a variety of nursing and scheduling staff, we developed a plan. Kind of.

During all the confusion, I thought, *Ya know what? I'm gonna ask Dr. Sethi. He's the one that put these legs back together (many times).* When he called me back, he was as kind as ever. (I thank God for that man on a regular basis.)

To summarize: "Sheila...you're the Bionic Woman! You're MRI compatible."

"Huh? It's okay for metal to be in an MRI machine?" I asked.

Unlike Superman (aka: The Man of 'Steel,') I'm Bionic (aka: Titanium). Cool! Sure wish I could run like Jaime Sommers. (If you're too young to know who Jaime Sommers is, Google her.)

Back to the day of the MRI.

As I lay stiff as a board, on a board, the pounding jack hammer sounds began, intermittently interrupted by the sound of a semi-automatic machine gun. Not all facilities provide decent ear protection. I'd had much better in the past. I should have taken with me the hearing protection I use on the firing range.

Within a few minutes of the first series, I started having intense, faa-ree-kee, phantom pains. Keep in mind, I couldn't move. Not good. I tried going to my "happy place" as I lay there. Not sure if the phantom pains were related to the magnetic field or strictly coincidence, but as soon as the series would end...so would the pain. Weird!

Next was the nuclear, full-body scan. While it's a much more peaceful test, as far as the noise goes, it was definitely more stressful. It's similar in set-up as an MRI, but without all the pounding racket. However, there is one rather uncomfortable drawback. You're lying on your back, on a table that has a slight upward curve to it and they have your arms, with your elbows, strapped tight and straight to your sides.

The tech asked, "Would you like a warm blanket?"

"Shoot, yeah!" Might as well be comfy and nap if possible. That's exactly what I did. I woke to the sound of the alarm and machine cutting off. I'm thinking, *Nice. That was a piece of cake.*

Then I heard this male voice, "Please don't move yet. We need to wait until the radiologist reviews the scans before we can let you up."

I couldn't move if I wanted to. Y'all have me bound to this thing!

What seemed like twenty minutes or more passed by. The tech then came in and said, "They want another couple of series." (Of course they did!)

As he adjusted the machine towards my right tibia, which is the area where they saw lesions, I let out a sigh of relief and told myself, *If they've scanned my whole body and only wanna see a little more in just that area...that's good news.*

The second series started and finished. Yeah! I could finally get out of there! That's when he came in and said, "We have just one more area."

It's then that he moved the machine towards my head again to take another series of scans. I heard his footsteps as he left the room. I laid there, head perfectly still, my eyes looking at the ceiling. The only thing I could move were my eyes. In the silence, those awful, fear-filled thoughts started to take over. *They must see lesions in my head if they need to take more scans...What does it mean?...Is it...cancer?* It was then that I felt my ears fill with tears—my tears. Big ones quickly rolled out the sides of my eyes, and filled up my EARS. I glanced up to see that there were less than ninety seconds until the series was complete.

Again, I tried desperately to find my "happy place," all the while, having a li'l talk with Jesus.

Since there was no way of drying my tears before the tech came back in, I decided, "It must be allergies," would be the best response.

The tech returned. He gently acknowledged my tears without saying a word. Thank you Lord for giving this man a kind and gentle spirit. He handled it perfectly.

As I sat on the bench outside, waiting for the Vanderbilt Valet service, I had a shiver run through my body from tip to top. At that moment, I was enveloped with a blanket of peace that said, *You must have had a muscle twitch when you fell asleep during the first head scan series and that's why they had to do another set.*

Call it what you like. For me...it's the flutter of the Holy Spirit that wraps Himself about me in comfort and peace. I absolutely LOVE those moments! They outweigh EARS full of tears...hands down.

It had been a long, hard couple of weeks. First coming to grips with potentially another surgery—knee replacement, then the possibility of bone cancer, then, the waiting for diagnostic testing, and finally, waiting for the test results.

After waiting an hour and fifty-eight minutes in the oncologists waiting area the day of my follow-up appointment, I was finally called into a treatment room. The oncologist, a lovely woman, came in and declared me "perfect." Her word.

"Thank You Jesus!" My words.

Dr. Sethi was right. What the radiologists saw on my X-rays was residual scarring in my tibia from where he took bone marrow out years ago.

~ ~ ~

The ongoing shrinkage and atrophy with Shortie continued. That meant the process of a new liner, new socket, new sleeve, etc., was also in repeat mode.

Physical therapy continued. There was always some part of my body that needed therapy—especially since I spent a significant amount of time non-weight bearing.

Mirror, Mirror, on the Wall…

To be accurate, it was more like, "Mirror, mirror, on the foot…"

I continued to have crazy phantom pains. Off the charts (literally), crazy pain in the lower left leg and foot.

While in a physical therapy session, I had what I would describe as medium phantom pains. As the medical profession would say, "On a scale of 1 to 10, what would you rate it?" (I still hate that question) What scale? Or better yet, who or what is the scale based on? Is it based on normal? If so, what and who is normal?

Anyway, I had an episode of fairly significant phantom pain while in physical therapy. Kind of freaked out my sweet, little physical therapist. Apparently, my sudden coming up off the table, lack of breathing, and look of intense pain can do that to a therapist.

That was the first day we briefly tried Mirror Imaging Therapy. I had previously tried it, at home…alone, with no real success. When I asked Mary, my rock star physical therapist, if we could concentrate on the Mirror Imaging, she was all in! I wanted to try it when I wasn't in the throes of heavy phantom pains. Since I was on "standby," if you will, for any weight bearing again (ugh!), it was perfect timing.

For those who don't know what Mirror Imaging Therapy is, let's see if I can help you understand.

I sit upright, with my legs extended in front of me. A long mirror is placed between my legs. The mirror is facing my long leg. I then shift or lean a bit in order to see into the mirror. The reflection I see is a mirror image of my long leg, tricking my mind into believing Shortie (my amputated leg) is still there. Talk about freaky!

Wait, it gets better. WAY better! I took my right boot off, and Mary began flexing and stretching the right foot and ankle. As she did, I looked into the mirror at the image reflecting back. I kid you not! I could feel the sensations in the missing limb. As her hands wrapped around my right foot and ankle, she proceeded with slow, deep tissue massage. Huge emotion overtook my senses. Tears began to fall…

The emotion that's evoked from a simple touch between two people is greater than most of us ever realize…let alone acknowledge. God created our body and mind to be able to interpret the nature of another's touch upon us. We've all been touched by another, be it in anger, frustration, desperation, control, hurt, fear, in sorrow, joy, excitement, endearment, friendship, or love. Without a word ever spoken, our senses tell us what's behind even the simplest touch.

I think maybe that's why I was overcome with such emotion during the Mirror Image Therapy. Albeit in my mind, I felt the warmth and kindness of another's touch on that which is untouchable…(Tears well up again as I type this). I pray I never again underestimate the power of touch.

Mirror Image Therapy was a slow process, but it turned out to be a huge benefit for me. It's amazing how powerful the mind is.

Too often we underestimate the power of a touch, a smile, or a kind word.
—Leo Buscaglia

Cooter Brown...

I tend to have a strut all my own, and some days, it's downright comical. For years, since the accident, I was told it was most likely positional vertigo and most likely, it would eventually subside. The real answer would be "No" to both of those. I did not have BPPV (aka: positional vertigo). I had something even more unique. Imagine that. I don't know the medical term for it, but it's basically motion induced drunkenness caused by one of two things:

A) A neurological brain injury from the lateral whiplash when my head hit the other driver's windshield or when my head hit the pavement and my helmet flew off.

B) The long term use of one of the IV Antibiotics had a history of causing damage to the inner ear fibers. That damage creates the sensation of being drunk.

I'm sure you've heard the term "simulator." It describes a machine designed to provide a realistic imitation of a vehicle, aircraft, or other complex system used for training purposes. Have you ever heard of a drunk simulator? I'm here to tell you, they have one at the Vanderbilt Bill Wilkerson Center. Obviously, that's not really what it's for, but that's what it did to me. It was the craziest thing—fascinating, but CRAZY!

The physical therapist operating the machine promised me that normal folks wouldn't have a bit of trouble with it. Ha! We all know I'm nowhere near normal.

She had me step-up into a booth-type box that had three sides, each about eight feet tall. The floor of the box would move as well. The inside of the box was painted with pretty skyline scenery. She attached around my waist a security belt that was designed to keep me from falling. She then attached a number of wires to me, mostly on my head, that would register brain activity. I felt like Frankenstein.

Once she started the machine, the walls began to move. Or at least I thought they moved. It could have been the floor I was standing on that moved. At one point or another, every part of the device moved, sometimes, one at a time, other times, together. It felt like a bad carnival ride—and I don't do carnival rides. The room was spinning. I thought I was going to puke when she said, "Only thirty more seconds." That was the longest thirty-second ride of my life. Several hours after the testing, I still felt hung over.

The test results revealed that my feet and legs were strong and surprisingly stable, especially for an amputee. Hip, hip hooray for the countless hours of continued physical therapy! Unfortunately, I failed miserably with the other part—my brain and/or my ears. The results meant I had to see another specialist.

This goofy journey never ends. At least I had confirmation that my "drunkenness" wasn't "all in my head."

Oh, wait. It kind of was.

The neurologist, who specialized in movement disorders, diagnosed me with "neurological ocular movement disorder." In layman's term the phrase means: When I moved my head too fast, or if my eyes were closed, I'd lose my balance. The specialist referred me to the Bill Wilkerson Neurology Center at Vanderbilt to work with a physical therapist that specialized in the field.

In just a few weeks of brain-eye physical therapy I had great improvement. I was amazed at how such a simple thing caused such massive issues.

I'd learned that, basically when I was immobilized from the waist down for four months after the accident, and using my hands to move around, my brain became lazy. I wouldn't make a move unless I'd first turned my head and looked where I needed to place my hands. In doing so, the brain-eye communication became weak. Combine that with lateral whiplash and the drug side-effects, I wobbled about like the town drunk.

Remember the drunk simulator booth? The first time I tested with it, I failed miserably. My score was in the mid-forties. Passing for my age range was seventy to seventy-five. After successful therapy, not only did I pass, I aced it with a score of eighty-four!

The really cool test was one that I was too severe even to do initially. It was another computerized gizmo where a goofy head piece was hooked up to a monitor. The therapist manually (and very quickly, I might add), moved my head from side to side. The monitor across the room quickly flashed letters that I had to identify and indicate which direction those letters were facing (i.e: up, down, left or right). Sounds confusing, huh? Kind of like patting your head and rubbing your belly at the same time. Only you need to add chewing gum or better yet, blowing bubbles with that gum.

The physical therapist said the same test was used in San Diego for fighter pilot training. Apparently most folks on a good day aren't fighter pilot material.

Again, when God shows up, He shows up BIG! While I had no plans of becoming a fighter pilot, my test results indicated I more than met fighter pilot status.

Woohoo!

Chapter Seventeen

New Legman...

While I adored my original legman, after nearly two years of trial and setbacks from various prosthetic options, I needed to seek out someone with more experience. I was referred to Aaron Sorrenson, owner of Restorative Health Services, Inc. by a military veteran who couldn't say enough great things about Aaron.

My first visit to Aaron's clinic was extremely encouraging. I'd been struggling for too long to get the right combination for my compound issues. He was beyond professional, had what sounded like a great plan to meet my specific needs and his many years of experience gave me the confidence I needed to move forward.

When I first saw Aaron, I was able to walk with my current leg, but only a hundred steps or so in a row. Then I'd have to undress, take the prosthetic off, take off the liner, readjust, put the liner back on, then add the prosthetic, and then redress.

The same process was required if I did a flight of stairs. While all of the added time consuming, not to mention frustrating, process could be done, it shouldn't have had to be that way. There were better prosthetic options available, and Aaron made sure I would get them.

After waiting months for insurance to approve a new leg, the building, rebuilding, test-driving, modifying, and adjusting of the new leg had finally taken place. In layman's terms, "We were oh, so close!"

I'd had the new prosthetic leg on loan, as trial arrangement, if you will, for about a week. Transitioning into a completely different way of walking had its moments, but in general, I was doing pretty well with it. I saw Aaron for a few minor modifications, then left the new leg with him so he could build the maintenance socket (the top part where

Shortie slides into, which I usually refer to as 'the vase').

The new prosthetic leg with its versatile mobility, shock absorbing, flexion, traction, suspension, hydraulic, and vacuum system created an amazing combination, which was customized to my unique situation. Needless to say, Aaron was excited to see it all come together—almost as much as I was.

Meet Mighty Warrior Samson…

It was a toss-up between MacGyver or Samson. For a brief moment I thought I'd combine the two and call my new prosthetic leg McSamson. That sounded like a cheesy drive-through hamburger stand. For obvious reasons, this being the strongest leg I'd ever had, I'd chosen Samson.

While we were still getting to know one another, I saw great strides in our future. (Strides, get it? Ha-ha!) The amount of simulated, albeit natural-like foot, ankle and calf movement, was beyond amazing. For nearly four years, I'd walked with a rigid, non-moving leg. The learning curve was a whole new game for me, but I'm no quitter.

According to my new legman, most amputees have one or maybe two components in their prosthetic. Some have three. Very few have four. In over twenty years of building legs, this was the first leg he'd built that had five. We both expected great results. So far, so good. One step at a time.

What a blessing to experience such advances in technology.

"Fifty for Fifty"…

The year preceding my half-a-century birthday was tough. Really tough. I needed something to look forward to. Something special. Something to distract me from getting depressed. Something to occupy the cycle of frustrations and setbacks I'd been living for years since the accident. I needed joy amidst the constant pain and struggles.

During the dreary winter months, sitting at home alone with way too much time on my hands and definitely way too much time for yucky thoughts to invade my mind, I came up with a plan. The theme for the full calendar year of my fiftieth year on earth would be "Fifty for Fifty." I wrote a list of things I'd like to do, experience, see, and accomplish during the fiftieth year of my life. Before long, my list had way more than fifty things on it.

The first thing I checked off the list was to "write fifty hand-written thank you notes to people who've made a positive impact on my life." Every day for the first fifty days of 2015, I wrote and mailed notes of gratitude. It's amazing how such a simple act can make such a profound difference in people's lives. I kept a copy of each one. I must say, it's one of the most memorable treasures I have.

My actual birth date is in April, and there was no way I was going to allow any of my friends to throw me an "Over the Hill" party. I'd suffered enough darkness. I needed no reminders. Instead, we celebrated with a wonderful "Celebration of Life."

The party theme was "Feed Fifty Families." I'd been deeply blessed by countless volunteers, helpers, and prayer warriors along my journey, and I wanted to somehow give back those blessings. Included with the party invitations was a shopping list for non-perishable food items. When combined, they created a full meal from beverage to dessert for a family of four. In lieu of gifts, guests were asked to participate by bringing the food items in a recyclable grocery bag. The goal was fifty, in honor of my fiftieth birthday, but more importantly, "to feed fifty families." We not only met the goal, we smashed it! It required a caravan of three SUV's to delivery seventy-three bags of food. Best birthday EVER!

Prior to the accident, on September 29, 2011, I'd never ridden in a helicopter. The Life Flight chopper ride was anything but memorable for me. Within seconds of being loaded into the chopper, I was knocked out. I remember nothing else. Riding in a helicopter, for fun, was on my "Fifty for Fifty" list. I wasn't sure how or if I'd accomplish it. I figured I'd look into a helicopter ride along the beach the next time I was there.

God had way bigger plans! After spending a few days in the Tennessee Smoky Mountains, I stopped, unplanned and suddenly, at a helicopter tour place as I started my drive home. Waiting in the lobby, while a young newlywed couple in front of me spoke to the clerk, I read the sign with the various tours listed on it. Yikes. This is a lot more expensive than I expected. The sales clerk turned to me, "Have you decided which tour you'd like to go on?"

"Well, I'm not sure yet. Actually, I'm not sure I'm able to ride." I responded.

"Why's that?" he asked.

I looked down, and lifted my skirt a bit to show him my prosthetic and said, "I'm not real stable, especially on un-level ground. Plus, I'm not sure I can climb up into the chopper."

Without delay he said to me, "Honey, don't you worry. If you wanna ride, we'll help you get inside. Even if I have to carry you and lift you in myself."

Well, at least that part was covered, but what about the cost?

The fella looked around and saw no one was in the lobby but us so he quietly asked, "Can I ask what happened?"

Not having a shy bone in my body, I shared a bit of my story. He asked "Why a chopper ride?"

"The first and last time I was in a helicopter it saved my life, but I don't have any memory of it," I answered.

"Young lady, how would you like to ride copilot on the next tour? The couple before you just bought our longest tour. They can ride in the bench seat in back, and you can be right up front and see everything."

"I'd love to do that, but I can't afford the longest tour package." I replied.

He briefly hesitated and then with a big ol' grin he said, "Oh, I forgot to tell you, the copilot only pays the cost of our shortest tour today."

"Deal! Thank you SO much!"

"Honey, it's our honor to serve a living miracle."

God is so good!

I actually checked two things off my "Fifty for Fifty" list that day—

a helicopter ride for fun and conquering my fear of heights. I had no idea that there's a window at your feet in the front of a chopper. (Obviously, I'd never looked before.) I won't lie. It was pretty eerie, especially if I looked straight down. Once I found a happy-medium place in the floor window to look through, combined with the front window views, it was breathtaking!

Baby Steps…

Life with Samson, my latest prosthetic, was progressing well. Slow, yes, but I was finally making forward momentum. I'd still need to use crutches on long distances, in crowds, or on unlevel ground. To this day, I take a crutch if I'm in a crowded environment. Folks may not realize it, but as a high trauma amputee, if I'm bumped into—even on accident, the potential for me to fall is huge. Walking with a prosthetic can be like walking on a stilt that I don't feel. Combine that with a bum long leg and it can be a recipe for who-knows-what.

Because Samson and I were getting along so well, I was able to be more active, more mobile. I was far from registering for a marathon, but I was more than ready to try walking for exercise. A beautiful, private high school near me granted me permission to walk on their soft track. It's made of a spring-like rubber composition. It was level, and it had the least amount of impact to all my joints. It took all I could muster to complete a single lap my first time on the track. Over time, I'd slowly add to it. I was gaining strength and endurance, but I knew I needed more. This world is not a soft, level, rubber composite ground to walk on.

I'd discovered that I walked better in a store when I held onto a shopping buggy rather than without. That got me to thinking, *If I could figure out something to hang onto while walking on uneven ground, maybe that's the practice I need.* Initially, I considered finding an old shopping buggy to use. *Na, I'm not really a bag lady. Hmm…what else would work? Oh! I know. A runner's baby stroller.*

Craigslist to the rescue. I found a cheap, lightweight stroller to practice with. My first few attempts inside the house failed miserably.

Without weight in the stroller, the front wheels kept popping up, which threw me off balance. I needed weight for the seat. I discovered that a two gallon bucket filled with sand was ideal.

My goal? One lap around my street. That doesn't sound like much, but believe me, it was. I lived on the side of a ridge and nothing about it was level.

As I s-l-o-w-l-y made my way around the complex, I started thinking, *I probably should have done this when folks were at work. I have no doubt my neighbors were thinking, 'That goofy lady with one leg has finally lost it! She's pushing a baby stroller with a bucket in it. Bless her heart.'*

Along my route, I picked up a piece of paper that'd blown into my path. Not until I got home did I turn the paper over and open it up. It was a bib number from a 5K race that read "Insane Inflatable 5K." I had to laugh. Prior to completing my tiny lap, I'd thought to myself *Dang, I'll never make a 5K with these legs at this rate!* While some folks may think my efforts were insane, I choose to believe God rewarded me that night with a special 5K bib number to say, *I'm so proud of you! The courage I give you is beyond insane. You go, girl!*

My efforts to carry on, eventually paid off. No, I haven't completed a marathon. Not even a 5K via these designer legs. I did, however, celebrate my five year accident anniversary by completing a one mile walk on foot. Woohoo! For this girl, who by all medical accounts shouldn't even be alive, walking a mile was a grand accomplishment. I was honored to share the event with a group of fun-loving friends who walked with me. Each of us had a nickel in our shoe to commemorate the celebration. I'm so grateful for the love and support of my village people!

I Danced, I Really, REALLY Danced…

Outside of a very wobbly attempt at a slow dance, at a friend's wedding, I hadn't danced since before the accident. For decades, I longed to attend our local social gala—the Heritage Ball. It's a gorgeous, black-tie fund-raising event. I was SO excited to finally attend. I'd known for a couple of months that'd I'd be going, and I worked extra hard to prepare for it. No, not with all the fluff of the perfect dress, the matching shoes, the right jewelry, the hair, and the makeup, but with the strengthening of my legs. I had every intention of dancing at the ball.

When the evening arrived, I felt like Cinderella dressed in a beautiful, vibrant blue gown I had found at a steal of a price. The best thing about the gown was that it was really comfortable, and the flowing length covered the orthopedic shoes I was wearing. Butterflies filled my tummy as I waited on my escort and prince, Stryker, to pick me up. I was SO excited. While I waited, my mind drifted back over the years of horrific struggle and heartache, the constant setbacks and the ongoing pain. I also remembered something I'd said not long after the accident: "I will dance again. One day...I'll dance!"

We spent more time on the dance floor than off. Stryker, being fully aware of my designer legs, protected me from zealous dancers around us, as he gently twirled me around the dance floor all night long. The lead singer of the band, after finding out I was an amputee, graced us with a spotlight dance. He said, "I have the perfect song for you." Moments later he serenaded us with a beautiful rendition of "My Girl" as tears of pure joy trickled down my face.

I awoke the next morning feeling more like Gumby than Cinderella. My entire body hurt. Especially my cheeks...from smiling all night long. It was way worth it!

Life can be a dance between love and fear. Don't be afraid to let love lead.

Let It Go, Let It Go...

While on a girls' trip to the beach with Tiffany, I had an opportunity to check a few more things off my "Fifty for Fifty" list. One of the items had been on my lifetime bucket list as well: swim with the dolphins. After watching the movie, *Dolphin Tale*, I had to do all I could to make that dream come true. I've used the same style of liner that was developed and designed as a result of scientists working with Winter, the amputee dolphin, whom the movie is based upon. It's a fabulous product for those of us who have sensitive skin.

After extensive research, and talking to the administrative staff and the trainers at a dolphin facility in Florida, I made my reservation. Tiffany was granted special permission, without extra payment, to accompany me into the water. I'd studied photos of the facility and the water tanks ahead of time, so I could be as prepared as possible. I was informed I would not be allowed to wear "Nemo," my water leg, into the tank, because the metal puts off a certain sound underwater that bothers the dolphins.

It turned out that Tiffany never had to get into the water with me. The entrance to the water had wide steps, allowing me to get into the water a step or two, then sit on the top step to take off Nemo. It couldn't have worked out better.

I'd often said, if I ever get the chance to swim with the dolphins, I'd buy an entire groups worth of tickets, so I could have the experience all to myself. Ha! Because I'm not independently wealthy, that never happened, which turned out to be a huge blessing. Oh, my gosh! Have you ever tried keeping your balance in rolling water, all while a three to four hundred pound dolphin is stirring the undercurrent like crazy...all while standing on one leg?!

I tried holding onto the side of the water tank to keep my balance when I wasn't directly engaging with the dolphins. It didn't take long before I would swim back to the steps and sit and rest while waiting for my next turn.

There's truly something inspiring about being in the water with dolphins. They emanate a peace, a calm, like no other animal I've been around. There were three trainers that particular day: one in the water with the guests, and two at the other end of the tank with two other dolphins. The tank was huge! It was used at other times for water shows.

One at a time, each guest would take a turn with one of the dolphins, with the guidance and assistance of the trainer in the water with us. She was adorable, very helpful, and so patient with me, just like she was with everyone else in the group.

After three or four individual sessions with various dolphins, one of the mammals—the eldest of the three, wouldn't go to the other end of the tank where she was being called to go. Her defiance meant we had two giant mammals stirring up the water. Yikes! I'd just finished one of my turns and headed to the edge of the tank when she, the eldest dolphin—Sally, I think was her name—very slowly glided past my legs. There was no fear for either of us. I'm a good swimmer, so if she got me off balance, I'd recover.

Sally circled again and made another pass. This time, grazing my upper legs. The trainers did their best to command her, via whistle, back to the other end of the tank. She wasn't having it. There was something she had to figure out first about me and my legs. Upon the third and final pass, her nose just barely touched Shortie as she floated by me. My heart did flip-flops as she "kissed" Shortie. It was as if she was saying "You're beautiful just the way you are."

As I sat on the edge of the tank, drying off and putting Nemo back on, Tiffany and I visited with the trainers. They said Sally never fails to follow orders. She's actually one of the dolphins who helped teach the others. One of the trainers was so sweet when she smiled and said, "She knows you're special."

My "high" continued through the evening as I couldn't stop talking about it. Tiffany and I both thought maybe Sally could "hear" the metal inside my legs and she needed to figure it out. Not sure if dolphins hear titanium or not. Regardless…it's a kiss I'll never forget!

Each and every one of us is born with a miracle inside.—*Winter's Tale*

Tiffany's and my girl time at the beach turned out to be extremely therapeutic for me. First the magical experience with Sally the dolphin, then we got matching tattoos. No, not permanent ones—I've had enough needles to last several lifetimes. They were small, delicate henna tattoos of the infinity circle to celebrate the unending friendship that we're blessed to share.

The other thing we shared together was rather ceremonial. I'd seen sky lanterns on the movie screen but not in person. I found lanterns that were one hundred percent biodegradable that would dissolve completely in water. I offered a couple to Tiffany, but ever so gracious, she said, "No, honey. You enjoy them. I'll go with you and help you, but this is your time."

For a wordsmith like myself, there is healing in writing. There's even greater healing in writing when releasing that which you've written. The sky lanterns were solid white. On one, I wrote every icky word I could think of to describe the hurts and burdens I'd been carrying. On the second one, I wrote words of gratitude. Although the first one was covered pretty well, the second one had WAY more written on it.

After dark, we headed down to the beach for the ceremonial send off. Tiffany was nervous, and truth be told, scared. I couldn't figure out why, but I'd soon find out. Once the first lantern was unfolded and the burner set in position, I asked Tiffany to light it while I held onto it. The breeze off the water made it difficult to light. Once lit, I proceeded to follow the directions by letting the lantern fill up with gases from the flame before releasing it. The lantern slowly filled up, and lifting my arms above my head I released it. It floated about ten feet and crashed into the sand and started tumbling down the shoreline, all while still lit. Obviously I couldn't run after it, I could barely walk on the sand.

Tiffany ran after it, all the while yelling "Oh crap, oh crap. Sheila, it's gonna catch something on fire!"

After several failed attempts, she finally captured it as I caught up to her. She was scared to death of it, and I still couldn't figure out why.

After the second attempt at releasing the lantern with the same repeated results, Tiffany shared something with me I never knew. If I did, I didn't understand, or remember the impact it had had on her life. (I hate the residuals from countless hours of anesthesia, years of narcotics, and prescription drugs.) My sweet friend of more than twenty years had survived not one but two house fires as a child. She had every right to be frightened. Even so, she stuck right in there with me like a true friend!

We finally got the first one released, only to see it float out about a hundred yards over the ocean before it nose-dived hard into the water. The second lantern release went much smoother. It was BEAUTIFUL. It drifted way up high before it slowly made its way over the water and out to sea.

Ironically, the first sky lantern was the one on which I'd written all the yuck—all my burdens, the hurts, and the struggles. No wonder it never took flight. It was weighted down with enormous negativity. The crashing destruction of it symbolized the letting go of all the yuck in my past.

The second lantern, the one I'd written all the beautiful words of gratitude on, soared! It went so high and so far—farther than I'd ever imagined it could.

They will soar on wings like eagles, they will run and not grow weary, they will run and not be faint.—Isaiah 40:31, NIV

Pedal Power...

I realize riding a bike is no big deal to most folks, but for this girl, it was a huge accomplishment.

I hadn't been on a bicycle in decades. Plus, I've got two rebuilt legs that have a mind all their own! I couldn't feel what Shortie was doing, let alone what Samson, my prosthetic, would or wouldn't do on a bicycle pedal. Throw in a good dose of constantly changing balance issues and "game on" takes on a whole new meaning.

There's no way I could have attempted the obstacle without my trusty side kick Tammy. Her sweet, supportive, "You've got this girl" approach made for nothing but success. She had a helmet, knee pads, gloves, and elbow pads for me, and a beach towel for herself. A beach towel, on a bike ride? Tammy explained that when she taught her kids to ride a bike, she'd wrap a towel around their waist and once they mastered the ride, she'd let go of the towel. What an amazing mom!

I had no doubt her neighbors thought we were replicating a *Laverne & Shirley* episode as Tammy held the bicycle seat and handle bars while I slowly mounted the bike. The old expression is (basically) true. Riding a bike is just like riding a bike. In some ways, it was easier than I thought it would be. Yet, in other ways, it was much harder.

My confidence kicked in when Tammy had to run faster to keep up with me. She started humming the theme song from *The Wizard of Oz* scene with the old lady peddling her heart out. I gained momentum and speed as I rounded a corner, leaving Tammy in the dust. As I started up an incline in the road, I knew I needed to switch to a lower gear. Not remembering how to switch gears on a bicycle, I yelled, "Where's the clutch?!" The only reply I got was uproarious laughter from behind me.

Tammy caught up to me about the time my uphill climb slowed me to a stop. Thank goodness, because she was able to help steady both me and the bike as I figured out how to get my prosthetic off the pedal and onto the ground. Both of us sucking air—her from running and me from straining to pedal uphill—she said, "You goofball!" I was trying to down shift on a bicycle as one would do on a motorcycle. Ugh!

In life, I watch every step I take. It was hard looking down and seeing what Shortie was doing, all while trying to steer a bicycle. While I didn't ride more than probably a combined total of a square city block, it was beyond rewarding not only to try but also to succeed. "Thanks, Tam for your precious friendship and your willingness to join in on yet another one of my goofy escapades!"

Thank you for being a friend...
Theme from *The Golden Girls*

My "Fifty for Fifty" year was incredible. Not only did I celebrate fifty years of my life, I celebrated life itself. I learned how to tie a man's neck tie (thanks Tom), completed twenty random acts of kindness, tried caviar (yuck!), learned how to sign "I Can Only Imagine" (thanks Teresa), took a swing dance lesson (thanks Mr. Ken), had my first experience with a bidet (oh, my!), rode in a sling-shot vehicle—so cool! (thanks Tom and Deb), took a train ride excursion (thanks DL), stripped and refinished my kitchen cabinets all by myself, finally got a stamp in my passport, and collected over a hundred different pinched pennies from around the world—thanks to friends and family for sending them to me so I could make two unique bracelets from them. These were just a few of the wonderful things that filled time and energy for me as I began a completely different kind of recovery.

Looking back, I realize how important it was to find light in the darkness. I'd endured such horrific pain and loss for years. I needed to replace those dreadful memories with happy, positive, joy-filled memories. My post-divorce counselor said something really profound: "Whatever you enjoy doing, do it. Do not let anyone steal your joy."

He was referring to the various events and activities I'd previously shared for decades in my marriage. He was honest when he said, "It may not be easy, especially the first year or the first time you do something, but it's important that you not stop doing something because of what others may say, think, or do—even if it stirs up bad memories."

He was so right. It's not always easy to keep on keeping on, but you know what? It was, and is, beyond worth it. I chose not to let anyone steal my joy.

Choose happy not crappy!
—Sheila Preston Fitzgerald

Chapter Eighteen

A Day in the Life of *One Foot in Heaven...*

It's rare that a day goes by that someone, somewhere, doesn't share their story with me. I'm not sure if it's because I'm an amputee who doesn't hide it, if I have a bumper sticker on my butt that reads "Tell me your story," or if it's an inner light that shines for all the world to see. I pray it's the latter.

It doesn't matter where I am or what I'm doing, folks want to chat with me. When it first started happening, after the accident, I wasn't all that prepared to handle it. Oh sure, I've always been a social butterfly. A friend once asked me, "You were born with confetti, weren't you?" This was different. People, strangers, began sharing their deepest, inner-most selves with me.

Helping others always leads to healing.

Can I Take a Picture of Your Feet?

After picking up a few necessities at a local market, I proceeded to my car. I heard a woman's voice.

Her: "Excuse me?"

Me: "Yes ma'am?"

Her: "I just had to tell you, I LOVE what you've done to your (hesitation) pretend leg."

Me: (thinking to myself, *Maybe she doesn't know the term "prosthetic"*). Trying not to laugh as I replay "pretend leg" over in my head, I smiled and replied, "Thank you."

Her: "The toenails painted—very pretty. Oh! Wow!! You even have a toe ring!"

Me: (still smiling) "Yes ma'am." Did I mention, she stopped me while she's driving and leaning out of the window of her (slow) moving SUV?

Her: (finally stopping) "Can I take a picture of your feet?"

Me: (wanting to laugh, but something tells me not to, so I continue to smile politely) "Sure."

At this point in the story, most folks would think the lady is nuts, odd, rude, bold, weird—whatever. For me…it's just another day in the life of the gal with *one foot in heaven*.

With her phone in hand, she leaned out her window, asking me to step a little closer. I giggled to myself as I tried to keep my face and the "girls" out of the picture.

After stepping closer, I noticed two really important things. There was a bouquet of flowers in the seat next to her, and as she took her sunglasses off to take the picture, tears filled her eyes.

This sweet stranger began to share her story with me in the middle of a market parking lot. Her dear friend had been struggling with health issues. The night before, her friend confessed her fears that her doctors were talking amputation if things didn't improve. The lady shared with me that she had prayed that very morning for God to give her the words of encouragement for her dear friend as she stopped at the market to get her flowers. With tears streaming down her face she said, "He answered my prayer when you walked across my path. Thank you for brightening my day so I can share it with my friend who truly needs it."

I love how God takes something so simple as toenail polish on a "pretend" leg and turns it into something awesome!

Me: "God is SO cool! I pray your friend receives healing and finds joy in the photo. She's blessed to have a friend like you!"

When I got to my car, I paused for a moment and chatted with God. Praying for her friend, thanking Him for picking me to be at the right place and at the right time to encourage another, and for sweet friends like this dear lady. Because, I too, am blessed with countless friends who continue to love, support, and encourage me in my journey.

Over the years, I've learned to embrace moments with strangers. Never knowing where the stories will lead me, or rather lead the one telling the story, I titled them GPS—"God Provides a Story." Like most adventures requiring a global positioning system, there's usually great reward, or at the very least great adventure waiting ahead.

Don't let God's Grace on you go to waste.

This One's for the Boys...

I'd gone to get my car emissions test completed. The young man, using hand signals, directed me into the bay. We exchanged pleasant greetings, then paper work and payment was exchanged. He completed a couple steps of the inspection before he asked me to step out of the vehicle. After opening my door, I gingerly began my departure from my car. As I did, the fella says, "Oh! You have a PROSTATE!"

Y'all, I've gotten pretty good at responding (or not acknowledging) goofy things people say. This poor fella didn't skip a beat. I'm not sure if he didn't realize he had just told a lady she had a prostate, or if he missed the day in Health 101 that he, a male, has a prostate. Not girls. He referred to my prostate more than once during our brief conversation. By all indications, he was an educated fella. I think he didn't realize he was using the wrong word...a really wrong word. I didn't have the heart to tell him.

As I sat less than six feet from the young man as he finished the test, it took all I had not to bust out in laughter. I got back into the car and pulled away. I didn't get a block down the street before I had to pullover and wipe the tears. Oh, the never ending life with *one foot in heaven.*

Techno-Dork, Party of One

In the wonderful world of prosthetics, things are always changing. Improvements and advancements are happening at warp speed—especially with global technology and research. It's all very fascinating, but sometimes difficult to keep up with.

The combination of a new legman and a completely new prosthetic system was working really well for me and Shortie. I was gaining greater strength and mobility and Shortie suffered fewer skin breakdown issues, creating much less stress overall. However, Shortie kept shrinking, which was expected. (I wish the rest of me would shrink!)

My legman, Aaron, introduced me to the option of a SmartPuck®—a new, computerized socket system. It's an elevated vacuum system that allows Shortie to suspend without moving inside the socket. This, in turn, allows for less rubbing of skin, creating a healthier Shortie. The coolest part is that it's controlled with a smart device—my iPhone.

Like everything that's the hottest technology, we had trouble getting the new system. It was backordered several times as the manufacturer pulled the system to reconfigure the unit with improvements. Then it was backordered yet again.

Once we finally received the SmartPuck® and Aaron installed it into my current prosthetic, Samson, I was able to give it a try. It felt SO good! The SmartPuck® has a manual operating option on it, though it's limited, and remains in one position unless changed via the smart device application. Basically, the app allows me to adjust the amount of vacuum within the prosthetic to compensate for changes in activity throughout the day without having to take the prosthetic off. In layman's terms, it has three basic settings: sit—walk—run, which I can customize, from one to ten in each setting, to fit my specific activity levels.

I've never claimed to be tech savvy. Learning the new application software was no exception. Because the SmartPuck® was new and exciting to all of us at my legman's clinic, we had a room full of staff learning about all it could do. We were having a little trouble figuring out how the app worked. As I sat watching, my mind couldn't help but wander...

If folks could see this!...How many highly educated and vastly experienced adults does it take to figure out this new-fangled thing?...I need to get pictures of this!...Where's my phone?...Oh, yea. We're using it for the software application...at least we're trying to use the app...

I couldn't help it. Laughter struck in the midst of it all. Between my awesome legman, his number one fabricator/designer, and the SmartPuck® rep on the phone, I estimated at least 75 combined years' experience were represented in the wonderful world of prosthetics. Yet, there we were, like a bunch of kids with the latest toy, trying to put it all together so we could see it in action. You could taste the energy in the room.

When I walked out of the clinic a couple of hours later (WAY after closing time), we all looked like real-life happy face emoji's. They had tackled and conquered a brand new computerized system in prosthetics, and I was blessed by receiving it. Definitely a "win-win."

For the next week or so, it was extremely important that I take Sampson off every few hours and inspect Shortie for any irritation, pulling or blistering. (Remember, I don't feel a lot of Shortie and don't know if there's damage until it's too late.) Not that we expected it to happen, but it was a potential risk.

Some learning curves are just that—a curve. If you're fortunate, it may only be a slight bend. For me, when it comes to technology, my learning "curve" is more like the dragon tail—full of twists and turns, yet always an exciting ride.

My first day wearing the new bionic leg was filled with many mishaps. Thank God, none were serious or unsafe.

First, I couldn't figure out why the new-fangled gizmo kept turning off. When that happens, the leg is still functional, just not accurate for whatever movement I'm currently engaged in. It took three hours to realize what I was doing wrong.

On an iPhone, when a bunch of apps are opened (draining the

battery), you swipe the apps closed. Yep! My due diligence backfired on me. Who knew?...When you close an app, it stops working altogether. Duh!

Once I corrected that blonde moment, it didn't take long for my tech-savvy confidence to plummet yet again. Randomly, as I was up moving about the salon, the designer system would shut down again. Repeatedly, I went through the checklist of do's and do not's—all with zero success. I had to go back through the app and start all over again each time—reconnecting, reconfiguring, entering in all defaults for my particular needs, etc. After the third or fourth time of doing this, I was ready to give the stinkin' thing back! "It may be comfy, but it's a royal pain to mess with," I said to a client. She started asking questions about it. I answered the best I could. Within a matter of minutes, she's giggling under her breath.

"It runs via Bluetooth, yes?" she asks.

"It does," I reply.

Still giggling, she asked "...and it shuts down when you walk around or step outside?"

A frustrated "yes" by me.

Her giggling is gaining momentum as she asked, "Are you taking your phone with you when you walk away?"

"Of course not. The phone's connected to the salon wi-fi."

"Honey...the phone is connected to the wi-fi, but your leg app is connected to Bluetooth." (She's STILL giggling.)

Me: "Yea" (I'm still not getting it.)

Her: "Bluetooth has a limited range. It's not like wi-fi. If your phone isn't on/near you, Bluetooth doesn't connect...at all."

Me: HUGE light bulb moment! "Ohhh! Kinda like when I'm on my Bluetooth ear piece and leave the room with the phone left behind and I lose whoever I'm talking to." She was nodding her head as she tried not to cry from laughing so hard! *Oh for Pete's sake! Really, Sheila? You're losing it!* The fun never ends!

Over time, Shortie and I adjusted really well to the new upgrade for Samson. I nicknamed the SmartPuck® device "Petunia" because when it was running, pulling air from the socket, it grunted like a little piglet. Typically, when I have a good tight seal and all the air has been sucked out, there are no snorting sounds. On occasion, while in public, Petunia snorts a bit, when doing her job. I've grown accustomed to the sound. From time to time, Petunia is overheard by someone else. More than once I've had to point to Petunia as folks blame me for the snort that can sound like a toot. "It's not me, I promise!"

My Fallen World...

Just as things were looking up, I hit rock bottom..."rock aggregate" to be exact. Ugh!

I'd been dog sitting for a sweet neighbor while she was on holiday. As I proceeded to complete the end-of-the-day-letting-out for my li'l Daisy and for my neighbor's dog, I had a doozie of a fall. Somehow when I hooked Daisy's leash to an outdoor table (so she could do her business while I went to let the neighbor's dog out) I got hung up in the leash. Trying desperately to protect Shortie, my right side took the blunt force impact. Mind you, it was dark, it was cold, and I was lying on the aggregate patio. I lay there a few minutes assessing myself. Parts were hurting, but the first question was, "Can I get up from here?" Getting down isn't the hard part. Not being able to use my knees makes getting up really hard.

Thank God it was dark because I'm certain my technique was everything but ladylike. Once upright, I began to s-l-o-w-l-y move about. Pretty much everything hurt.

I still had a mission to accomplish—my neighbor's dog. Gingerly, I made my way to her place, hooked her dog up to the tie-out and then sank into one of her patio chairs. Then came the throbbing, followed by the frustration. It dawned on me: I hadn't fallen in months and months, maybe even a year. As I sat there in the cold night air, my frustration turned to anger, which brought on tears. BIG ol' tears! In moments like those the hard, cold reality of my physical limitations smacked me in the face! Before I knew it, I was cold, my face was freezing because of the wet tears, I heard my li'l Daisy crying (she was probably freezing, too), and I had yet to finish the task at hand. The short time I sat there seemed to make things go from bad to worse for my aching body. Once the neighbor's dog was taken care of, I wobbled my way home. Then came the stairs…ugh…sigh…ugh…sigh…ugh…

There were only three steps leading to my back door, but at that moment, it felt like ten flights. Inside the safety and warmth of my sanctuary, I lost it.

Tears upon tears fell. I really just wanted to curl up in a ball and cry myself to sleep. Not being able to lie on my left side because of the metal hardware in the left hip, and after falling on my right hip, there was no curling up in a ball. That brought on more frustrating tears.

Maybe I need to go back outside and cool off, I thought to myself. I opened the door, took a deep breath, looked up, and began to pray.

It was then that I realized that we all live in a fallen world. At times it's literal. Yet, for most of us, most of the time, it's the mental or emotional part of life where we take the hardest falls.

No clay has become a beautiful pot without first going through the fire.

Dream On…

I was once asked "When you dream, do your dreams have you with one or two legs?"

Great question! The simple answer is "Yes." I tend to be a rather vivid dreamer. My mind works a lot like a movie or a detailed story that becomes a movie in my head. It's not uncommon for me to dream in full-color, with huge emotion, complete with smells. Most of the time, I have phenomenal dreams. I also tend to wake with full recollection of the dream.

I had two fully functioning legs for forty-six years, so yes, I sometimes still dream having two legs. In the beginning, those dreams were tough to process. I'd grieve and grieve for my previous legs mourning the loss of all the things I miss doing. In time, my two-legged dreams gave me hope. Hope for Heaven, and for the new (amazing) body I'll one day have.

Even years later, there are days when I awake, pull back the covers, look down at my legs, and say to myself, "Aww, crap! It wasn't a dream. It's still not there."

Randomly, I have unpleasant dreams involving my rebuilt designer legs. Fortunately, that doesn't happen often. When it does, it's easy for me to identify the unpleasant dream with an unpleasant situation I'm dealing with.

Conquering the unpleasant results in greater rest.

Happy AMP-iversary Baby...

Every year I celebrate the AMP-iversary and the anniversary of the accident with a little "looking back" and a healthy dose of "launching forward." I reflect on how far I've come and then reward myself with a fun outing or a cool day trip.

It's not easy walking out this journey. Life is hard enough without adding major physical limitations to it. I make a conscious effort, every moment, to surround myself with uplifting, positive, encouraging, supportive options—within and around me. I don't watch television unless it's a good football game or an upbeat movie. I listen to contemporary Christian music, I read favorable books, and surround myself with happy, hope-filled, encouraging people. I believe the old saying is true—garbage in, garbage out. I've had plenty of garbage in my life. I need no more. I choose joy!

My story provides me with a constant reminder of what God does when He allows circumstances to be used to transform, to renew, to give life again. It's in the spiritual growth, through grace, that's been my greatest reward.

If there's one thing I've learned, it's this: being a traumatic amputee is never "done." You're never "healed." You don't ever reach an—

"Okay, good, that fits, so now we're done forever"—moment in life. A body in motion is constantly changing, and that means the man-made components must constantly change as well.

Ironically, that same life lesson applies to our spiritual journey. We're never "done." We never stop growing, learning, reaching for a deeper intimacy with God. Like my physical journey, it's not always easy. Setbacks, falls, failures, and mistakes happen, but...it's in those trials, we learn and grow in our faith walk.

Setbacks are simply opportunities for great comebacks.

I continue to be a learning tool for different specialists in the industry, which is another blessing—especially since the number of high compound trauma female amputees is super low compared to the male population of traumatic amputations. Yep, you guessed it. A woman's body responds differently than a man's. Imagine that.

In spite of the constant roller coaster ride being a traumatic amputee involves, I wouldn't trade it for brand new Barbie doll legs or a bazillion dollars. Don't get me wrong...I wouldn't wanna go through it all again in the least. However, what I've learned, how God has refined and defined who I am today—that's priceless!

Grit—Grace—Gratitude

Life Lessons...

I don't consider myself a Bible scholar by any stretch of the imagination. I have, however, read and studied it on a daily basis for years. I admit, there's much I don't understand.

For most of my life I've known there is a God, yet not until after the accident did I know Who He was. Knowing about someone is comparable to reading about them. Actually knowing them comes after you've met and developed a relationship with them.

My first real meeting with God was the night of the accident when He held me in His arms—protecting and comforting me in my darkest hour, showing me intimate love to the depths of my being. He captured my heart. Yes, He rescued me physically the night of the accident, but out of that physical rescue, the greatest spiritual journey began. His presence penetrated the very core of my soul. Over the years, as I spend time with Him in prayer, meditation, study, and worship, our relationship has continued to grow and flourish.

When God held me, and Jesus told me not to be afraid, I wasn't. It was that simple. I felt no fear, whatsoever. I truly wish I could fully and accurately describe the love and peace I experienced. I can tell you there is NOTHING like it. I'm given reminders of that kind of love every single day. I call them "Heaven's confetti"—sprinkles of hope and joy from above. It's what carries me through this journey.

It's taken me years to nurture our relationship—years for me to learn to trust Him, years for me to understand Him, and years for me to accept all He freely gives. Like any relationship, the more time, attention, and commitment you put in—the stronger the bond.

I'm often asked, "Would you ever get back on a motorcycle?" In a heartbeat! I miss it every day, but I know my designer legs aren't strong enough to hold up a bike anymore. I tried an inverted trike—it was fun, but not my style. Maybe one day I'll try a regular trike. "You could always passenger with someone," I'm often told. "Na, that's not really my style." Plus, it'd take a lot for me to trust another on a bike. That, and I'm not stupid. I'd never ride now in the area where I live. It's become insanely congested with traffic in middle Tennessee.

~ ~ ~

Since the accident, when people hear about my miraculous survival, most respond with some form of "WOW! God's not done with you. He must have saved you for something really special."

Why me? I can't answer that. I won't pretend to know God's plans. I do know that He picked me to walk out this journey, my journey, and by golly, I'm gonna do all I can to make Him proud. While I was working on my legs…He was working on my heart. I'm not about to let God's Grace on me go to waste!

Is it easy because I choose to trust Him? HARDLY! I live in varying degrees of pain every single moment of every single day, and even though I pray constantly for Him to take the pain away—so far, He's chosen to answer my prayer with strength to endure instead of complete healing.

Yes, bad things happen. I don't believe for one second that the driver who crashed into me did it on purpose. What I do believe, is that it's my choice how I respond. Only by the Grace of God, because of His Son's sacrifice and gifting me with the Holy Spirit, am I able to endure.

There are better options than getting even, staying mad, giving up, or living a life of bitterness. It's up to us to make the choice. Like any good habit created—choosing "happy" over and over and over again, in spite of loss, hurt, shame, regret, fear, etc.—a life of continually choosing "happy" eventually becomes second nature. When that happens…true joy is born!

Will there be folks who choose not to believe my personal encounter with the Trinity? Maybe. I mean no disrespect, but that's their issue, not mine. Nothing, nor no-one, will convince me otherwise.

Choose to believe, receive, and achieve all He has planned for you!

It's taken me years to trust God enough to share my incredibly miraculous journey with the world. The spiritual encounter, the night of the accident, is unwavering. It's me who's changed. I've been refined, not just by the life altering physical changes, but by the life-giving changes within me. I'm no longer bound by fear.

I've learned to rely on God for everything. In spite of the ongoing struggles, I no longer fear. Jesus told me, "Don't be afraid…We've got you." He was the first to say, "You're gonna be okay." Chad, one of the first responders at the scene of the accident, said the same thing as they loaded me into the helicopter. Tammy, my dear friend, also confirmed it when she whispered it into my ear in the hospital later that same night.

You're gonna be okay.

Epilogue

His Story...His Glory

I struggled for weeks in an attempt to complete the ending of *One Foot in Heaven*. How does one write "The End" when their life and story continues? I have yet to pass away (to Heaven) and unlike Cinderella or Sleeping Beauty my "Happily Ever After" has yet to happen.

The book ending was all God.

I had a scheduled writing day, but arose that particular morning with zero creativity. I did everything possible to avoid my office. I cleaned house, I groomed the dog, I made phone calls, and made a double batch of homemade soup. It was early afternoon when I told myself, "Stop avoiding, Sheila! If you'll read the last ten pages or so, maybe you'll be inspired to write the ending."

Dragging myself to the office, I began reading the manuscript. I didn't get far before the various bits and pieces of notes I had scattered on my desk came to life like an animated Disney movie. Without direction or thought, I picked up a pen and within minutes, the multitude of scattered notes fell into place like puzzle pieces completing a masterpiece.

Once the final words were penned, I slumped back into my chair letting out a huge sigh. The next thirty to forty-five seconds were filled with a myriad of emotions.

Oh my gosh! Is it REALLY finished Lord? You sure??

I cried tears of joy, exhaustion, anxiousness, reservation, excitement, and more. My emotions, like a first-time mom giving birth to a new life, were like that of a pinball machine bouncing all over the place.

Something told me to check the date. I looked up at my computer screen that indicated the time—3:25 p.m. The techno-dork that I am, I couldn't find the date on my computer. I reached over and tapped my cell phone for the date. It was March 25th...3/25.

Oh, that's SO cool! (God knows I play brain games with myself to help remember things.)

For the rest of the day, I was on an emotional roller coaster. Truth be told, it was exhausting. One moment I'd cry because the manuscript was completed. The next, I'd cry tears of *What now, Lord?*

Off and on all evening I'd be reminded of the numbers three-two-five. I've never studied Biblical symbolic numerology. One of my girlfriends, Tammy Rene, has a huge connection to Biblical numerology. Unfortunately, by the time I thought to call her it was past her bedtime. I couldn't sleep so I started researching Biblical numerology. It was fascinating! The number two made sense to me as it symbolizes witnesses. The number three was easy—it symbolizes the Trinity. I would have never guessed number five, but I really liked it when I read it's symbolism. Numeral five symbolizes God's goodness and Grace poured out on mankind's weakness.

Hmm...interesting, I thought to myself.

Not until I read it out-loud, in order of three-two-five, did it shake me to my core. Gods perfect confirmation:

The Trinity witnessed me at my weakest moment and poured out their Grace on me...*One Foot in Heaven* is Their story.

We are all beautifully broken.
When God pours into us,
may we leak Him.

Appendix

Prosthetics for Dummies 101—Version Sheila

Like most people, I had NO IDEA what and how prosthetics worked. Ignorant me thought I'd be fitted for a new leg one week, pick it up the next week, and walk out never to return. That is NOT how it works—for any amputee.

In an ideal, clean amputation, the initial process can take as little as sixty to ninety days for an amputee to walk with a new prosthetic. That's if the individual is healthy, and has a scheduled surgical amputation. For most amputees, even those who have scheduled surgical amputation, the process isn't that simple. There's usually contributing factors such as: a weakened immune system, disease, illness or infection, all of which cause delays for the amputee in physical healing and regaining strength and mobility.

Then, there are those of us with high trauma amputations. One of my surgeons once told me, "It's as if someone put your leg in a blender and pulled it out. That's how damaged your residual limb is." That alone is a challenge for me and my prosthetic team to overcome. Add to that challenge all the other damages on both of my legs, and the obstacles can be extremely difficult. Notice I didn't say impossible. Thank God, I've got an awesome legman, who like me, sees the word impossible and chooses to say, "We're just gonna have to try harder!"

Sheila's Prosthetic Application Instructions

1. Apply resilience balm on any/all raw, calloused, or weakened skin on Shortie.

2. Apply a very thin layer of hypo-allergenic massage cream on the thin skin graft areas to keep them from being pulled and torn when inside the socket.

3. Gently roll on the liner-liner. The liner-liner is a special liner that is worn inside a regular liner. It's made of a clear gel composite material that acts as a SPANX® girdle for all the redundant tissue on Shortie. I must pay special attention to the custom-built padding (the distal end "heel-pad" that was created from one of my abdominal muscles) that's been attached to the bottom end of what remains of my fibular and tibia bones. Because of all the loose, redundant tissue, the plastic surgeon built "heel-pad" tends to shift and move about if it is not first manually put into the proper position and then secured with the SPANX®-style liner-liner.

4. Place a silicone gel bumper pad outside the distal end of the liner-liner for extra padding.

5. Gently roll on the liner, while keeping the liner-liner and gel bumper pad in position, making certain there are no wrinkles or air pockets in either liner. Air pockets create blisters and/or open wounds. Wrinkles create hickies and/or tearing of the thin grafted skin.

6. Typically, though not always with a new socket, at least a three-ply sock is put on over the second liner. The wool blend socks are used to help fill the space inside the socket when Shortie shrinks. A residual or compromised limb continues to atrophy over one's lifetime. In general, the majority of atrophy is within the first twelve to eighteen months for most amputees. Unfortunately, Shortie is nothing like most amputations. It's been seven years since my amputation, and Shortie continues to shrink and change.

7. While balancing on my long leg, I gently slide Shortie into the socket (the upper part that looks like a vase).

8. Checking alignment of Shortie in the socket, making sure I'm not hitting bottom or twisted inside the socket in any way, I

stand for a minute or so to allow Shortie to settle in the socket. Most days, it takes me at least two attempts. Somedays when I'm struggling with a poor fitting socket, I can go through the process four, five, six, or more times in an effort to get a comfortable, or least tolerable, fit.

9. Once Shortie and the socket have found their happy place, I then roll up the outer sleeve. The sleeve is a thick silicone gel covered in a heavy, flexible material—similar to a wetsuit. The outer sleeve acts as a conduit seal over the outside of the upper part of the socket, and over the upper part of the outer liner and my thigh. Once again, it's imperative that there's no air pockets or wrinkles, especially in the fold of the leg behind the knee. In a matter of a few steps, blisters and tugging of skin can and does occur if not properly sealed.

10. I stand, gently distributing my body weight between both legs, further allowing Shortie to settle down into the socket. If all is good, I take a few steps to test the fit. If pain or more than normal early-morning-discomfort exists, I have to take everything off and start all over again.

11. Once a decent fit is achieved, I pull up my tights or leggings that were put on the prosthetic the night before. In an attempt to limit 'wardrobe malfunctions' I put out my clothes the night before. There's nothing more frustrating than to finally get a great fit with limb and prosthetic only to realize you have the wrong shoe on!

12. After I take thirty or forty steps, and the overall fit feels good, I turn on the computerized elevated vacuum system via my smart device. The SmartPuck® was the industry's first intelligent socket system with constant vacuum technology. It's been the most comfortable and secure system I've ever had. When all components are functioning together, I have little to no skin breakdown issues, which is HUGE for Shortie! The SmartPuck® allows me to adjust the vacuum pressure settings to accommodate my activity levels throughout the day—all

without having to remove the prosthetic.

13. At the end of my day, bedtime, I complete the entire process backward. The only thing I add is daily cleaning of all components. A must to keep infections at bay.

Answers to Frequently Asked Questions

How long does it take to build a new prosthetic?

Unfortunately, there's not a simple answer. There are fully computerized digital imaging systems that build sockets nowadays, but they're more expensive and are rather new to the industry. As with anything machine-made versus hand-made, the machine-made product is much faster. Personally, I've not yet experienced a digitally made socket.

For me, it can take several months to get a new prosthetic. First, there's the measuring and casting of Shortie (my residual limb). Then a test socket is made from the casting. If the test socket fits well, a permanent socket is built. Because I have so much redundant, flexible tissue on Shortie, I've yet to get a good fit from the first test socket. It's usually two or three before we get the right fit. It's no one's fault, it's just how it is because of Shortie's extensive permanent damages. Once we get a good fit with a test socket, the permanent socket is made. The prosthetic industry calls it a 'permanent' socket, but that's not entirely accurate. It's only permanent until something changes—and things are always changing!

How long does a prosthetic last?

Again, not a simple answer. I've been an amputee not quite seven years. I've had more than 30 sockets. Most were in the first three years after amputation. I've yet to have one last three years. I'm told that clean amputees recover and stabilize much quicker. I've also been told that my situation is so unique that I shouldn't expect anything to be "normal." Sockets basically last until the residual limb shrinks so much, that even with added socks, the fit becomes sloppy causing potential falls. The hardware components last, on average, three to five years. When I found that out, it blew my mind! The best analogy I can give you is this: if you drove your car sixteen hours a day at fifty mph, that's nearly 300,000 miles in one year. Obviously, like drivers, the more activity or the higher the speed, the quicker it'll wear out.

What's the difference between the socket and the hardware of a prosthetic?
The socket is the upper component that looks like a vase—the part where Shortie slides into. The hardware is the various components that make up the rest of the man-made leg. For me, that includes a metal rod (aka: shin), the computerized SmartPuck® elevated vacuum system, an internal shock absorber, a computerized ankle with an internal microprocessor, a heel that resembles a mini version of the amputee runners blade, a metal foot plate that looks a bit like a split hoof, and finally, a flesh tone foot shell giving the appearance of a real foot— actually, more like a mannequin's foot. There are also various other pieces of titanium that hold all the components together. I believe I've had seven full (socket and hardware) prosthetic legs thus far.

What do you do with old prosthetics?
Initially, most were recycled or donated to programs for those without insurance or the financial means to afford one. A few of my old prosthetics have been reconfigured for either a backup leg or a water leg (aka: Nemo).

Can you get your prosthetic wet?
My daily use prosthetics are not designed to be immersed in water. Think about it this way—your car can withstand the rain, but it's not designed to drive it into the lake.

Do you shower with your water leg on?
I've tried it several times, but find I get more water on the floor once I'm done showering then when I don't wear a prosthetic. Nemo, my

water leg, holds water and it's hard to empty out the water and dry it off. Water of any amount on the floor is a huge fall risk for me.

Does Shortie sweat inside the prosthetic?

YES! I didn't realize how much moisture our body eliminates into the air through our pores. Because Shortie is basically inside multiple layers of gel, fabric, and carbonite, it sweats. With exercise and on hot humid days, I have to completely undress Shortie, pour out the puddled up sweat that's pooled inside the bottom of the liner-liner, clean Shortie and the liner-liner and then redress. If I don't, the pooled-up sweat at the bottom of the liner-liner can and does create soggy skin that quickly breaks down. The added fluid inside the liner-liner also creates an unstable fit, creating a poor gait and potential fall.

What if Shortie shrinks during the day?

If it's ever so slight shrinkage, I can adjust my SmartPuck® vacuum system to accommodate the change. If I find that Shortie is hitting the bottom of the socket, which is hard for me to tell because I don't really "feel" that part of Shortie, I add another sock. With added physical activity, Shortie shrinks due to internal body fluids being pushed upward. The fluids get pushed up, and the residual limb drops further into the socket—hitting bottom is a big no-no for amputees.

Is there a male versus female prosthetic?

For me, yes. For most of the industry, no. I'll never forget when Aaron, my legman, presented me the first prosthetic he designed for Shortie and I. I was so excited about the various new components. Then I saw the foot shell. He noticed the confused look on my face and asked what was wrong. "Why'd you put a 'dude' foot on it?" I asked. Bless him!

He looked at me, then looked at the foot shell and said, "It's a unisex foot."

Without skipping a beat I replied, "Do I LOOK unisex?"

We both busted out laughing. Needless to say, that was a start to a wonderful working relationship. He made sure to order a split-toe female foot shell for me. I may have lost a leg, but by golly, God made me a girl and a girl I'm gonna be—split toe, nail polish, and a toe ring…even on a fake foot!

How many kinds of prosthetics are there?
I'm familiar with at least a dozen different styles of lower limb prosthetics. There's probably a dozen more I'm unaware of. They vary based on individual needs and preferences. Because of my extensive damages, I'm not an ideal candidate for a majority of the options available.

How much does a prosthetic cost?
Are you sitting down? This question is always a tough one to answer. They're not cheap. Mine are customized specifically for my unique physical needs. The national average cost for a lower limb prosthetic is $20,000.00 to $50,000.00. Because of my extensive, bilateral compound issues, mine have been on the higher side of average. Yes, insurance helps, depending on the policy benefits. It's safe to say, it's costly to be an amputee, and the costs only increase over time.

Do you sleep with your prosthetic on?
No, it's WAY too heavy, bulky, and cumbersome. On random occasions, I've fallen asleep with it on. I always wake with hip and back joint pain. It's not worth it. Unfortunately, if I have to use the restroom in the middle of the night, I have to hobble via crutches on one leg, but not before first turning on all the lights—having to completely wake up.

Can you feel anything through the prosthetic?
I can't "feel" it if someone touches the prosthetic. However, I can more than feel it if someone accidentally bumps or kicks it. If I'm sitting down, and someone steps over my prosthetic and in the process

kicks it, I feel it. Sometimes it's not a big deal, it's simply vibration. Sometimes it's a painful twisting inside the socket on Shortie. When I sit or stand still, Shortie isn't moving, but when kicked, the prosthetic wrenches and twists the thin skin inside. Most of the time the result is a simple rub resulting in what looks like a big hickie. Other times I've had torn skin. Just because it's not causing a problem on the outside doesn't mean it's not causing a problem on the inside. That's kind of like people, isn't it?

Can you drive with a prosthetic?

It's still legal to drive with a valid driver's license as an amputee. A vehicle may need to be modified to meet each individual need. For me, as a left leg amputee, I'm able to use my right leg to drive. Because of the extensive damages to my right leg, I have to monitor my time behind the wheel, making frequent stops when I travel long distances. Speaking of driving, parking as an amputee can be really frustrating. I have to use handicap parking, not because I can't always walk the extra distance, but because I need the extra white-lined area to get in and out of my car. In order for me to get the prosthetic out of the car, I have to have the car door opened all the way—it's nearly perpendicular with the SUV I currently drive. It's the only way I can get my legs in and out of the car without hurting them. I love y'all, but those white lines in and around handicap parking are there for a purpose, and it's not for shopping buggies, motorcycles, or overflow parking.

What's one thing you do differently now that you wear a prosthetic, that you didn't have to do before?

Oh my goodness. Way too much to list in these pages. However, there is one thing I learned the hard way. For safety's sake, it's extremely important to have what I call "my long leg out." I now must sleep with my long leg on the outside edge of the bed. If I'm in bed, I'm on the right side of the bed, which allows my long leg to be on the outside edge. For 46 years I had two legs. When suddenly awaken from a deep sleep, my mind defaults back to the past. I've bolted out of bed during a storm, fully expecting to hop out of bed and seek shelter in my safe place, only to fall flat on the hardwood floor because I didn't have my long leg hit the floor first. Lesson learned! The same application is applied to showering.

How much does a prosthetic weigh?
There are many, many variables to consider when it comes to the weight of a prosthetic. Mine tend to average four to five pounds for my every day leg. My current water leg, Nemo, weighs in at about eight pounds. I've had prosthetics in the past that were much heavier—ten pounds or more. While that might not seem like much, think about it like this: a gallon of water weighs eight pounds. Lugging around a gallon of water, or a ball and chain when the fit is too big, can quickly take its toll on Shortie and my entire body.

Can you wear high heels?
After the first amputation, I could still wear a small heel—less than two inches. Unfortunately, after the second revision amputation, I'm no longer able to wear a heel elevation higher than about 3/4 of an inch.

Do you have a different prosthetic for different shoes?
No. My foot shell is a standard woman's size eight—the same size as my right foot. I'm so grateful shoe sizes are standardized. (Unlike clothing—ugh!) I used to love shoes, still do. Sadly, big shoe stores are a giant no-no for me. That's one place I break down every time I go in.

Do you wear a leg shell over your prosthetic?
I've never worn one. Years ago, I asked about them. I was curious how they worked. It sounded like they are more trouble than they're worth. Over the years, I've learned how important it is to not hide my prosthetic to the world. It's become my light, my 'foot in the door' to share His incredible story through my journey of *one foot in heaven*.

Let your light shine!
Matthew 5:14–16, NIV

I've found The Amputee Coalition to be an excellent resource for amputees, as well as for friends and family of amputees. Visit www.amputee-coalition.org or call 1-888-267-5667.

Acknowledgments

First and foremost, thank You, Jesus! You are my everything!

I am so grateful to my parents for their love, commitment, and sacrifice to our entire family. I love and miss y'all. Hug Jesus for me!

To my siblings and extended family...I love y'all!

To my pastors and church family...you are my family as I have none locally...thank you for being the hands and heart of Jesus!

To the mighty prayer warriors far and near: family, friends, neighbors, churches around the globe, small groups, church leaders, colleagues, clients, and more...thank you!

There's NO WAY I could have endured this journey without the precious love poured out on me from my village people. I am beyond blessed by multitudes of friends who've walked this journey with me. I wish I could list each of you by name. If I did, I'd be certain to miss someone. To my amazing tribal leaders, Tammy and Tiffany, words can't express the love I have for y'all. What priceless gifts you are to me!

To the massive number of volunteers who've walked this journey with me: those who brought meals, the babysitters, the personal shoppers, the Daisy keepers, the errand runners, the doctor-visit chauffeurs, the hospital advocates, the home remodelers, the lawn caretakers, and the blood donors...thank you! My heart smiles when I think of you!

To the incredible self-sacrificing first responders: Franklin, Tennessee Firefighters and Paramedics, Franklin, Tennessee Police Department, Williamson County Sheriff's Department, Williamson County Ambulance and Vanderbilt Life Flight...y'all ROCK! Thank you!

To all who contributed to the Sheila Fitzgerald Recovery Fund: Franklin Firefighters Association, Franklin Noon Rotary, Tennessee Chiropractic Association, Franklin BBQ Society, and all the generous individuals who made the initial financial burdens easier to bear. Thank you!

To Tim and Deb Knight for sharing their beautiful beach home with me. This book wouldn't be complete without your generous support. Your beach home is truly a writers paradise! Thank you!

To all the healthcare personnel especially Dr. Manish Sethi and Dr. David Pence. Thank you Dr. Sethi for stepping out in faith and allowing God to use your gifted surgical hands to put me back together when others couldn't see the possibility. Thank you Dr. Pence for keeping me structurally aligned before, during, and since the accident. God truly placed me in the hands of two fine physicians!

To my editor, the beautiful and gifted Lisa Blevins May, you make my words make sense. Thank you!

To my publishing editor, the incredible Loral Robben Pepoon, you are a talented grammatical wordsmith. Thank you!

To my incredible book mentor, Mr. Norman Rohrer, and his precious wife, Virginia, God certainly blessed me big when He put y'all in my life. Thank you both for your prayer, love, support and encouragement!

To Larry and Barbara Adamson, your constant support and encouragement to share my journey with the world has been huge! Thank you for stepping in when my parents were unable to. I love y'all!

To Brian Nock, without your encouraging email years ago, this would be a title-less book. Thank you! I cherish your and Janet's dear friendship!

To Jason Thompson my website designer guru. I can't thank you enough for bringing this techno-dork into the 21st Century. You rock!

To Kayla, Loral, and Seth at Selah Press for your incredible gift of page layout and formatting. What a joy it's been working with y'all!

To Christine Dupre of Vida Graphic Design, graphics artist extraordinaire, thank you for capturing the vision!

Thank you ALL for making *One Foot in Heaven* a reality! May every reader be blessed by your talents and generosity.

About the Author

Dubbed "sweet and sassy" by her friends, Sheila Preston Fitzgerald's love of people, love of life, and most importantly her love for God radiates Jesus, the Light of Life.

As a highly-sought-after professional manicurist by day, Sheila finds great joy in helping others not only look beautiful but also feel beautiful.

Sheila also shares her incredible passion for life through various speaking engagements. While women's ministry and church communities tend to be her most common audience, she is quick to note that she shares her miraculous true story wherever she's called to encourage, inspire, and give hope. Sheila has also spoken to civic groups, non-profit organizations, schools, and a juvenile detention center.

Her speaking topics cover a wide array of subjects from her vast life experiences. Some of her inspirational messages have been entitled: "Overcoming Fear," "Learning to Trust Again," "Finding Hope," "Growing Your Faith," "Living a REAL Life in a Virtual Society," "The Importance of Being a Donor," "Never Ever Give Up," "Rewards of Redemption," "Delighting in Physical Disabilities," and "Letting Go of Guilt, Shame, and Regret."

Sheila's service and commitment to others has led to prestigious awards from the Tennessee Chiropractic Association and the American Red Cross. The Rotary Club of Franklin, Tennessee, also awarded Sheila the coveted Paul Harris Fellow Award for her exemplary service to the community even though she is not a Rotary Club member.

Sheila's heart smiles when she's able to spend time building up others, having intentional quiet time with God in prayer and meditation, and lovingly serving her church family as a part of the prayer ministry team.

She admits to having a love affair with all things pen and paper—from devout journaling to working on a second book to sending hand-written notes of encouragement via snail-mail.

When there's not a pen in her hand, Sheila cherishes her time with friends and family, relaxing with a good book that renews her soul, sharing her God-given gift of hospitably by hosting guests in her home, and of course, loads of snuggles with her little dog Daisy.

Sheila resides in the beautiful, rolling hills just south of Nashville, Tennessee.

Follow

One Foot in Heaven
Sheila Preston Fitzgerald

Facebook: One Foot In Heaven
Instagram: 1FootInHeaven
www.OneFootInHeavenOnline.com

To book Sheila Preston Fitzgerald for your next event:
1FootNHeaven@gmail.com

Coming Soon
One Foot in Heaven—Daily Encounters with Jesus

Made in the USA
Columbia, SC
11 September 2019